Pro SQL Server Always On Availability Groups

Uttam Parui

Vivek Sanil

Apress®

Pro SQL Server Always On Availability Groups

Uttam Parui
Mooresville, North Carolina
USA

Vivek Sanil
San Antonio, Texas
USA

ISBN-13 (pbk): 978-1-4842-2070-2
DOI 10.1007/978-1-4842-2071-9

ISBN-13 (electronic): 978-1-4842-2071-9

Library of Congress Control Number: 2016955944

Managing Director: Welmoed Spahr
Lead Editor: Jonathan Gennick
Development Editor: Corbin Collins
Technical Reviewer: Rahul Deshmukh
Editorial Board: Steve Anglin, Pramila Balan, Laura Berendson, Aaron Black, Louise Corrigan, Jonathan Gennick, Todd Green, Robert Hutchinson, Celestin Suresh John, Nikhil Karkal, James Markham, Susan McDermott, Matthew Moodie, Natalie Pao, Gwenan Spearing
Coordinating Editor: Jill Balzano
Copy Editor: Karen Jameson
Compositor: SPi Global
Indexer: SPi Global
Artist: SPi Global

Distributed to the book trade worldwide by Springer Science+Business Media New York, 233 Spring Street, 6th Floor, New York, NY 10013. Phone 1-800-SPRINGER, fax (201) 348-4505, e-mail orders-ny@springer-sbm.com, or visit www.springer.com. Apress Media, LLC is a California LLC and the sole member (owner) is Springer Science + Business Media Finance Inc (SSBM Finance Inc). SSBM Finance Inc is a Delaware corporation.

For information on translations, please e-mail rights@apress.com, or visit www.apress.com.

Apress and friends of ED books may be purchased in bulk for academic, corporate, or promotional use. eBook versions and licenses are also available for most titles. For more information, reference our Special Bulk Sales–eBook Licensing web page at www.apress.com/bulk-sales.

Any source code or other supplementary materials referenced by the author in this text are available to readers at www.apress.com. For detailed information about how to locate your book's source code, go to www.apress.com/source-code/. Readers can also access source code at SpringerLink in the Supplementary Material section for each chapter.

Printed on acid-free paper

Contents at a Glance

Contents

About the Authors

Uttam Parui is a Senior Premier Field Engineer at Microsoft, based out of Charlotte, North Carolina. He has worked at Microsoft for more than 16 years and has been working with the SQL Server product since SQL Server 6.5. As a Premier Field Engineer, he delivers SQL Server consulting and support for designated strategic Fortune 500 customers. Also, he has been developing content, speaking at events, as well as authoring books, white papers, and articles related to SQL Server administration, high availability, disaster recovery, and more. Uttam is the coauthor of *Microsoft SQL Server 2008 Bible* (Wiley Publishing) and technical editor for *Pro SQL Server 2008 Failover Clustering* (Apress). He has trained and mentored engineers from the Customer Support Services and Premier Field Engineering teams, and was one of the first to train and assist in the development of Microsoft's SQL Server support teams in Canada and India. Uttam received his master's degree in Computer Science from the University of Florida at Gainesville. He can be reached at uttam_parui@hotmail.com.

Vivek Sanil is a Senior Premier Field Engineer at Microsoft. Vivek has been working extensively with SQL Server since joining the industry more than 16 years ago. He has been with Microsoft since 2005. Vivek currently works in a support and consulting role in a dedicated capacity with a few large Fortune 500 customers. Areas of specialty include Database Engine internals, SQL Always On, and performance troubleshooting. He has architected and developed numerous PFE workshops that Microsoft delivers to its customers. Vivek has also moderated in several worldwide Microsoft Virtual Academy events. He can be reached at vivek_sanil@hotmail.com.

About the Technical Reviewer

Rahul Deshmukh works as an SQL Server Premier Field Engineer at Microsoft. He helps Fortune 500 companies with the design, implementation, and performance tuning of SQL Server HA DR solutions and has helped architect some of the biggest Availability Groups deployments. He also has more than 1000 hours of experience teaching SQL Server internals, administration, and Always On technologies to customers from all over the continent.

Rahul has presented at SQL Server user groups and contributed to one of the most successful PASS Pre-Con sessions on Always On.

Rahul has SQL Server and Azure certifications from Microsoft. He holds a master's degree in Information Science from the University of North Carolina at Chapel Hill.

You can reach Rahul at www.RahulDeshmukh.info and follow him on Twitter @sqlrahul.

Acknowledgments

From Uttam Parui.

My first thank you goes to my loving wife, Shyama; and my two doting daughters, Nika and Rika, for their encouragement, understanding, patience, and love while I spent many nights, weekends, and holidays working on the book. I'd like to thank my parents for their endless love and support and for giving me the best education they could provide, which has made me successful in life.

A very special thank you goes out to my coauthor Vivek Sanil and technical reviewer Rahul Deshmukh for their contributions, feedback, and support. I truly believe that the book came out as good as it has due to their professionalism and passion for quality and perfection. I could not have asked for a better team.

A warm thank you goes out to the Microsoft SQL Server Always On experts for sharing their knowledge, best practices, tips, and solutions: Kevin Farlee, Luis Carlos Vargas Herring, Elden Christensen, Juergen Thomas, Shon Knoblauch, Charles Mathews, Robert Dorr, Trayce Jordan, Luís Canastreiro, David Levy, David Browne, and Balmukund Lakhani. My sincerest apologies if I missed anyone.

Last but not least, I want to thank everyone at Apress who I worked directly or indirectly with on this book: Jonathan Gennick, Jill Balzano, and Corbin Collins.

From Vivek Sanil.

I am grateful for the opportunity to have worked on this book. I am all the more grateful for the help and encouragement that I have received from so many wonderful friends and colleagues.

First, my considerable thanks go to Uttam Parui, the coauthor of this book. Having him on the same team while writing this book made it a fun and fulfilling experience. I hope that the work that we have put into it is appreciated by all who read it.

Thanks to Rahul Deshmukh (technical reviewer) for his hard work in reading the chapters, testing the solutions and code, and providing feedback. I truly believe that his input helped make this book even better than what we had initially envisioned.

Heartfelt thanks goes to the team at Apress that helped make this book happen. Jonathan Gennick had faith in our idea, Jill Balzano managed the project efficiently, and Corbin Collins helped edit and polish the prose that helped us create a professional product in the end.

A special thank you to all the Always On experts at Microsoft, who shared their knowledge and helped answer our questions and clarify our doubts. Throughout the year, there have been many people that have influenced me greatly, generally without knowing just how much I was influenced by them. Thanks to all of you and what you have done for me.

Last, but not least, I thank my wife, Ajita, and my son, Reyansh. Without your support, I would not have been able to participate in this book. I would also like to thank my parents for providing me the support, love, and education to be successful in life.

PART I

Getting Started

PART 1

Getting Started

■ ■ ■

CHAPTER 1

High Availability and Disaster Recovery Concepts

In a perfect world, data will always remain available no matter what. But in the real world, we know that there can be multiple problems that can cause data to become unavailable.

For example, hospitals depend on patient data to be available all the time; otherwise patient care can be affected. Let's say that a surgeon is in the operating room and needs to refer to some of the patient's critical information. If the surgeon is unable to access the patient data in a reasonable amount of time, it could result in the loss of the patient's life. Another example is a 24/7 online retailer such as Amazon.com whose customer-facing website must be up and running at all times. If the customer cannot see the merchandise on the website or cannot place an order, the website is considered unavailable from the customer's point of view and may cause a loss of sale and revenue.

What Is High Availability?

One of the most important goals for critical business applications is ensuring that the data is highly available. To achieve high availability, you need to formulate a proactive strategy that will mitigate the threats to availability and also minimize the downtime to users.

The main goal of *high availability* (HA) is to minimize and mitigate the impact of downtime to end users and maximize availability. High availability solutions aim to mask the effects of failures (hardware, software) or natural disasters and have the critical data available as soon as possible in the event of a failure or disaster. High availability is about putting together people, processes, and technologies in place before a failure occurs to prevent the failure from affecting the availability of the data. Most often, people and processes are forgotten, and technology is given the most importance. It should be the other way around as most downtimes are caused due to people and process issues. To achieve high availability, you need support from all three pillars: people, process, and technology.

Figure 1-1 shows the three pillars of a high availability solution.

© Uttam Parui and Vivek Sanil 2016

U. Parui and V. Sanil, *Pro SQL Server Always On Availability Groups*, DOI 10.1007/978-1-4842-2071-9_1

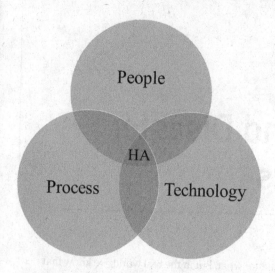

Figure 1-1. *Pillars of a high availability solution*

It is very important to have people with the right skill set, roles, responsibilities, and leadership in place. Processes play a very important role, too. Processes should be documented, followed, have clear ownership, and be practiced and updated as the business application and workload changes with time. Technology needs to be able to meet the business goals for achieving high availability, be easy to deploy, and supported and maintained.

Calculating Availability

Availability is usually expressed as a percentage of uptime in a given year and is calculated as the following:

$$Availability = \frac{Actual\ uptime}{Expected\ uptime} \times 100\%$$

The resulting value is expressed by the *number of 9's* that the solution provides. For example, let's say that the total downtime in a given year (365 days x 24 hours = 8760 hours) for a particular high available SQL Server application is one hour. Then, let's calculate the following:

$$Availability = \frac{8760 - 1}{8760} \times 100\% = 99.9\%\ or\ three\ nines$$

Table 1-1 shows the translation from a given availability percentage to the corresponding time a system would be unavailable.

Table 1-1. *Availability Percentage*

Availability Percentage	Number of 9's	Maximum Annual Downtime
90%	1	36 days, 12 hours
99%	2	3 days, 15 hours
99.9%	3	8 hours, 45 minutes
99.99%	4	52 minutes, 32 seconds
99.999%	5	5 minutes, 15 seconds
99.9999%	6	31.5 seconds
99.99999%	7	3.15 seconds

■ **Note**   As the requirement for the number of 9's or uptime increases, the cost of the system increases, and vice versa. In order to achieve a maximum annual downtime of 5 minutes, 15 seconds (i.e., 5 nines) or 31.5 seconds (i.e., 6 nines), you need to eliminate all single points of failures and allow online replacement of all production-related resources.

We have seen customers interpreting availability in many different ways. For example, for some applications, scheduled downtime may not affect the end users. For such applications, customers exclude the scheduled downtime from the availability calculations. By doing this, they claim to have very high availability that may seem to give an impression of continuous availability, which in reality is rare and very costly.

Another example is a scenario where the SQL Server may be up and running for all the days in a year but the end users could not access the data for 5 hours due to a network outage. In this scenario, the SQL Server is up but the services are not available for 5 hours due to the network outage. The database administrators (DBAs) may claim 100% uptime. However, using the above formula for calculating availability, the application will be 99.9% available, or 3 nines.

Causes of Downtime

Every minute of downtime affects the business either directly (such as loss in sales, revenue, decreased productivity) or indirectly (loss of goodwill). Figure 1-2 shows some common causes of downtime.

Figure 1-2. *Common causes of downtime*

There are mainly two types of downtime:

- Planned downtime
- Unplanned downtime

Planned downtime, also referred to as planned maintenance, is a duration of time that is planned in advance for activities such as these:

- Maintenance,
- Upgrades (software, hardware),
- Patching service packs or hotfix (cumulative or security updates).

Planned downtime typically does not cause data loss but can make the data unavailable from the users unless preventive steps are taken in advance to minimize the effects of the downtime. *Unplanned downtime,* also referred to as an unplanned outage, is an event that you cannot predict in advance:

- Datacenter failure caused by natural disasters, fire loss, or power loss, to name a few;
- Server failure due to software or hardware failures;
- Storage subsystem failure;
- Human error (such as dropping a table by mistake or shutting down the server).

Unplanned downtime not only will make the data unavailable but in many cases may also cause data loss. In most cases, data loss can be prevented or minimized by investing in planning for such events in advance.

What Is Disaster Recovery?

Disaster recovery is not the same as high availability although the terms are often mistakenly interchanged. Earlier in this chapter, we discussed that high availability is about putting together people, processes, and technologies in place *before* a failure occurs to prevent the failure from affecting the availability of the data. *Disaster recovery* is about using people, processes, and technologies to recover any lost data and make it available again after a failure occurs. Figure 1-3 shows some common causes of natural disasters such as fire, storms, tornadoes, and man-made disasters like bugs, failed changed implementations, spills, and terrorism, to name a few.

Figure 1-3. *Common causes of disaster*

Many customers use high availability and disaster recovery interchangeably because it is possible to have a solution that provides both high availability and disaster recovery. However, it is not necessary that if a solution provides high availability, it will also provide disaster recovery and vice versa. In fact, it is common to see most of our customers have some form of high availability. However, disaster recovery is mostly on their to-do project list, which is often never implemented and paid attention to until a disaster actually occurs.

Recovery Objectives

Before implementing a disaster recovery plan, it is important to understand what costs that a disaster can incur to the business. For example, say your datacenter is destroyed by a hurricane. How long will it take to recover and return to normal operations? How much data loss can your business accept? To design a disaster recovery plan, you have three main requirements for the business unit:

- *Recovery Time Objective* (RTO). It is the maximum allowable downtime when a failure occurs. In other words, it is the maximum acceptable amount of time by business to restore normal operations after a failure. After a failure occurs, your primary goal is to restore normal operations to the point that business can continue normally.

- *Recovery Point Objective* (RPO). It is the maximum acceptable level of data loss after a failure occurs. It represents the point in time to which the lost data can be recovered.

7

- *Recovery Level Objective* (RLO). It defines the granularity with which the data needs to be recovered after a failure occurs. For an SQL Server, it will define whether you must be able to recover the whole instance or database or a group of databases or tables.

RTO, RPO, and RLO requirements must be documented in the service-level agreements (SLAs) and should be reviewed periodically and changed as your environment changes. For example, let's say your database size increases from 250 GB to 2.5 TB in a year. This will significantly change the RTO as now you need to work with a database that is 10 times larger as compared to when the original RTO was documented.

Most DBAs are not aware of RTO, RPO, or RLO requirements. Without knowing these requirements, DBAs risk a huge mismatch between what they are able to recover after a failure occurs and what a business needs to effectively survive a failure. Therefore, it is very important to understand the RTO, RPO, and RLO requirements before a disaster occurs and proactively design a disaster recovery plan and test it periodically.

Planning for Disaster Recovery

Disasters are unpredictable and recovering from them can be stressful, time consuming, and expensive – especially for businesses that have not proactively thought about such a situation. On the other hand, businesses that have planned for DR in advance are better able to deal with the disaster and are able to resume normal operations with comparatively minimal or no loss of data, productivity, and revenue.

The main goal of a disaster recovery plan is to recover any lost data and resume normal operations after a failure has occurred. When you are creating a DR plan, management and IT personnel should identify scenarios for different types of disasters that can affect your business, document the steps that are required for each scenario, and agree to follow the plan when a disaster occurs. For DR of your SQL Servers, the steps should be written by your senior-most DBAs in such a way that they can be implemented by your junior-most DBAs or third party with very little help. The plans should not only include detailed technical steps; it should also include what steps each person involved in the recovery needs to implement. This type of documentation is normally referred to as a *run-book* or a *cook-book*. Once the steps are written, it is highly recommended to simulate the disasters and test the steps to ensure it will work when you have a real disaster.

■ **Note** To ensure that the DR plans are up to date; complete; and can meet your RPO, RTO, and RLO requirements, they should be periodically tested and updated (at least once every six months). DR plans should be practiced by the same people who will be involved in the recovery process should a disaster occur.

Summary

High availability and disaster recovery solutions differ from each other but are often erroneously interchanged. While HA solution is about preventing a failure from affecting the availability of data, DR solution is about recovery from a failure and resuming high availability of data. Most customers spend their time and resources in prevention and have some form of HA solution but only 50% of them have a DR plan. Out of the 50%, only half have ever tested their DR plans, which is equivalent to not having one at all. While prevention is important, it is equally important to have a solid DR plan that you can follow to recover with minimal loss of data, productivity, and revenue should a real disaster occur.

In the next chapter, we will discuss the common SQL Server solutions that are available to build end-to-end HA and DR solutions for your mission-critical applications.

CHAPTER 2

■ ■ ■

Introduction to Always On

In today's fast evolving business and commerce landscape, businesses need to be up all the time. Downtime equates to revenue loss, and businesses are looking for ways to increase availability and improve their disaster recovery capability. The IT professional architecting solutions and the IT professional supporting such solutions are increasingly feeling the heat from businesses to implement cutting-edge technologies to achieve their uptime goals.

A recent incident, where the New York Stock Exchange (NYSE) was shut down, caused huge trading losses as trades could not be made for almost four hours. This incident highlights the importance of high availability and the impact of downtime on businesses. There are numerous such incidents happening every day and the IT professionals have to use all the options they have in their arsenal to mitigate such risks. To cater to this need, Microsoft introduced and provided a new high availability and disaster recovery solution called Always On in SQL Server 2012. This feature was further enhanced in SQL Server 2014 and then in SQL Server 2016.

Common Solutions before Always On

SQL Server provides several options for creating high availability and/or disaster recovery for a server or database. Let's assume you are in the market to buy new phones for yourself and your family. You go to the electronics shop nearest to your home and pick up the cheapest smartphone they have to offer. This shop provides great deals but they do not have a return policy. You go back home happy with your purchase. The next day, you are surfing the Internet and you find that the biggest online retailer had a buy one, get one free deal going on for the same phone. If only you had done your research and looked at all your options before heading out to the electronics store, you could have bought two phones for the price of one. Similarly, investing into a particular HA/DR solution without exploring all the alternatives that the product (SQL Server in this case) has to offer can cause buyer's remorse and limit you from meeting your SLA goals.

Let's take a brief look at the high availability and disaster recovery solutions that were available before Always On was released (i.e., before SQL Server 2012). The options we discuss in this chapter are still available in SQL Server 2016.

Failover Cluster Instances (FCI)

Failover Cluster Instance (FCI) is a single instance of SQL Server that is installed across *Windows Server Failover Clustering* (WSFC) nodes. Imagine you are traveling on an airplane and during the flight, the pilot starts feeling dizzy. The co-pilot takes over immediately without any disruption to the service, and the passengers won't even notice that someone else is now flying the plane. The two pilots flying the plane are like two nodes in a cluster. When the main pilot becomes unavailable the co-pilot takes over without any disruption to the service. Similarly, when one node becomes unavailable the other takes over the services.

© Uttam Parui and Vivek Sanil 2016
U. Parui and V. Sanil, *Pro SQL Server Always On Availability Groups*, DOI 10.1007/978-1-4842-2071-9_2

FCI can also be stretched across multiple datacenters residing in the same or different subnets. On the network, an FCI appears to be an instance of an SQL Server running on a single computer. The clients connect to a single *virtual network name* (VNN) for the FCI. When FCI fails over from one WSFC node to another, the clients use the same VNN to connect to the SQL Server instance even after a failover. SQL Server data for the instance is stored in the shared storage. On failover the second node connects to the shared storage and presents the data back to the user. There is no data duplication/redundancy within the failover cluster configuration.

Figure 2-1 shows a typical SQL failover cluster setup. The client PCs connect over the public network and the cluster nodes communicate with each other over the private network(optional). You do not need to have two separate networks. Both public connectivity and intracluster communication can occur over one network provided there is redundancy for the network.

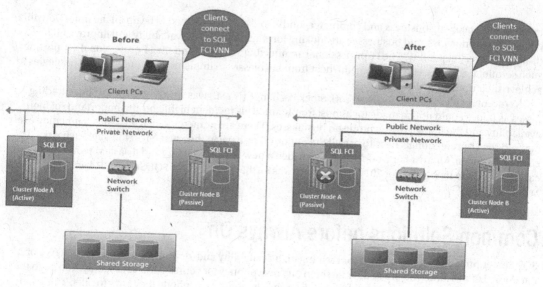

Figure 2-1. *SQL failover cluster diagram*

■ **Note** FCI is now a part of the SQL Server Always On Offering and renamed/rebranded as Always On Failover Cluster instance.

Database Mirroring

FCI provided an instance and node level failover. *Database mirroring* is a solution to increase database availability by supporting almost instantaneous failover at the database level. As the name suggests, a mirrored database is an exact copy of the database that has been mirrored. Objects outside the database are not copied to the mirror server as part of the database mirroring synchronization process. Database mirroring can be used to maintain a single standby database, or mirror database, for a corresponding production database that is referred to as the principal database. For automatic failover capability, a witness server can be added to the configuration along with synchronous mirroring. Both synchronous and asynchronous mirroring can be set up within the same datacenter or across datacenters.

Figure 2-2 shows a typical database mirroring setup. Asynchronous mirroring is typically set up between two SQL Server instances in separate datacenters for disaster recovery purposes. And synchronous mirroring is typically set up between two SQL Server instances in the same datacenter for high availability. Witness provides the automatic failover capability.

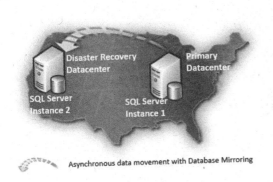
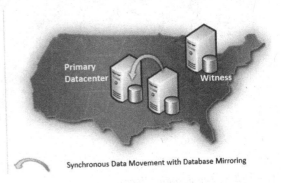

Figure 2-2. Database mirroring diagram

■ **Note**   Database mirroring feature is deprecated and will be removed in a future version of SQL Server. Avoid using this feature in new development work, and plan to modify applications that currently use this feature. It is recommended that you use Always On Availability Groups instead.

Log Shipping

Similar to database mirroring, *log shipping* operates at the database level. You can use log shipping to maintain one or more warm standby databases (referred to as secondary databases) for a single production database that is referred to as the primary database.

Imagine you are driving a car and suddenly you realize that you have a flat tire. You are in luck — you have a spare tire in the trunk. You pull over and replace the flat tire with the spare one. Log shipping standby databases are like spare tires. If the primary database becomes unavailable for some reason, you can failover to your secondary database. If the secondary database needs to be kept up to date using transaction log backups, then the following things need to happen:

- Transaction log backups need to happen periodically on the primary database (recovery model needs to set to full recovery model on the primary database for transaction log backups to be allowed).

- The transaction log backups need to be copied over to the secondary.

- The transaction log backups need to be restored on to the secondary database.

In log shipping, the backup, copy, and restore activities are managed through SQL Server agent jobs that are created when log shipping is configured. In newer cars nowadays, sensors notify the driver if the tire air pressure drops below a certain limit. Similarly, in log shipping, a monitor server does the job of the sensors by monitoring the health of the backup, copy, and restore jobs. And if they are not healthy, they can be configured to raise alerts and notify administrators.

Figure 2-3 shows a typical log shipping setup. Log shipping is typically set up between multiple SQL instances in separate datacenters for disaster recovery purposes.

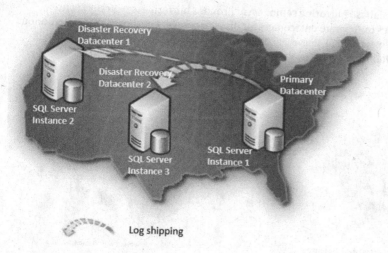

Log shipping

Figure 2-3. *Log shipping diagram*

Replication

Replication is like a magazine subscription. People subscribe to magazines (articles) and get the latest copy weekly, biweekly, or monthly (depending on the frequency that they choose). The magazines are distributed by agents. Similarly, in SQL Server, the objects being replicated are called articles, and articles make up a publication. The SQL Server instance hosting the publication is called the publisher. SQL Server or non-SQL Server targets requiring data updates from the publisher and the publication are called the subscribers. The multiple agents (snapshot, log reader, distribution agents) within SQL Server do the job of replicating the data from the publisher to the subscriber. The magazine example is just to provide a simple overview of replication.

There is a lot more to replication. There are different types of replication that implement different methods of moving data from the publisher to the subscriber and in some cases getting the changes from the subscriber back to the publisher. In replication, you do not have to necessarily replicate the entire database. You can choose the tables/objects that you want to replicate from within a database. When replication was first introduced, it was with the intention to provide a read/write copy for reporting purposes, where the reporting applications would connect to the copy of the production data on the subscriber and not have to go against the production database itself. Replication has evolved over the years and new types have been added for scalability and high availability. Since it's an additional copy of the data, it can be leveraged for high availability/disaster recovery in certain scenarios.

- Snapshot replication

  Snapshot replication is the most basic type of replication. As the name suggests, it distributes data exactly as it appears at a specific point in time (snapshot). Changes to data are not monitored; hence when data synchronization happens, a snapshot of the entire publication is generated and sent to subscribers. Snapshot replication is ideal if the data changes infrequently and if you are replicating small volumes of data or if a large volume of changes occurs over a short period of time.

- Transactional replication

    This is the most common type of replication used by our customers. *Transactional replication* typically starts with a snapshot of the publication database objects and data. Subsequent data changes at the publisher are monitored and delivered to the subscriber as they happen. Basically, incremental changes are propagated to subscribers as they occur. This replication type is ideal, where the application requires low latency between the time that changes are made at the publisher and when the changes arrive at the subscriber. This replication type is also useful in the case where the publisher has a very high volume of insert, update, and delete activity.

- Merge replication

    Just like transactional replication, *merge replication* typically starts with a snapshot of the publication database objects and data. However, in this case, the data changes to both the publisher and the subscriber are monitored with the help of triggers. The changes from the publisher are delivered to the subscriber and vice versa. Conflicts can occur; however it has the ability to detect and resolve them. It allows multiple subscribers to update the same data at various times and propagate those changes to the publisher and to other subscribers.

- Peer-to-Peer replication

    Out of all the different replication types, *Peer-to-Peer*(P2P) *replication* is the most likely to be used for high availability purposes. P2P replication was built on transactional replication. It provides a scale-out and high availability solution by maintaining copies of data across multiple server instances, also referred to as nodes. As data is maintained across the nodes in near real time, P2P replication provides data redundancy, which increases the availability of data.

Figure 2-4 shows a typical peer-to-peer replication setup. Read/write data is replicated across multiple server instances in geographically separate locations.

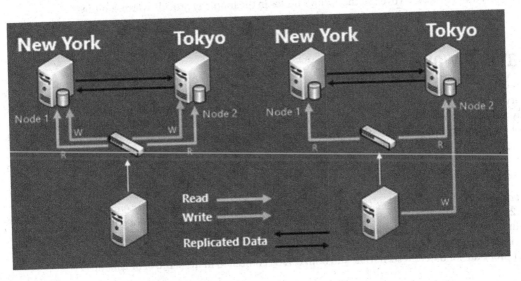

Figure 2-4. Peer-to-Peer replication diagram

During the holiday season, I was shopping around for a TV. My simple expectation was a high definition display and amazing surround sound. Unfortunately, I could not find one TV that had both. Every TV had either great display or great sound. So I settled for a cheaper TV and also got a sound bar. The combination of TV and sound bar was my solution for the TV viewing experience that I was looking for. Similarly, many times one high availability/disaster recovery solution may not meet your business needs. In such situations, you can use more than one solution.

For example, a very common high availability and disaster recovery solution that organizations use is to use Failover Cluster Instances (FCIs) to protect SQL Server instances within each datacenter, combined with asynchronous database mirroring, to provide disaster recovery capabilities for mission-critical databases. Another common high availability and disaster recovery solution that organizations incorporate (when they need more than one secondary datacenter or if they do not have shared storage) is database mirroring with a witness within the primary datacenter combined with log shipping to move data to multiple locations.

Limitations and Concerns

The solutions discussed so far achieve high availability and disaster recovery. However, these solutions are fragmented and have some limitations:

- Database mirroring does not allow multiple secondaries.

- Database mirroring solution is a one-to-one mapping, which means multiple databases cannot fail over as a group.

- Log shipping might lose data and does not fail over automatically.

- From a cost perspective, investments are not used to their full potential because the passive servers mostly run idle.

- Offloading of reporting and maintenance tasks from the primary server is not easy.

- SAN is a single point of failure in failover clustering.

- Peer-to-peer transactional replication does not automatically detect a failure or automatically fail over, so the various nodes in the topology provide warm standby copies of the published data.

What Is Always On?

Always On is a collection of high availability and disaster recovery functionality with the goal to minimize recovery point objective (RPO) and recovery time objective (RTO) further below the times that can be already achieved with the above solutions. *Always On* was introduced in SQL Server 2012 and addresses most of the above-mentioned limitations. There are two solutions included under the Always On umbrella:

1. Availability Groups

2. Failover Cluster Instances

Availability groups were first introduced in SQL Server 2012 and then got further enhanced in SQL Server 2014 and 2016. Failover Cluster Instances were the existing FCI feature that got enhanced when it got rolled under the Always On umbrella. For the purpose of this book, we will be focusing on availability groups and diving deep into the technology in the later chapters. Each solution has different characteristics, making them appropriate for different scenarios, and both can be combined in the same deployment.

You can consider Always On Availability Groups as a greatly enhanced version of database mirroring. Availability groups address most of the limitations that database mirroring had and enhances the high availability and disaster recovery capability. It does this by providing an integrated set of options, including automatic and manual failover of a *group of databases*, multiple secondaries, active secondaries, fast application failover, and automatic page repair.

Always On Failover Cluster Instances enhance the existing SQL Server failover clustering and support multi-subnet clustering, which helps enable cross-datacenter failover of SQL Server instances. Fast and predictable *instance* failover is another key benefit, which helps ensure fast application recovery. Table 2-1 below provides a quick summary of the differences between the two Always On solutions.

Table 2-1. *Always On Solutions*

Failover Cluster Instances (FCI)	Availability Group (AG)
Enhanced under Always On	Introduced in SQL 2012
Server Failover	Multi-database failover
Shared Storage	Direct attached storage
Passive Secondary Nodes	Active Secondary Replicas
Failover takes 30s to a couple of minutes (server restart)	Failover takes less than 30s (secondary replicas are online)
Both solutions require Windows Server Failover Cluster	

Always On Availability Groups have been enhanced quite a bit since they were first introduced in SQL Server 2012. In SQL Server 2012 it supported up to five availability replicas per availability group (one primary and up to four secondary replicas). We will be discussing the concepts and the specifics in detail in later chapters. Let's take a look at some of the enhancements in the various versions over the years.

SQL Server 2014

- Number of secondaries increased to eight replicas;
- Increased availability for readable secondaries through reduction in the events that caused the readable secondaries to be unavailable;
- New wizard added for adding an Azure replica;
- Enhanced diagnostics through new functions like "is_primary_replica" and new DMVs like "sys.dm_io_cluster_valid_path_names";
- Simplified dashboard with addition of the "add/remove column" button for the hidden columns. This made DBAs click on it and discover all those hidden columns that they didn't know existed before.

SQL Server 2016

- Improvement in log transport performance
- Improvement in database level failover trigger
- Load balancing in readable secondaries

- Group-managed service account support

- Microsoft Distributed Transaction Coordinator (MSDTC) support

- More than two automatic failover targets

- Basic Availability Group (BAG) in Standard Edition

- SQL Server 2016 and Windows Server 2016 – Better together

- Domain-Independent Availability Groups

- Automatic Seeding

- Distributed Availability Groups

- Support for encrypted databases

- Support for SSIS Catalog

- Updatable columnstore index support on secondary replica

Summary

As you can see, SQL Server offers a gamut of HA/DR solutions. Understanding their benefits and limitations will equip you with making the right decision when it comes to designing your enterprise SQL Server environment for HA/DR. Of these solutions, we will focus on availability groups for the remainder of this book. Availability groups offer both HA and DR and so much more. A lot of improvements were made in SQL Server 2016. Don't worry if you are not familiar with some of the terms used in this chapter; it's okay. This chapter is just to provide an overview on Always On. We will be looking at the terms, terminology, concepts, and implementation specifics in detail in the upcoming chapters. In the next chapter, we will take a look at the availability group concepts and common topologies.

PART II

Planning Always On Availability Groups

CHAPTER 3

■ ■ ■

Concepts and Common Topologies

Always On Availability Groups (AGs) provide the best in class and cost-effective, high availability (HA) and disaster recovery (DR) solutions for on-premises and cloud applications. Availability group solutions are significantly improved as compared to previous SQL Server solutions like database mirroring and log shipping. It provides an integrated set of options, including automatic and manual failover of a group of databases, multiple secondaries, active secondaries, fast application failover, and automatic page repair.

Availability Group Concepts

The basic concept of an availability group solution is simple. An availability group solution supports a set of primary user databases and one to eight sets of corresponding secondary user databases. The secondary databases are kept up to date with the primary databases by transferring transaction log blocks from each primary database to every secondary database either synchronously or asynchronously over the network. Figure 3-1 shows a typical availability group solution.

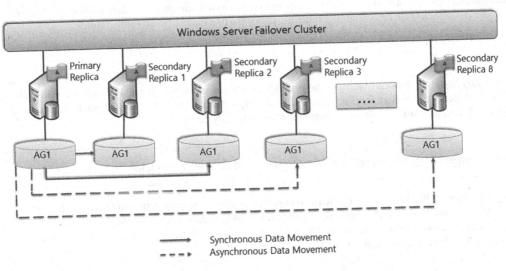

Figure 3-1. Typical availability group solution

As we are building the foundation for Always On Availability Group solutions, in this chapter we want to define the terms that we will be using many times in the next chapters.

© Uttam Parui and Vivek Sanil 2016
U. Parui and V. Sanil, *Pro SQL Server Always On Availability Groups*, DOI 10.1007/978-1-4842-2071-9_3

Availability Group and Replicas

An *availability group* (AG) is a container for a set of discrete user databases known as *availability databases* that fail over together as a group. The *unit of failover* is the availability group. Any object that resides outside the availability databases like logins, jobs, and linked servers do not fail over with the availability group.

Each availability group defines a set of two or more failover partners known as *availability replicas*. An availability replica hosts a copy of the availability databases.

■ **Note** There is *no enforced limit* on the maximum number of availability groups (AGs) or availability databases. Microsoft has extensively tested with 10 AGs and 100 databases per physical replica. The maximum number depends on your specific environment (hardware, workload, etc.), and you need to thoroughly test the solution in a test environment before deploying it in the production environment.

For a given availability group, the availability replicas must be hosted by separate instances of SQL Server running on different nodes of the same Windows Server Failover Cluster (WSFC). Availability groups rely on Windows Server Failover Cluster for health monitoring, failover coordination, and server connectivity. Each SQL Server instance can be used for many availability groups, but each availability group can host only one copy of a user database on an SQL Server instance.

■ **Note** Even though availability groups require Windows Server Failover Cluster, it does not require the SQL Server instance to be clustered nor does it require shared disks. SQL Server instance can be stand-alone or clustered. Most availability group solutions use stand-alone SQL Server instances and local hard disks.

An availability group is a WSFC role, previously referred to as a resource group. It defines a set of two or more failover partners known as availability replicas. There are two types of availability replicas:

- Primary replica

- Secondary replica

Primary replica is the replica that hosts the primary databases and makes them available for read-write connections to clients. *Secondary replica* is the replica that maintains a secondary copy of each primary database and serves as a potential failover target for the availability group.

■ **Note** An availability group supports one primary replica and up to eight secondary replicas.

The secondary replica is an active replica as it supports read-only access to the secondary databases for your reporting workload. Also, it allows performing backups and maintenance tasks such as database integrity checks on the secondary database without impacting the production workload on the primary replica. Figure 3-2 shows the availability replicas.

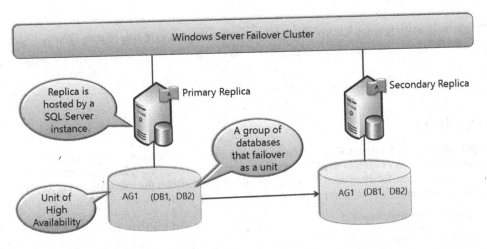

Figure 3-2. *Availability replicas*

Each of the readable secondary replicas can be configured using one of the following three options:

- *Yes* – The secondary replica allows all connections with read-only workload.

- *No* – The secondary replica denies all connections. This is the default option.

- *Read-intent only* – The secondary replica allows connections to be made from applications that explicitly specify the *'ApplicationIntent=ReadOnly'* connection string option.

Availability Group Listener

An *availability group listener* is similar to the virtual network name (VNN) and virtual IP (VIP) address(es) created in an SQL Server failover clustering instance (FCI). An availability group listener allows the clients to connect to an availability group database in a primary or secondary replica without needing to know the physical name of the SQL Server instance that it is connecting to. This means that the clients and applications only need to know about one entry point.

■ **Note**   An availability group listener is dedicated to a single availability group. Different availability groups cannot share the same listener.

Availability group listener consists of a Domain Name System (DNS) listener name, listener port number, and one or more IP addresses. Availability group listeners rely on the Windows Server Failover Cluster (WSFC) to redirect the client connections in the event of availability group failures. When you create an availability group listener, it becomes a cluster resource with an associated VNN, VIP address(es), and availability group dependency.

When a primary replica goes offline and a secondary replica takes the role of the primary replica, the availability group listener enables the clients to connect to the new primary replica. Also if read-only routing is configured on the readable secondary replicas, read-intent client connections to the primary replica are automatically redirected to the readable secondary replica. We will discuss read-only routing and readable secondary replicas in detail in the chapter about readable secondary.

■ **Note**   Although an availability group listener allows failover redirection and read-only routing, client connections are not required to use them. They can directly connect to the SQL Server instance without using the listener.

Availability Mode

The primary replica also sends the transaction log blocks for each primary database to every secondary database. The *availability mode* of each availability replica determines whether the primary replica waits to commit the transactions on the database until the secondary replica has written the transactions log record to disk. Availability groups have two availability modes:

- Synchronous-commit mode

- Asynchronous-commit mode

In *synchronous-commit mode*, the primary replica waits to send the transaction confirmation to the clients until the secondary replica writes the transaction log records to disk. This mode allows zero data loss at the cost of increased transaction latency. This mode is recommended when business requirements are to have zero data loss and high availability.

In *asynchronous-commit mode*, the primary replica does not wait for the secondary replica to write the transaction log records to disk. The primary replica sends the transaction confirmation to the clients as soon as the transaction log blocks are persisted on the primary database. In this mode, the transaction latency is reduced as compared to synchronous-commit mode, but since the transaction log blocks may arrive later, it does not guarantee zero data loss. Asynchronous-commit mode is recommended for disaster recovery solution where the availability replicas are separated by considerable distances. We will discuss the data synchronization workings in detail in chapter on data synchronization internals.

■ **Note**   Availability groups support one primary replica and up to eight secondary replicas. All the replicas can run under asynchronous-commit mode, or up to three of them can run under synchronous-commit mode.

Failover and Failover Modes

An availability group *failover* is a process during which the failover target takes over the primary role, recovers the databases, and brings them online as the new primary databases. When the former primary is available, it takes over the secondary role and its databases become the secondary database. The failover process may be triggered by the DBA for administrative purposes or it could occur automatically if the primary replica is not healthy.

The type of failover that the availability replicas supports depends on the availability mode and failover mode. There are two types of failover modes:

- Automatic

- Manual

Synchronous-commit replicas support both automatic and manual failover modes. Asynchronous-commit replicas only support manual failover mode.

There are three types of failover:

- Automatic failover (without data loss),
- Planned manual failover (without data loss), and
- Forced manual failover (with possible data loss).

Automatic failover (without data loss) occurs on the loss of the primary replica. Automatic failover causes a synchronized secondary replica to take over the primary replica role with guaranteed data protection.

■ **Note**   Starting with SQL Server 2016, automatic failover replicas have been increased from two replicas to three replicas. This new enhancement increases the resiliency and scale of the availability groups solution.

Automatic failover is supported only when the below conditions are satisfied:

1. Both the primary and secondary replicas are running under synchronous-commit mode with the failover mode set to automatic.

2. Each secondary database is synchronized with its corresponding primary database.

3. Windows Server Failover Clustering (WSFC) has quorum.

4. A failure condition defined by your flexible failover policy of the availability group are met.

Do not worry if you are not familiar with WSFC quorum or flexible failover policy – we will be discussing them in detail in Chapters 5 and 9, respectively. Table 3-1 shows the conditions required for automatic failover (without data loss).

Table 3-1. Automatic failover (without data loss)

Replica Property	Primary Availability Replica	Secondary Availability Replica
Failover Mode	Automatic	Automatic
Availability Mode	Synchronous-commit	Synchronous-commit
Synchronization State	Synchronized	Synchronized

Availability group health monitoring in SQL Server 2012 and 2014 only monitored the health of the primary SQL Server instance. This means that if the primary SQL Server instance is online and healthy but an availability database goes offline or becomes corrupt, automatic failover will not be triggered.

■ **Note**   Starting from SQL Server 2016, an availability group allows us to optionally configure the health monitoring to also consider the health of the availability databases. This means that now an automatic failover can be triggered when an availability database goes offline or becomes corrupt.

Planned manual failover (without data loss) occurs when an administrator manually initiates the failover to cause a synchronized secondary replica to take over the primary replica role with guaranteed data protection. Manual failover is supported only when the below conditions are satisfied:

1. Both the primary and secondary replicas are running under synchronous-commit mode.

2. Each secondary database is synchronized with its corresponding primary database.

3. Windows Server Failover Clustering (WSFC) has a quorum.

Table 3-2 shows the conditions required for planned manual failover (without data loss).

Table 3-2. *Planned manual failover (without data loss)*

Replica Property	Primary Availability Replica	Secondary Availability Replica
Failover Mode	Automatic/Manual	Automatic/Manual
Availability Mode	Synchronous-commit	Synchronous-commit
Synchronization State	Synchronized	Synchronized

Forced manual failover (with possible data loss) is the only type of failover that an administrator can initiate when the primary replica is lost and the secondary replica is not failover ready or no secondary replica is synchronized. This is the only form of failover supported by asynchronous-commit replicas because they are never synchronized. Forcing failover requires that the WSFC cluster has quorum. Forced manual failover is also referred to as *forced failover*. Table 3-3 shows the conditions required for forced manual failover (with possible data loss).

Table 3-3. *Forced manual failover (with possible data loss)*

Replica Property	Primary Availability Replica	Secondary Availability Replica
Failover Mode	Automatic/Manual	Automatic/Manual
Availability Mode	Synchronous or Asynchronous-commit	Synchronous or Asynchronous-commit
Synchronization State	Synchronized or Synchronizing	Synchronizing

■ **Note** If you issue a forced failover on a synchronized secondary replica, all secondary databases are suspended. You need to manually resume each suspended database individually on all secondary replicas.

Forced manual failover is a disaster recovery option that allows an administrator to use a secondary replica as a warm standby replica after a failure occurs. As there is a potential for data loss, the forced manual failover option should be used with caution. The amount of data loss depends on whether any transaction log blocks were not sent to the secondary replica before the failure. Table 3-4 shows the possibility of data loss for a particular database on the replica after a forced manual failover.

Table 3-4. Possibility of data loss after forced manual failover

Availability mode of Secondary Replica	Database Synchronization State	Is data loss possible?
Synchronous-commit	Synchronized	No
Synchronous-commit	Synchronizing	Yes
Asynchronous-commit	Synchronizing	Yes

Common Topologies

Now that we have defined the most common terms, let's discuss the commonly used Always On Availability Groups topologies and their advantages and limitations. The most common topologies that we see in the field are the following:

- Stand-alone to Stand-alone
- SQL Failover Clustered Instance (FCI) to Stand-alone and vice versa
- SQL FCI to SQL FCI
- Extend on-premises Always On Availability Groups to Microsoft Azure
- Always On Availability Groups in Azure Virtual Machines (VMs)
- Distributed Availability Groups (introduced in SQL Server 2016)

Stand-alone to Stand-alone

This is the most commonly used Always On Availability Groups topology. In fact, more than 90% of the Always On Availability Groups solutions that we see in the field use this topology. In this topology, we have a two or more node Windows Server Failover Clusters (WSFCs) with stand-alone instances of SQL Server running on each cluster node. Figure 3-3 shows the simplest form of an Always On Availability Groups solution implementation. The figure shows a two-node WSFC with two stand-alone instances of SQL Server each running on separate nodes of the cluster.

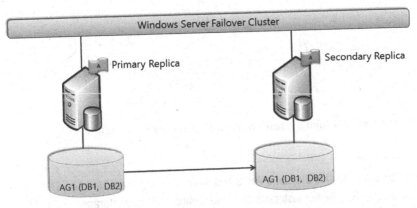

Figure 3-3. Stand-alone to Stand-alone AG Topology using two-node WSFC

■ **Note** Since the SQL Server instances are stand-alone, there is no shared storage required in this topology. Each stand-alone SQL Server instance has its own copy of the data stored in local storage.

In the simplest form, the above topology will have both the cluster nodes in the same datacenter and the replicas running under synchronous-commit mode with the failover mode set to automatic. With this configuration, you will achieve a highly available solution with automatic failover (without data loss). You also have disaster recovery as there are two sets of databases (one on each node). Additionally, you can configure the secondary replica as readable and offload the reporting workload to the secondary replica without impacting the primary workload running on the primary replica.

The disadvantage to this configuration is that since both the nodes are in the same datacenter, there is no datacenter level disaster recovery available. As Availability Groups support one primary replica and up to eight secondary replicas, you can easily add more replicas and configure them to achieve the HA and DR business requirements for your applications. One popular configuration to achieve high availability and datacenter level disaster recovery is to add a third node in a disaster recovery datacenter. Figure 3-4 shows a similar topology. The replicas (primary replica and secondary replica 1) in the primary datacenter are running under synchronous-commit mode with automatic failover to provide high availability. The third replica (secondary replica 2) is in a disaster recovery datacenter and is running under asynchronous-commit mode to provide datacenter level disaster recovery. Also, since the third replica is running under asynchronous-commit mode, the performance of the Availability Groups solution will not be affected by the network latency between the two datacenters.

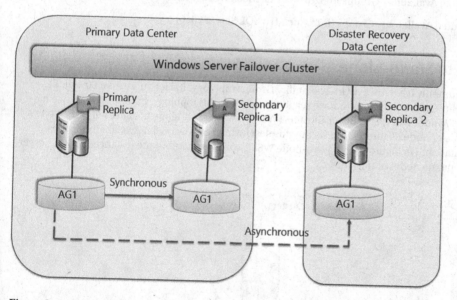

Figure 3-4. Stand-alone to Stand-alone AG Topology using three-node WSFC for HA and DR

■ **Note** All the three nodes are participating in the same WSFC and do not use any shared storage. This is a non-shared solution as the stand-alone SQL Server instances store the databases in local storage.

If your budget does not allow adding a third replica but you still need to provide datacenter level disaster recovery, then you can place the second replica in the disaster recovery datacenter. In this configuration, you will need to set the availability mode appropriately based on the network latency between the two datacenters. For example, you may have to set the availability mode to asynchronous-commit mode when the datacenters are far apart and network latency is a problem.

As you can imagine, there are a lot of possibilities in the stand-alone to stand-alone topology to deploy a complete HA and DR solution based on your business requirements.

SQL Failover Clustered Instance (FCI) to Stand-alone and Vice Versa

Always On Availability Groups solutions are not limited to using stand-alone SQL Server instances. SQL Server Failover Clustering Instance (SQL FCI) for the primary or the secondary replica is also supported. Figure 3-5 shows a two-node SQL FCI configured as a primary replica of an availability group with a stand-alone SQL Server secondary replica. Typically, the SQL FCI is placed in the primary datacenter to provide high availability and the stand-alone SQL Server replica is placed in another datacenter for disaster recovery purposes.

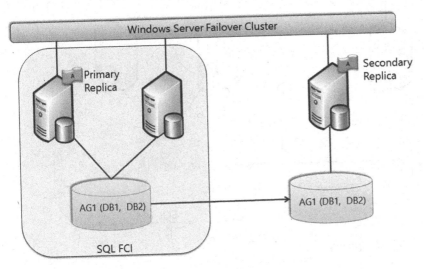

Figure 3-5. SQL FCI to Stand-alone AG Topology

There are a couple of things that you need to know if you use SQL FCI in an AG topology.

1. The SQL FCI and stand-alone SQL Server are all members of the *same* Windows Server Failover Cluster.

2. Always On Availability Groups do not support automatic failovers to and from an SQL FCI. SQL Server enforces this behavior by disabling the option for automatic failover for any replica that is an SQL FCI. You can still have automatic failover from one node to another node within the SQL FCI, but the availability replica on the FCI can only manually fail over to or from another replica in the availability group. Typically, this is not a problem as you do not want automatic failover from the primary datacenter to the disaster recovery datacenter.

3. SQL FCI can host only one replica for a given availability group across all its cluster nodes. When an availability replica is running the SQL FCI, the possible owners list for the AG will contain only the active SQL FCI node.

4. SQL FCI replica uses a shared storage solution. The shared storage solution is shared only by the nodes within the SQL FCI and not between the availability group replicas.

SQL FCI to SQL FCI

In this topology, both the primary replica and the secondary replicas are SQL Server FCIs. Figure 3-6 shows SQL FCIs used as primary and secondary replicas in primary and secondary datacenters, respectively, to provide an HA and DR solution.

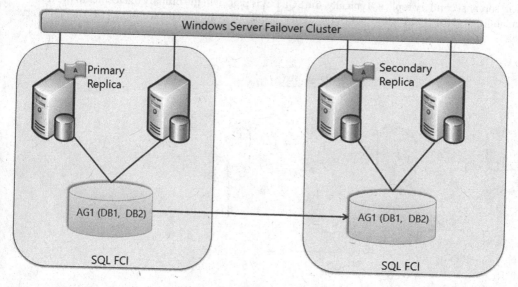

Figure 3-6. *SQL FCI to SQL FCI AG Topology*

As mentioned earlier, Always On Availability Groups do not support automatic failovers to and from an SQL FCI. So in this topology, similar to the previous topology, automatic failover will only be that of the SQL FCI from one node to another within the SQL FCI.

Although Always On Availability Groups support SQL FCIs as availability replicas, it is not very commonly used by our customers. Most customers are able to meet all their high availability and disaster recovery requirements using the stand-alone to stand-alone availability group topology. We have seen this topology used by customers who already had an SQL FCI and wanted to extend the environment to another datacenter using a secondary replica purely for disaster recovery scenarios.

Extend On-Premises Always On Availability Groups to Microsoft Azure

What if one of the business requirements is to achieve cross-site disaster recovery but the IT department does not have a cross-site datacenter? Microsoft Azure Virtual Machines (VMs) can help us achieve cross-site disaster recovery by extending our on-premises Always On Availability Groups to Azure. Figure 3-7 shows two replicas in a stand-alone to stand-alone AG on-premises topology and a third replica in Microsoft Azure making it a *Hybrid IT* high availability and disaster recovery solution. This solution requires a virtual private network (VPN) connection between on-premises network and Microsoft Azure. Also, it requires a *multi-subnet* Windows Server Failover Cluster (WSFC) as all the AG replicas are required to be in the same WSFC.

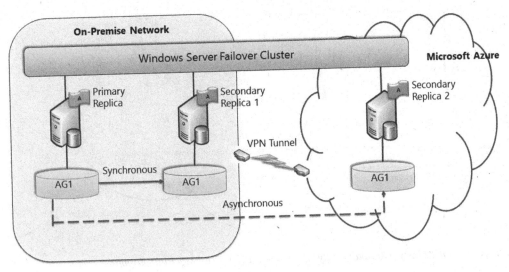

Figure 3-7. *Hybrid IT: Extend on-premises Always On AG to Microsoft Azure Topology*

You can use the built-in 'Add Azure Replica Wizard' in SQL Server Management Studio to extend the on-premises Always On Availability Group solution to include Azure replicas. Below are some benefits that such a hybrid solution provides:

1. Microsoft Azure secondary replica will protect your application from issues impacting your on-premises datacenter.

2. Microsoft Azure provides high availability mechanisms, such as service healing for cloud services and failure recovery detection for the VMs that further improves the availability of your replicas.

3. This solution will in most cases eliminate the need of an expensive disaster recovery (DR) site, which will eliminate costs associated with DR site hardware, maintenance, and operational costs.

4. Also, there is no charge for network traffic going into Microsoft Azure VMs. So, the synchronization traffic from an on-premises primary replica to a Microsoft Azure replica will be free of charge.

Always On Availability Groups in Azure Virtual Machines (VMs)

You can build a high availability (HA) and disaster recovery (DR) solution for your SQL Server databases in Microsoft Azure using Always On Availability Groups. Figure 3-8 shows an Azure-only: HADR solution using Always On Availability Groups.

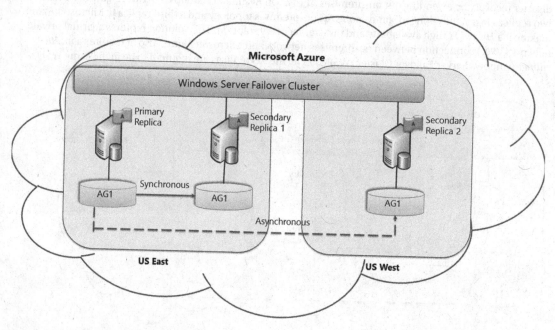

Figure 3-8. Azure-only: Always On Availability Groups in Azure Virtual Machines Topology

To achieve high availability, the primary replica and secondary replica 1 are running in Azure VMs within the same region under synchronous-commit mode. To achieve disaster recovery, the secondary replica 2 is running in a different datacenter in Azure VMs under asynchronous-commit mode. This solution provides cross-region disaster recovery.

■ **Note**   In the Azure Management Portal, there is a new gallery setup for Always On Availability Groups with a Listener. This allows you to configure everything you need for an Always On AG solution automatically.

Distributed Availability Groups

Let's say that you need to implement an HA and DR solution for a mission- critical application using SQL Server 2016 Always On Availability Groups. You need to use the existing two-node Windows Server 2012 R2 failover clusters in your primary and secondary datacenters that are in different domains without making a lot of big changes.

After reviewing the preceding topologies, you may have realized that they all need one single Windows Server Failover Cluster (WSFC). But here one of the requirements is to use the two existing WSFCs. Another requirement is to implement the solution without making a lot of big changes. That means you cannot work with your infrastructure team to make both the datacenters in the same domain. Nor can you upgrade the clusters to Windows Server 2016 and then create a single multi-domain cluster. So how can you accomplish the goal of implementing an HA and DR solution using SQL Server 2016 Always On Availability Groups?

Before discussing the solution, let's consider another scenario. Say you have two geographically dispersed datacenters and there are different applications (App1 and App2) in each datacenter using Always On Availability Groups for high availability. You have been asked to include disaster recovery for the applications in each datacenter by using the other datacenter for disaster recovery.

One of the ways to implement a solution for both the scenarios is by combining Always On Availability Groups with Log Shipping or Replication but you want to use Always On exclusively to make the solution simple to deploy, administer, maintain, and troubleshoot.

SQL Server 2016 introduced a new feature called a *Distributed Availability Group* that will enable you to accomplish both the above scenarios with minimal work. Distributed availability group lets you associate two availability groups residing on different WSFC. Figure 3-9 shows the architecture of a distributed availability group.

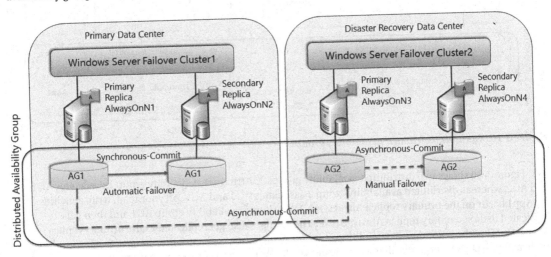

Figure 3-9. Distributed availability group

In Figure 3-9, there are two separate clusters (WSFC1 and WSFC2). WSFC1 is in the primary datacenter and WSFC2 is in the secondary datacenter. Each cluster has its own availability group (AG1 and AG2) with a matching configuration of databases. AG1 and AG2 are associated to each other with a distributed availability group. AG1 is the primary availability group in this figure and AG2 is the secondary availability group. All your read-write activities occur on the primary replica AlwaysOnN1, and then get replicated to its secondary replicas (AlwaysOnN2). The changes are also replicated to the primary replica (AlwaysOnN3) on the secondary availability group AG2 on WSFC2. The primary replica (AlwaysOnN3) replicates those changes to its secondary replicas (AlwaysOnN4).

■ **Note** In a distributed availability group, the secondary availability group (AG2 in Figure 3-9) automatically becomes read-only and read/write activities can occur only on the primary replica of the primary availability group (AG1 in Figure 3-9).

The topology shown in Figure 3-9 can be used to implement the solution for scenario 1 discussed in this section. To implement a solution for scenario 2, you can create distributed availability groups for each application (App1 and App2) as shown in Figure 3-10.

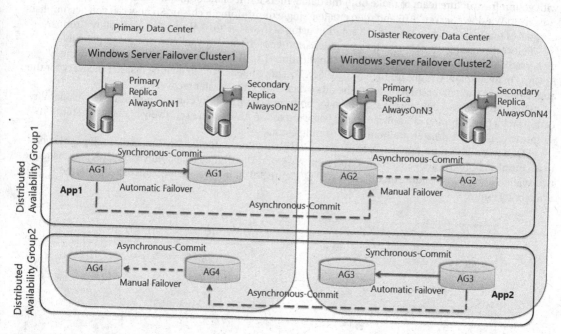

Figure 3-10. *Multiple distributed availability groups*

Figure 3-10 shows two distributed availability groups. Distributed availability group 1 associates AG1 and AG2, whereas distributed availability group 2 associates AG3 and AG4. All your read/write activities for App1 occur on the primary replica AlwaysOnN1 of primary availability group AG1 and then gets replicated to its secondary replica AlwaysOnN2. The changes also get replicated to the primary replica AlwaysOnN3 of the secondary availability group AG2, which then replicates the changes to its secondary replica AlwaysOnN4. Similarly, all read/write activity for App2 occurs on the primary replica AlwaysOnN4 of primary availability group AG3. The changes then get replicated to its secondary replica AlwaysOnN3 and then to the primary replica AlwaysOnN2 of the secondary availability group AG4.

■ **Note**   Figures 3-9 and 3-10 show asynchronous-commit mode between the primary and secondary availability groups as typically this topology is used for geographically dispersed sites. If you have a high-speed, reliable network between your sites then you can configure synchronous-commit mode between the availability groups.

The following are some key differences between a regular availability group and a distributed availability group:

- Since the distributed availability group has two WSFCs and each cluster maintains its own quorum mode and node voting configuration, the health of the secondary cluster does not affect the primary cluster. In a regular availability group topology, we would need to exclude the cluster nodes at the DR site for voting to ensure that the health of the cluster nodes in the DR site does not affect the health of the primary site cluster nodes.

- In a distributed availability group, changes are replicated once over the network to the secondary WSFC and then replicated within the cluster. In a regular availability group with a single WSFC, the changes are replicated to each and every individual replica. This makes distributed availability groups very efficient for geographically dispersed sites.

- Automatic failover from primary availability group to secondary availability group is not supported since automatic failover functionality is provided by WSFC, and there is no single WSFC between the two sites in a distributed availability group.

- The operating system version on the primary and secondary WSFC can be different. In a regular availability group, as there is only one WSFC, the operating system version on all the cluster nodes has to be the same. Due to this advantage, you can use distributed availability groups as one of the methods to perform rolling updates/upgrades of the operating system.

- A distributed availability group is limited to two availability groups. However, an availability group can be a member of more than one distributed availability group. So, you can have distributed availability group 1 contain AG1 and AG2 and distributed availability group 2 contain AG2 and AG3, with AG1 replicating to AG2 and AG2 replicating to AG3.

Summary

This chapter introduced the concepts and topologies that are important to understand in order to effectively build, configure, and manage SQL Server 2016 Always On Availability Groups High Availability (HA) and Disaster Recovery (DR) solutions.

In the next chapter, we will discuss how transaction log blocks are replicated from the primary replica to a secondary replica in synchronous and asynchronous modes.

CHAPTER 4

■ ■ ■

Data Synchronization Internals

Now that we have looked at the Availability Groups concepts and common topologies, it's time to dive deeper into the internals. We have already seen that, Always On Availability Groups support two availability modes (i.e., asynchronous-commit mode and synchronous-commit mode). In this chapter, we will try to understand how the replication of a transaction log blocks work from the primary replica to a secondary replica in *synchronous-commit* and *asynchronous-commit* modes.

Trade-offs and Opportunity Cost

Haven't we all heard the saying, "you can't have it all"? For example, "You can't have all the advantages of the single life and be married." And, "You can't have a busy weekend and get lots of rest."

Similarly, when it comes to choosing the right data synchronization mode for Always On Availability Groups, you have to weigh the trade-offs and the opportunity cost.

In synchronous-commit mode, the emphasis is on high availability over performance, at the cost of increased transaction latency. Primary replicas wait to send the transaction confirmation to the client until the secondary replica has hardened the log to disk.

Asynchronous-commit mode runs with minimum transaction latency at the cost of high availability. The primary replica does not wait for any of the secondary replicas to harden the log. Rather, immediately after writing the log record to the local log file, the primary replica sends the transaction confirmation to the client.

To paraphrase a wise person, The bad news is that you can't have it all. The good news is that when you know what's really important, you don't want it all anyway.

Synchronous-Commit Mode

Figure 4-1 gives an overview of how the replication of transaction log blocks from the primary replica to a secondary replica works in synchronous-commit mode. For synchronous-commit to occur, both the current primary replica and the secondary replica in question must be configured for synchronous-commit.

© Uttam Parui and Vivek Sanil 2016
U. Parui and V. Sanil, *Pro SQL Server Always On Availability Groups*, DOI 10.1007/978-1-4842-2071-9_4

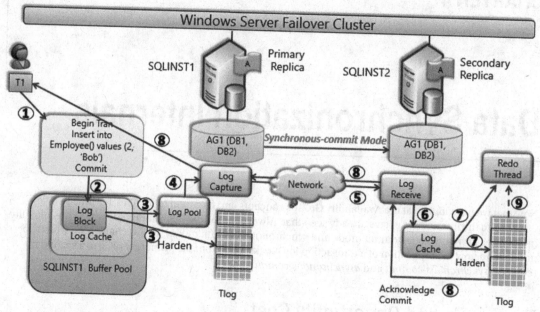

Figure 4-1. *Data synchronization in synchronous-commit mode*

Data synchronization in synchronous-commit mode works as follows:

1. A client issues a transaction against the database participating in the availability group on the primary replica.

2. Primary replica generates transaction log blocks. In the background, the secondary replica initiates a request to the primary, asking for the *log blocks* to be shipped. The secondary and primary will negotiate the proper log sequence number (LSN) staring point and other necessary information. Primary replica's log cache gets filled with these log blocks.

■ **Note** Log block is a contiguous chunk of memory (often 60K) and maintained by the Log Manager.

---

3. When the log block becomes full or the primary replica issues a commit operation, the log blocks from the log cache are flushed to the log file to make it persistent. In an Always On Availability Group configuration, when the log block is being flushed to the disk on the primary replica, it also gets copied to the *log pool.*

4. The log blocks in the log pool are read by a thread called *log capture,* and its job is to read the log blocks from the log pool and send them to the secondary replica. In case of multiple secondary replicas, there is one log capture thread for each replica that ensures that the log blocks are sent across multiple replicas in parallel. The log content gets compressed and encrypted before being sent over to the secondary replicas.

5. On the secondary replica, a thread called *log receive* receives the log blocks from the network.

6. It writes to the log cache on the secondary replica.

7. There's one redo thread per database that is always running on the secondary replica. While the log blocks are being written to the log cache, it reads those log blocks and applies those changes to the data pages and the index pages in the database on the secondary to bring it up to date with whatever has happened on the primary replica. When the log block on the secondary replica becomes full, or it receives a commit log record, it hardens the content of log cache onto the log disk on the secondary replica.

8. If the secondary replica is configured to run in synchronous mode, it will send an acknowledgment on the commit to the primary node indicating that it has hardened the transaction, and so it is safe to tell the user that the transaction is committed. And because the log has been hardened on the secondary, there is a guarantee that in case there is a failover, there will be no data loss.

9. The redo thread runs independently of how log blocks are being generated on the secondary or being copied and persisted. If the redo thread is a running few minutes behind, those log blocks may not be available in the log cache. In that case, the redo thread will pick up those log blocks from the log disk, and that is what is shown in the dotted line on the right side of the figure above.

■ **Note** Availability group replicas ping each other to signal that they are still active. If a replica receives a ping back from the other replica during the *session-timeout* period (default 10 seconds), it indicates that the replicas are up and running and are communicating to each other. If the primary replica does not get a ping response from the secondary replica within the session-timeout period, the primary replica temporarily shifts into asynchronous-commit mode for that secondary replica. When the secondary replica reconnects with the primary replica, they resume synchronous-commit mode.

Asynchronous-Commit Mode

Figure 4-2 gives an overview of how the replication of transaction log blocks from the primary replica to a secondary replica works in an asynchronous-commit mode. The process is similar to synchronous mode except that the acknowledge message of a successful commit is sent after the log blocks are persisted on the primary replica's transaction log.

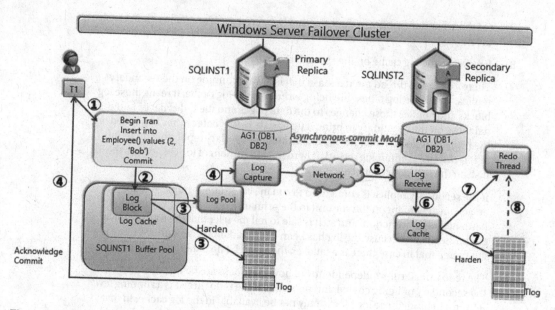

Figure 4-2. *Data synchronization in asynchronous-commit mode*

1. A client issues a transaction against the database participating in the availability group on the primary replica.

2. Primary replica generates transaction log blocks. In the background, the secondary replica initiates a request to the primary, asking for the log blocks to be shipped. The secondary and primary will negotiate the proper LSN staring point and other necessary information.

3. When the log block becomes full or the primary replica issues a commit operation, the log blocks from the log cache are flushed to the log file to make it persistent. In an Always On Availability Group configuration, when the log cache is being flushed to the disk on the primary replica, they also get copied to the log pool.

4. If all secondary replicas are in an asynchronous availability mode, the success of this step is good enough to send an acknowledgment message of a successful commit back to the application when the I/O to the local transaction log has completed. At the same time, the log blocks in the log pool are read by a thread called log capture. Its job is to read the log blocks from log pool and send them to the secondary replica. In case of multiple secondary replicas, there is one log capture thread for each replica that ensures that the log blocks are sent across multiple replicas in parallel. The log content gets compressed and encrypted before being sent over to the secondary replicas.

5. There is a thread called log receive that is running on the secondary replica. It receives the log blocks from the network and it starts writing to the log cache.

6. It writes to the log cache on the secondary replica.

7. There's a redo thread that is always running on the secondary replica. While the log blocks are being written to the log cache, it reads those log blocks and applies those changes to the data pages and the index pages in the database on the secondary to bring it up to date with whatever has happened on the primary replica. When the log cache on the secondary replica becomes full, or it receives a commit log record, it hardens the content of log cache onto the log disk on the secondary replica.

8. The redo thread runs independently of how log blocks are being generated on the secondary or being copied and persisted. If the redo thread is running a few minutes behind, those log blocks may not be available in the log cache. In that case, the redo thread will pick up those log blocks from the log disk, and that is what is shown in the dotted line on the right side of the figure above.

■ **Note** Starting with SQL Server 2016, the synchronization throughput of Availability Groups has increased ~10x due to improvements in the data synchronization process. The performance improvements include parallel and faster compression of log blocks on the primary replica, an optimized synchronization protocol, and parallel decompression and redo of log records on the secondary replica. In SQL Server 2012 and 2014, the redo process is executed serially by a single thread and therefore bound to a single CPU core. For high-write workloads the secondary replicas are no longer able to keep up, resulting in long downtimes during a failover. In SQL Server 2016, the redo is executed in parallel to make use of all the available CPU cores. The database recovery times on failover has improved, and the freshness of data on the secondary has increased due to these improvements.

Synchronization Behavior in Various Scenarios

Let's take a look at how data synchronization is affected when the primary or secondary replica fails or if they get disconnected and what happens when they recover.

Scenario 1: Secondary Replica Goes Offline

While a secondary replica is unhealthy (i.e., it goes offline or gets disconnected), it is still part of the availability group. This means that any transaction log entries that are not hardened by all the replicas in an AG are retained by the primary replica database. This ensures that when the secondary replica comes back online, it can receive all the log blocks that it hasn't hardened yet. This can cause the transaction log on the primary and other healthy secondary replicas to grow and fill the disk.

If this happens, either you have to fix the secondary replica and bring it back online so it will start accepting those log blocks or you need to remove the replica from the availability group. Once the unhealthy replica is taken out of the availability group, the primary replica database doesn't have to hold those log blocks anymore and can overwrite them, thus reusing the transaction log.

The same rules apply if a secondary replica database becomes unhealthy. If a secondary replica database is taken out of the availability group or if a whole secondary replica is taken out of the availability group, while adding it back, every secondary replica database must have the latest full backup, latest differential log backup, and all the transaction log backups since the last backup was applied to it. This ensures that any transaction log entries that were truncated from the transaction log of the primary replica database after the secondary replica database was taken out of the availability group have been applied to the secondary replica database before it is introduced back in the availability group. For a very large database or a busy database with frequent transaction log backups, this could be difficult to achieve during business hours. In such cases, it may be beneficial to add the databases back during off hours.

How Does a Synchronous Secondary Replica Resynchronize with the Primary Replica?

1. When the synchronous secondary replica goes offline, its status changes from Synchronized to 'Not Synchronizing'. As soon as it changes its status, the primary replica stops waiting for an acknowledgment that the secondary has hardened a commit and starts treating it as an asynchronous replica. This ensures that commits on the primary replica won't be delayed by an unhealthy synchronous secondary replica.

2. Once the secondary replica is brought back online, it establishes a connection with the primary replica and sends its *End of Log* (EOL) LSN to the primary replica.

3. On receiving this, the primary then starts sending it the log blocks that it hardened after the EOL LSN.

4. As soon as the secondary starts receiving and hardening these log blocks, its status changes to Synchronizing. This indicates that the secondary replica is connected to the primary and is catching up (i.e., it is essentially behaving as an asynchronous replica).

5. The secondary replica keeps hardening the log blocks, keeps applying the hardened transactions with the REDO thread, and keeps sending this information back to the primary replica.

6. This goes on until the Last Hardened (LH) LSN of the primary and secondary replica match. As soon as they do, the status of the secondary replica changes to Synchronized and from that point onwards, primary replica starts treating it as a synchronous replica.

7. Primary replica starts waiting on an acknowledgment for the commit from the secondary replica before letting the user know that the transaction has been committed successfully.

How Does an Asynchronous Secondary Replica Resynchronize with the Primary Replica?

1. When the asynchronous secondary replica goes offline, its status changes from Synchronizing to 'Not Synchronizing'. Primary replica responds in the same way.

2. Once the secondary replica is brought back online, it establishes a connection with the primary replica and sends its End of Log (EOL) LSN to the primary replica.

3. On receiving this, the primary then starts sending it the log blocks that it hardened after the EOL LSN.

4. As soon as the secondary starts receiving and hardening these log blocks, its status changes to Synchronizing. This indicates that the secondary replica is connected to the primary and is catching up.

Scenario 2: Primary Replica Goes Offline

When a primary replica goes offline, the failover target takes over the primary role, recovers its databases, and brings them online as the new primary databases. The former primary replica, when available, switches to the secondary role, and its databases become secondary databases.

We saw in the last chapter that there are three types of failover:

- Automatic failover (without data loss)

- Planned manual failover (without data loss)

- Forced failover (with possible data loss)

Table 4-1 summarizes which forms of failover are supported under different availability and failover modes. For each pair of availability replicas, the effective availability mode and failover mode is determined by the intersection of the modes of the primary replica plus the modes of one or more secondary replicas.

Table 4-1. Forms of failover and availability modes

	Asynchronous-commit mode	Synchronous-commit mode with manual failover mode	Synchronous-commit mode with automatic failover mode
Automatic failover	No	No	Yes
Planned manual failover	No	Yes	Yes
Forced failover	Yes	Yes	Yes*

* If you issue a forced failover command on a synchronized secondary replica, the secondary replica behaves the same as for a manual failover.

Automatic Failover Sequence of Actions

To support an automatic failover, the conditions for automatic failover discussed in the previous chapter on Availability Groups concepts and common topologies must be met. An automatic failover initiates the following sequence of actions:

1. The state of the primary databases is changed to DISCONNECTED, if the primary replica is still running and all the clients are also disconnected.

2. The secondary database rolls forward any log waiting in the recovery queue on the secondary database.

■ **Note**   *Recovery queue* is the amount of log records in the log files of the secondary replica that has not yet been redone. The amount of log in the recovery queue, speed of the system, and the workload would determine the amount of time required to complete the roll forward process in the secondary database.

3. At this point, the secondary replica becomes the new primary replica. Its databases become the primary databases. The new primary replica rolls back any uncommitted transactions (the undo phase of recovery) as quickly as possible. Rollback occurs in the background while clients use the database. Committed transactions are not rolled back as part of this process.

4. Until the secondary databases connect and resynchronize to the new primary database, the databases are marked as *NOT SYNCHRONIZED*. Before the rollback recovery starts, secondary databases can connect to the new primary databases and quickly transition to the *SYNCHRONIZED* state.

5. The original primary replica becomes the secondary replica and its databases become secondary databases when the replica comes back online again. And it resynchronizes with the corresponding primary replica and the databases. After the databases have resynchronized, failover is possible again, however in the reverse direction this time.

Planned Manual Failover Sequence of Actions

To support a planned manual failover, the conditions for planned manual failover discussed in the previous chapter on Availability Groups concepts and common topologies must be met.

You can manually fail over an availability group using SQL Server Management Studio, T-SQL, or PowerShell. A planned manual failover, which must be initiated on the target secondary replica, initiates the following sequence of actions:

1. A request is sent to the primary replica by the WSFC to go offline in order to ensure that there are no new user transactions occurring on the original primary databases.

2. The secondary database rolls forward any log waiting in the recovery queue on the secondary database.

3. At this point, the secondary replica becomes the new primary replica, and the original primary replica becomes the new secondary replica.

4. Any uncommitted transactions are rolled back by the new primary replica and the databases are brought online as the primary databases.

5. Until the secondary databases connect and resynchronize to the new primary database, the databases are marked as *NOT SYNCHRONIZING*. Committed transactions are not rolled back as part of this process.

6. The original primary replica becomes the secondary replica and its databases become secondary databases when the replica comes back online again. And it resynchronizes with the corresponding primary replica and the databases. After the databases have resynchronized, failover is possible again, however in the reverse direction this time.

Forced Failover Sequence of Actions

You can manually fail over an availability group using SQL Server Management Studio, T-SQL, or PowerShell.

Forcing failover involves the following sequence of actions:

1. Change of role for the target secondary replica to primary role is initiated from RESOLVING or any other state.

2. The failover target becomes the new primary replica and immediately makes its copies of the databases available to clients.

3. The original primary replica becomes the secondary replica and its databases become secondary databases when the replica comes back online again. However, all secondary databases (including the former primary databases, when they become available) will be in the SUSPENDED state. This suspended secondary copy might be suitable for recovering missing committed data for the primary database. However, recovering missing data would depend on the previous data synchronization state of the suspended secondary database.

4. If a secondary replica is configured as readable, then you can query the secondary databases to manually discover missing data. T-SQL statements can be then issued on the new primary databases to make any necessary changes.

■ **Note**   We recommend forcing failover only if you must restore service to your availability databases immediately and are willing to risk losing data.

How a Forced Failover Can Cause Data Loss

It is critical to understand that forcing failover can cause data loss. Data loss is possible because the target replica cannot communicate with the primary replica and, therefore, cannot guarantee that the databases are synchronized.

Figure 4-3 gives an overview of how a forced failover causes data loss on the primary replica and how it can propagate to a secondary replica.

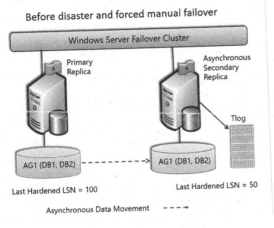
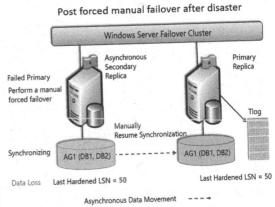

Figure 4-3. Forced manual failover impact

1. In the above example, before the primary replica goes offline, the last hardened LSN on the primary replica is 100 while that of the asynchronous secondary replica is 50.

2. After the primary replica goes offline and a forced failover is initiated, the secondary replica becomes the new primary replica and marks its last hardened LSN as 50.

3. Once the old primary replica is brought online, it shows its synchronization as suspended.

4. If the synchronization on the old primary is resumed, it synchronizes with the new primary; sends its last hardened LSN as 100; and when it sees that the last hardened LSN of the new primary is 50, it rolls back its transaction log to LSN 50 and from that LSN onwards, starts accepting the transaction log blocks from the primary replica. Thus data loss is propagated from the primary to the secondary replica if the synchronization is resumed.

Summary

This chapter should have helped you understand the internal workings of data synchronization within Availability Groups. In the next chapter, we will take a look at one of the key requirements for Availability Groups: that is, Windows Server Failover Clustering.

■ ■ ■

CHAPTER 5

Introduction to Windows Server Failover Clustering

In the previous chapters, we mentioned that Always On solutions leverage the Windows Server operating system and Windows Server Failover Cluster (WSFC) as a platform technology. For a given Always On Availability Group, the availability replicas must be hosted by separate instances of SQL Server running on different nodes of the same WSFC. Availability groups rely on WSFC for health monitoring, failover coordination, and server connectivity. Hence it's crucial that SQL Server database architects and administrators have a better understanding of WSFC.

Overview of a Failover Cluster

A failover cluster is a group of independent servers that work together to increase the availability and scalability of mission-critical applications such as SQL Server, Exchange, SAP, File Server, and Virtual Machines. Even though a group of independent servers are working together in a failover cluster, the failover cluster appears as a single system to the clients. Figure 5-1 shows a typical failover cluster.

© Uttam Parui and Vivek Sanil 2016
U. Parui and V. Sanil, *Pro SQL Server Always On Availability Groups*, DOI 10.1007/978-1-4842-2071-9_5

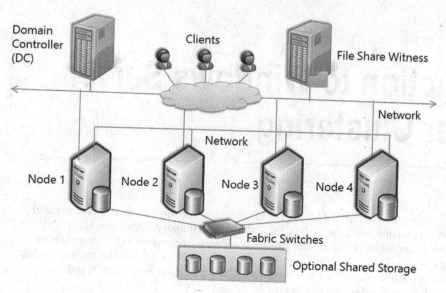

Figure 5-1. *Typical Windows Server failover cluster*

To understand the various components that make up the Windows Server failover cluster, we will define the most common failover clustering terms.

Cluster Node

The independent servers that work together in a failover cluster are referred to as a cluster node. Each cluster node has a working installation of Microsoft Windows Server operating system.

■ **Note** In Windows Server 2012 R2 and earlier versions, all the cluster nodes were required to be members of the same domain. Starting with Windows Server 2016, you can create failover clusters without active directory dependencies.

You can now create failover clusters in the following configurations:

- *Single-domain clusters* – cluster nodes joined to the same domain.

- *Multi-domain clusters* – cluster nodes joined to multiple domains.

- *Workgroup clusters* – cluster nodes that are member servers/workgroups and not joined to any domain.

Networks

To ensure smooth cluster operations, it is important to have redundant and reliable communications among all cluster nodes. Properly configured connectivity between the cluster nodes is required to provide access to the highly available services required by the clients and to guarantee the internal cluster communications.

To avoid a single point of failure, two or more independent networks must be connected to all the cluster nodes. A network component failure (NIC, router, switch, hub, etc.) should not cause the cluster communication to break down and communication should continue to make progress in a timely manner. If cluster communication cannot proceed on one network, the switchover to the other cluster-enabled network is automatic. This is why the cluster nodes must have multiple network adapters available to support cluster communications and each one should be connected to a different switch.

■ **Note**   Starting with Windows Server 2008 clustering, there is no concept of a public and private network.

In previous versions of Windows failover cluster, the public network provided clients with access to the highly available cluster services and the private network was used for internal cluster communications. Starting from Windows Server 2008 clustering (and above), cluster communications go over all networks that can communicate between the nodes. It's part of the cluster health process to see if the network is up and can talk to the other node.

Cluster Resource

A cluster resource is a physical or logical entity that can do the following:

- be managed by a failover cluster,

- be brought online or taken offline,

- be hosted (owned) by only one cluster node at any point of time.

Examples of cluster resources are a network name, IP address, disk, and Availability Group listener.

Resource Dependency

Resource dependency is a two-way association between resources. If a resource A depends on resource B, then resource B is a dependency of resource A. As an example, a network name resource depends on an IP address resource. This means that for a network name resource to be online, an IP address resource needs to be online first. Also, if you take the network name resource offline, the IP address resource will be first taken offline followed by the network name resource. A resource can be dependent on multiple resources using *AND* or *OR* logic.

Role

A *role*, previously referred to as resource group, is a collection of resources that are required to run a specific application or service. An Availability Group is a role.

Failover

Failover is the process of moving a group from one cluster node to another in the case of a failure. Windows server failover cluster attempts to perform a failover of a group when the following happens:

- A cluster node failure or a resource failure occurs and the restart threshold is hit

Or

- An administrator performs a manual failover

Failback

Failback is the process of moving a group to the preferred owner. When a node becomes inactive for some reason, the failover cluster fails over the groups hosted by the node. When the node becomes active again, the failover cluster can fail back the groups originally hosted by the node. By default, failback is disabled on the groups. The default setting is useful as you do not want the groups to be in a ping-pong situation when they fail over from one node to another and then fail back to the original node as soon as it is active and then again fail over if the original node becomes inactive again. It is better to first evaluate the cause of the original failure and remediate the issue and only after ensuring that the node is healthy is when you should manually fail back the groups to the original node.

■ **Note**   Even though the default failback settings work for most scenarios, you can configure the failback to occur during a specific time period, say between 8 p.m. to midnight. If you do configure failback, it is important to set the failback time such that failback does not happen during peak business hours.

Preferred Owner

Preferred owner (also referred to as *preferred node*) is the cluster node where you want the resource group to run. Most customers do not set the preferred owner for a group because it does not matter where the group resides. All that matters is that the group is running on one of the cluster nodes. When a node fails, the remaining nodes take over the groups from the failed node. This will increase the load on the other nodes and unless it has the capacity to take on more loads, performance will be affected. Hence, it is important to design the failover cluster such that the nodes can host the groups in case of failover with minimum performance impact. Failback does not occur if a preferred owner is not configured for the group.

■ **Note**   One strong motivation to use preferred owners with availability groups is due to licensing. Availability groups (AG) does not require a SQL Server license for one disaster recovery (DR) replica as long as it is truly passive and the primary SQL Server instance is covered by active Software Assurance (SA). In this case, Microsoft usually places a limit on how many days you can run the AG on the DR replica in a year. To ensure that the limit is not exceeded, you can utilize preferred owners and scheduled failbacks.

Possible Owner

Possible owner (also referred to as possible node) is a cluster node that can run a resource. By default, all cluster nodes are possible owners so that the resources can run on any node. In most cases, we use the default settings. But if you have a scenario where you have a multi-node cluster and you do not want a particular node to not run some resources, you can remove the node from the possible owners list of the resource.

Heartbeat

The failover cluster keeps track of the current state of the cluster nodes within a cluster and determines when a group and its resources fail over to another cluster node. The communication takes place in the form of messages that are sent regularly between each cluster node. These messages are called *cluster heartbeats*. The cluster heartbeats let all nodes know which node is up and down. The cluster heartbeat mechanism uses port 3343 and is unicast in nature and uses a Request-Reply type process. This provides for higher security and more reliable packet accountability.

Table 5-1 shows the heartbeat configuration settings along with default and maximum values.

Table 5-1. Heartbeat Configuration Settings

Parameter	Windows Server 2012 R2 (default)	Windows Server 2016 (default)	Maximum
SameSubnetDelay	1 second	1 second	2 seconds
SameSubnetThreshold	5 heartbeats	10 heartbeats	120 heartbeats
CrossSubnetDelay	1 second	1 second	4 seconds
CrossSubnetThreshold	5 heartbeats	20 heartbeats	120 heartbeats
CrossSiteDelay	NA	1 second	4 seconds
CrossSiteThreshold	NA	20 heartbeats	120 heartbeats

■ **Tip**   To be more tolerant of transient failures on Windows Server 2012 R2 and below, it is recommended to increase the SameSubnetThreshold and CrossSubnetThreshold values to the higher Windows Server 2016 values.

The *delay* parameter is the frequency at which the cluster heartbeats are sent between cluster nodes. It is the number of seconds before the next heartbeat is sent. By default, for single subnet (SameSubnetDelay) and multi-subnet clusters (CrossSubnetDelay), a heartbeat is sent every one second.

The *threshold* parameter is the number of heartbeats that a cluster node can miss before the failover cluster takes recovery action. By default, for single subnet (SameSubnetThreshold) and multi-subnet (CrossSubnetThreshold) clusters, if a node misses a series of five heartbeats, the cluster considers the node to be unreachable and takes recovery action.

CrossSiteDelay and CrossSiteThreshold are new parameters for Windows Server 2016 failover clusters that have nodes in different fault domain sites.

It is important to understand the following:

1. Both the delay and threshold have a cumulative effect on the total health detection. For example, setting SameSubnetDelay to send a heartbeat every 2 seconds and setting the SameSubnetThreshold to 10 heartbeats missed, means that the cluster can have a total network tolerance of 20 seconds before recovery action is taken.

2. Increasing the network resiliency to network hiccups comes at a cost of increased downtime when there is a complete loss of server also referred to as 'hard' failures.

3. Increasing the thresholds to higher values does not resolve the transient network issue: it simply masks the problem by making health monitoring less sensitive.

The cluster heartbeat configuration settings are advanced settings and are exposed only via PowerShell. These settings take effect immediately and can be run any time without causing any downtime.

Quorum

Mission-critical workloads hosted on failover clusters are considered highly available if the cluster nodes that are hosting the resources are up. However, the cluster generally requires more than half the nodes to be up and running, which is known as having *a quorum*. The quorum of a failover cluster determines the number of failures the cluster can sustain while still remaining online. If an additional failure occurs beyond this threshold, the cluster will stop running.

Quorum is extremely important for any high availability solution and is designed to handle the scenario when there is a communication problem between sets of cluster nodes, so that two nodes do not try to simultaneously host a resource group and write to the same disk at the same time. This is known as *split-brain syndrome*, and you need to prevent this to avoid any potential corruption to a disk by having two simultaneous disk owners. The failover cluster forces the cluster service to stop in one of the subsets of nodes to ensure that there is only one true owner of a particular resource group. Once the stopped nodes can communicate with the main group of nodes, they will automatically rejoin the cluster and start the cluster service.

Quorum is based on a voting algorithm where more than half of the voters must be online and be able to communicate to each other. The concept is similar to a parliament house or committee. If there are too few members present, then the committee does not have a quorum (required number of votes) and cannot hold an election. More than half of the total votes is required to achieve quorum to avoid having a tie in the number of votes in a partition, since majority will mean that the other partition has less than half the votes. In a five-node failover cluster, three voters must be online; yet in a four-node failover cluster, three voters must also remain online to have majority. Because of this logic, it is recommended to have an odd number of voters in the cluster. A voter in a cluster can be the following:

- A cluster node – every cluster node has one vote.

- Disk witness, file share witness, or cloud witness – either a disk witness, file share witness, or a cloud witness can have one vote in the cluster but not multiple disks, multiple file shares, multiple cloud witnesses, nor any combination of the three. *Cloud witness* is only available in Windows Server 2016.

▪ **Note** If a healthy failover cluster loses quorum, failover cluster is designed to stop the cluster services causing our mission-critical applications such as Always On Availability Groups to shut down. Therefore, it is critical to ensure that Quorum is always maintained or the cluster service will be stopped.

Dynamic Quorum

To understand this concept, let's assume you have a five-node failover cluster. If you lose three nodes, the remaining nodes would go offline even though there are two nodes remaining. To avoid this scenario, starting from Windows Server 2012 failover clustering, a new functionality called *dynamic quorum* was introduced. As the name implies, dynamic quorum adjusts the quorum dynamically. This allows the failover cluster to continue to function when less than 50% of the nodes are active.

Dynamic quorum works only if the nodes are shut down sequentially. So, in the five-node failover cluster scenario above, assuming you didn't lose all the three nodes at the same time, as cluster nodes went offline, the number of votes in the quorum would adjust dynamically. When the first node failed, you would in theory have a four-node cluster. When the second node failed, you would then have a three-node cluster, and so on. If you continued to lose cluster nodes one by one, you could go all the way down to a one-node cluster also referred to as *Last Man Standing* and still remain online.

▓ **Note**   Dynamic Quorum is enabled by default when a Windows Server 2012 (or above) failover cluster is created.

Dynamic Witness

Even with dynamic quorum functionality, the administrator had to determine whether to add a quorum witness (disk or file share) or not depending on the number of nodes to make it always an odd number. The administrator had to monitor and manually keep changing the value as nodes were added or evicted from the cluster. To relieve this burden from the administrator, starting with Windows Server 2012 R2, *dynamic witness* is enabled by default when the failover cluster is created. As the name suggests, dynamic witness automatically takes care of when to use the quorum witness or not, relieving the burden from the administrator.

▓ **Note**   The new recommendation for Windows Server 2012 R2 (and above) failover clusters is to include the quorum witness and the cluster will decide when to use its vote or not. Windows Server 2012 R2 has two types of quorum witnesses (disk and file share) and Windows Server 2016 has an additional witness type (cloud witness).

If there is an even number of nodes in the cluster, then the cluster will consider the witness as a vote (1) and will make the total votes an odd number. If there is an odd number of nodes in the cluster, then the cluster will not consider the witness vote (0) as you already have an odd number. If the witness goes offline, then the cluster makes the witness vote as 0 to prevent any unnecessary issues due to quorum failures.

Benefits and Limitations of Failover Cluster

Now that you are familiar with the most common cluster terms, we will discuss the benefits and limitations of failover cluster. This will help you understand what a cluster is capable of doing and what it cannot do.

As discussed earlier in this chapter, if one cluster node fails, a process called failover automatically shifts the workload of the failed node to another working node in the cluster. This ability of a failover cluster to handle failures allows the cluster to meet two important requirements:

- *High availability* – the ability to provide the end users access to a service for a high percentage of time while reducing unscheduled outages.

- *High reliability* – the ability to reduce the frequency of system failures.

Because the mission-critical services are not bound to any specific cluster node, interruption to any such node only has a minor impact on the overall availability of the service. On the other hand, a single server solution would be completely offline during a patch window or disaster that affected the host. On a multi-node cluster, the hosted mission-critical services can be easily moved from the node that needs to be taken offline for maintenance or disaster recovery, which greatly improves the overall uptime of the mission-critical application.

Another benefit of failover cluster is *Scalability*. Starting with Windows Server 2012 (and above), failover clustering supports up to 64 cluster nodes. This helps to easily *scale out* the solution by adding nodes to it. For example, if you have a two-node failover cluster hosting applications that is getting close to hitting a node-specific capacity limit such as CPU or memory, it is very easy to add a third node and redistribute the load.

The total cost of ownership (TCO) has been reduced for failover clusters as the failover clustering feature is now included (starting from Windows Server 2012 and above) in Standard Edition. With this change, small- and medium-size businesses can take advantage of high availability in their standard server deployments.

Although failover clustering has a lot of benefits it is important to understand its limitations, too. Failover clustering does not protect from these:

- Shared storage failures,

- Network failures,

- Hack attacks,

- Operational errors.

Failover clustering does not provide load balancing and fault tolerance. Fault tolerant servers are those that have complete redundancy across all components. If one component fails, the secondary component takes over in a process that is seamless to the application running on the server. This is different from a failover cluster where a hardware or software failure causes the workload to move from the failed node to a healthy node. During the failover process, the end users are disconnected briefly and there is minimum downtime incurred.

Summary

In this chapter, we provided an overview of Windows Server failover cluster and covered all the basics of failover cluster. We defined the most common failover cluster terms and discussed the benefits and limitations of failover cluster. In the next chapter, we will discuss the requirements and considerations for deploying Always On Availability Groups.

CHAPTER 6

■ ■ ■

Prerequisites

Chapter 5 looked at Windows Server Failover Cluster (WSFC), one of the key requirements for Always On Availability Groups. In this chapter, we will look at the prerequisites for deploying availability groups.

Windows Requirements

To support the Always On Availability Groups feature, ensure that every computer that is participating in one or more Availability Groups meets the following fundamental requirements:

- OS is Windows Server 2008 or later
    - Each computer should be running either x86 (non-WOW64) or x64 Windows Server 2008 or later versions.

■ **Note**   Server Core version is supported for availability groups.

- OS edition supports Windows Server Failover Clustering (WSFC) feature
    - For Windows Server 2008 and 2008 R2, the failover clustering feature is available in Enterprise and Windows Datacenter editions.
    - For Windows Server 2012 and 2012 R2, the failover clustering feature is available in Standard and Datacenter editions.
    - At the time of writing this book, Windows Server 2016 edition features have not been announced. But in all probability, the failover clustering feature will be available in Standard and Datacenter editions.
- Members of the same domain (only for SQL Server 2012 and SQL Server 2014)
    - Each computer participating in the SQL Server 2012 or 2014 availability groups should be a member of the same domain.

© Uttam Parui and Vivek Sanil 2016
U. Parui and V. Sanil, *Pro SQL Server Always On Availability Groups*, DOI 10.1007/978-1-4842-2071-9_6

- In Windows Server 2012 R2 and previous versions, a cluster can only be created between member nodes joined to the same domain. However, starting with Windows Server 2016, you can now create a Failover Cluster without Active Directory dependencies, as discussed in Chapter 7.

  Failover clusters can be created in the following configurations:

  - Single-domain Clusters - Clusters with all nodes joined to the same domain.

  - Multi-domain Clusters - Clusters with nodes that are members of different domains.

  - Workgroup Clusters - Clusters with nodes that are member servers / workgroup (not domain joined).

- Hence SQL Server 2016 on Windows Server 2016 is supported in the following environments:

  - Cross domains (with trust)

  - Cross domains (no trust)

  - No domain at all

■ **Note**   Windows Server 2016 clusters use certificates for intra-cluster authentication. Management of SQL Server does not change; it uses certificate-secured endpoints internally like database mirroring.

- Not a domain controller
  - The computer should not be a domain controller.
- Install Windows Server updates and hotfixes

  - The SQL Server product group provided a list of hotfixes to be installed on the operating system if it were to host an availability group. Refer to the recommended hotfix list documented in books online in the link below:

    `http://msdn.microsoft.com/en-us/library/ff878487.aspx#WinHotfixes`

■ **Note**   Windows Server 2012 includes all the fixes recommended for availability groups on Windows Server 2008 R2.

- Is a node of the same Windows Server Failover Cluster (WSFC)
  - Each computer should be a node in a WSFC.

■ **Note** Distributed Availability Groups can be set up between availability groups in different WSFCs as seen in Chapter 3. However, the nodes participating in the individual availability groups should be in the same WSFC.

- Sufficient nodes to support your Availability Group configuration

    - For a given availability group, a WSFC node can host only one availability replica. However, on a given WSFC node one or more instances of SQL Server can host availability replicas for many Availability Groups. So make sure you have sufficient nodes to support your availability group configuration.

Recommendations

Now let's take a look at some recommendations for the computers that host availability replicas:

- OS - Windows Server 2012 or above

    - Windows Server 2012 and above works best with availability groups and includes all the fixes for Availability Groups.

- Can handle comparable workload

    - For a given availability group, all the availability replicas should run on comparable computers that can handle identical workloads.

- Sufficient disk space

    - Every computer on which a SQL Server instance hosts an availability replica must possess sufficient disk space for all the databases in the availability group.

- Dedicated network adapters

    - Use a dedicated network adapter (NIC) for availability group data synchronization to achieve best performance. The same network links should be used for communications between WSFC cluster members and communications between availability replicas. If separate network links are used, then it can cause unexpected behaviors in case some of the links fail.

SQL Server Instance Requirements

To support the Always On Availability Groups feature, ensure that every SQL Server instance that is to participate in one or more availability groups meets the following requirements:

- Windows Server Failover Clustering (WSFC) host

    - The computer hosting the SQL Server instance must be a Windows Server Failover Clustering (WSFC) node.

- Reside on separate nodes of a single WSFC

    - The SQL Server instance that host availability replicas for a given availability group must reside on separate nodes of a single WSFC cluster.

> ■ **Note** In case of a distributed availability group, the SQL instances can reside on nodes in different WSFCs, as a distributed availability groups can be set up between availability groups in different WSFCs. However, the SQL Instances participating in the individual availability group should still be on the nodes of a single WSFC.

- Enterprise Edition
  - Use SQL Server Enterprise Edition to configure availability groups on SQL Server Instances.

> ■ **Note** Basic Availability Groups do not need SQL Server Enterprise Edition and is supported on SQL Server Standard Edition.

- Same SQL Server collation
  - All the SQL Server instances that host availability replicas for an availability group must use the same SQL Server collation.
- Enable availability groups feature
  - On each SQL Server instance that will host an availability replica for any availability group, enable the availability groups feature.
- For Kerberos support with the Availability Group:
  - Use the same SQL Server service account for all the SQL Server instances that host an availability replica for the availability group.
  - Manually register a Service Principal Name (SPN) with Active Directory on the SQL Server service account for the virtual network name (VNN) of the Availability Group listener. Domain administrator permissions are required to perform this operation.
- For FILESTREAM support for databases in the availability group:
  - Make sure that the FILESTREAM feature is enabled on every SQL Server instance that will host an availability replica for the Availability Group.
- For contained databases, support for databases in the Availability Group:
  - Make sure that the contained database authentication server option is set to 1 on every SQL Server instance that will host an availability replica for the availability group.

Availability Database Requirements

To support the availability groups feature, ensure that every database that is to participate in the availability group meets the following requirements:

- It should be a user database

> ■ **Note** System databases cannot be part of an availability group.

- It should be a read-write database

- It should be a multiuser database
- It should not have AUTO_CLOSE option enabled
- It should have its recovery model set to full recovery
- It should have at least one full backup
- It should not belong to an existing availability group
- It should not be configured for database mirroring

Availability Group Interoperability

There are scenarios where you need to use certain other SQL Server features along with availability groups. The following features interoperate with Always On availability groups in SQL Server 2016:

- Analysis Services
- Change data capture
- Change tracking
- Contained databases
- ColumnStore Indexes (support for updatable columnstore index on the secondary replicas was introduced in SQL Server 2016)
- Cross-database transactions between databases hosted on two different SQL Server instances
- Database encryption
- Database snapshots
- FILESTREAM and FileTable
- Full-text search
- In-Memory OLTP
- Log shipping
- Remote Blob Store (RBS)
- Reporting Services
- Service Broker
- SQL Server Agent
- Stretch Database
- Server instances
- Replication

Only certain types and certain components of replication are supported. Following is the support matrix for the different types and components of replication:

	Publisher	Distributor	Subscriber
Transactional	Yes	No	Yes (No automatic failover)
Peer to Peer	No	No	No
Merge	Yes	No	Yes (No automatic failover)
Snapshot	Yes	No	Yes (No automatic failover)

■ **Note** Bidirectional and reciprocal transactional replication is not supported.

Summary

This chapter should have helped you understand the requirements and considerations for deploying Availability Groups. You might want to use the above as a checklist for your availability groups deployment. Now that you have a good understanding of the requirements and considerations for deploying availability groups, in the next chapter we will take a look at how to create a WSFC.

PART III

Deploying Always On Availability Groups

■ ■ ■

CHAPTER 7

Create a Windows Server Failover Cluster

After reviewing the requirements and considerations for creating Always On Availability Groups in chapter 6, you understand that one of the key requirements for creating Always On Availability Groups is creating a Windows Server Failover Cluster (WSFC). In this chapter we will provide step-by-step instructions to create a Windows Server 2016 failover cluster using Failover Cluster Manager interface and Windows PowerShell.

The setup environment used in this book simulates an almost real-life production environment. It consists of five servers:

- One Domain Controller (DC) named AlwaysOnDC.

- Two member servers named AlwaysOnN1 and AlwaysOnN2 in the primary datacenter for high availability.

- Third member server named AlwaysOnN3 in the secondary datacenter for disaster recovery.

- One client machine named AlwaysOnClient in the primary datacenter.

■ **Note** Most real-life production environments typically will have at least two domain controllers to provide high availability and fault tolerance.

All the servers (AlwaysOnN1, AlwaysOnN2, and AlwaysOnN3) are members of the same domain CORPNET.CONTOSO.COM and have Windows Server 2016 Standard Edition and stand-alone instances of SQL Server 2016 Enterprise Edition installed. To provide a high availability and disaster recovery solution using Always On Availability Groups, we will create a three-node Windows Server 2016 Failover Cluster. Figure 7-1 shows the setup environment that we have used in the book.

© Uttam Parui and Vivek Sanil 2016
U. Parui and V. Sanil, *Pro SQL Server Always On Availability Groups*, DOI 10.1007/978-1-4842-2071-9_7

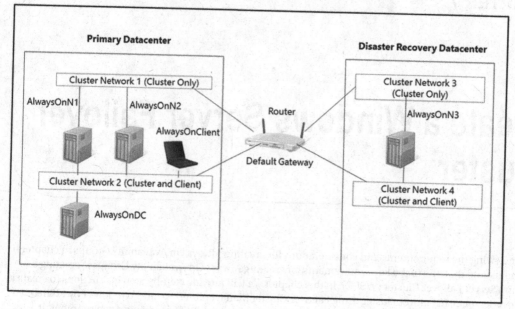

Figure 7-1. Setup environment used in this book

■ **Note**   Before proceeding to create the failover cluster, ensure that the *setup account* that will be used to create the failover cluster has membership in the local *Administrators* group on all the servers that will become cluster nodes and active directory *Create Computer Objects* and *Read All Properties* privileges in the organization unit (OU) to create the computer objects.

Create a Windows Server Failover Cluster Using Failover Cluster Manager

We first discuss the steps to create a Windows Server Failover Clustering using the Failover Cluster Manager graphical user interface (GUI). By default, the Failover Cluster Manager interface is not installed on the operating system. In the first step, you will install the failover clustering feature during which you will also install the failover clustering tools including the Failover Cluster Manager interface.

Step 1: Install Failover Clustering Feature

Before you can create a Windows Server 2016 Failover Cluster, you need to install the Failover Clustering feature on the servers that you want to include in the cluster. In this step, we will show you how to install the Failover Clustering feature on the servers using the Add Roles and Features Wizard.

■ **Note**   The minimum permissions required to install the Failover Clustering feature on a server is membership in the local *Administrators* group.

Open Add Roles and Features Wizard

Using the setup account, log on to the server that you want to include in the failover cluster. Right-click Start menu and select Control Panel. In Control Panel, select Administrative Tools and then Server Manager. In Server Manager, click the Manage menu and select Add Roles and Features from the list as shown in Figure 7-2.

Figure 7-2. *Accessing Add Roles and Features Wizard from Server Manager*

This will invoke the Add Roles and Features Wizard as shown in Figure 7-3. Review the Before you begin screen and then select Next.

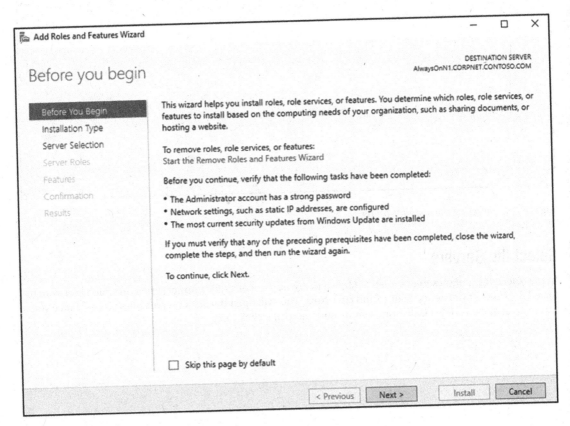

Figure 7-3. *Add Roles and Features Wizard*

Select Installation Type

In the Select installation type screen, you can install roles and features or virtual machines. To install the Failover Clustering feature, select Role-based or feature-based installation as shown in Figure 7-4 and click Next.

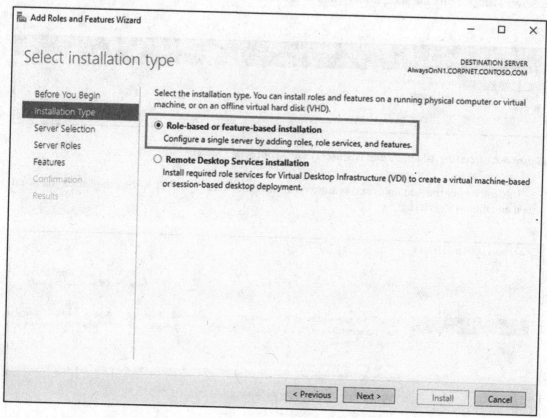

Figure 7-4. *Selecting the installation type*

Select the Servers

In the Select destination server screen as shown in Figure 7-5, select the correct server on which you want to install the Failover Clustering feature and click Next. This will open the Select server roles screen. Since you want to install the Failover Clustering feature and not a role, click Next.

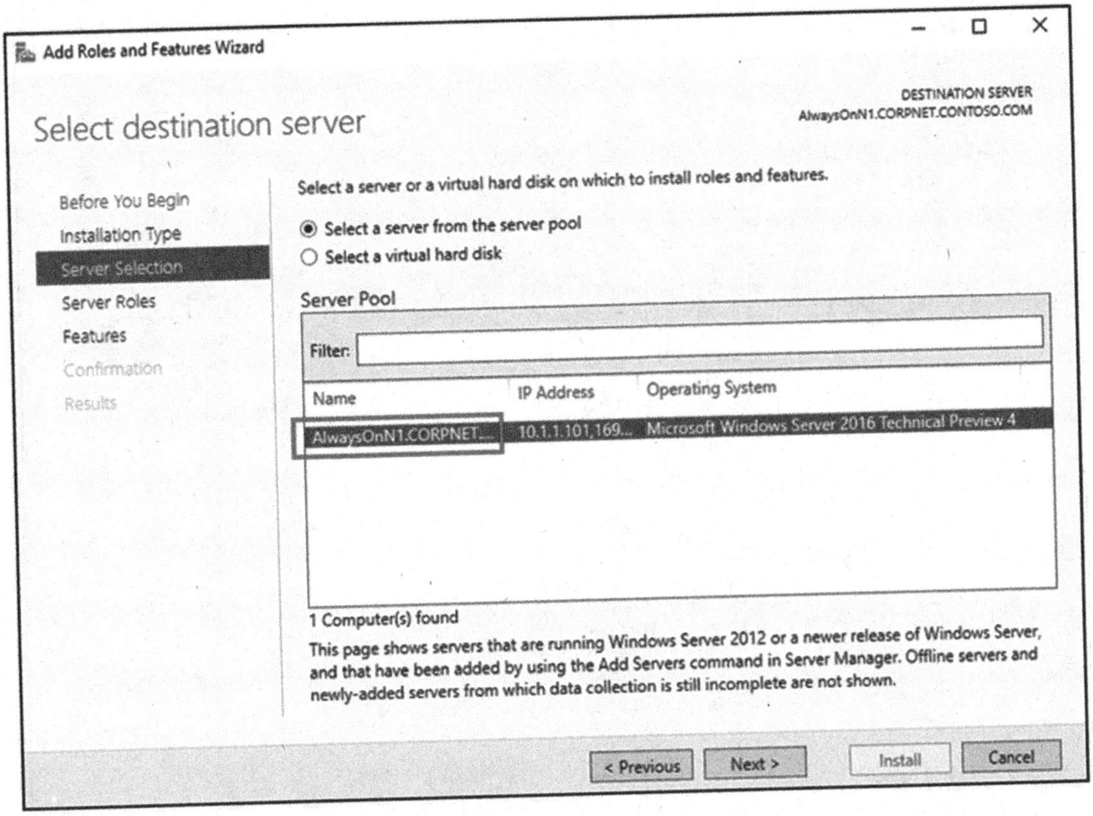

Figure 7-5. Selecting the server to install the Failover Clustering feature

Select Failover Clustering Feature

In the Select features screen, click Failover Clustering as shown in Figure 7-6. A pop-up screen will appear with additional tools to manage the Failover Clustering feature as shown in Figure 7-7. Click Add Features to install the Failover Cluster Management Tools and Failover Cluster Module for Windows PowerShell. Click Next.

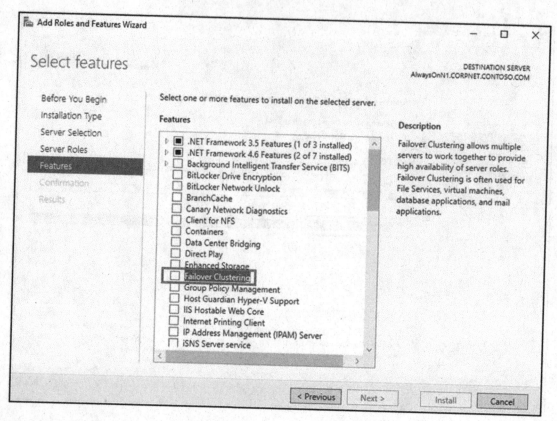

Figure 7-6. *Selecting the Failover Clustering feature*

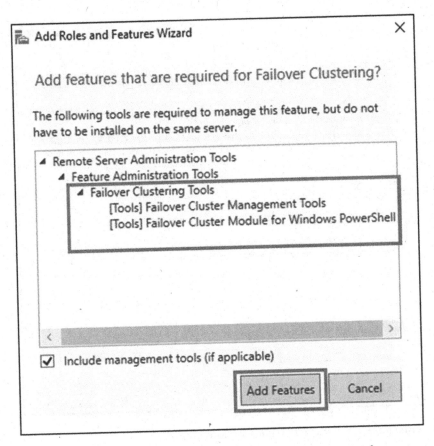

Figure 7-7. Adding additional tools to manage the Failover Clustering feature

Confirm Installation Selections

In the Confirm installation selections, review your selections and click Install as shown in Figure 7-8.

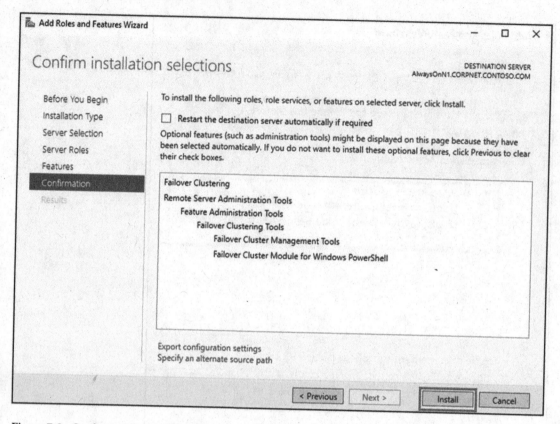

Figure 7-8. *Confirming the installation selections for the Failover Clustering feature*

■ **Note**   The installation of the Failover Clustering feature does not require a reboot, making it unnecessary to check the Restart the destination server automatically if required check box.

When the Failover Clustering feature is installed, you will see the Results screen shown in Figure 7-9. Click Close.

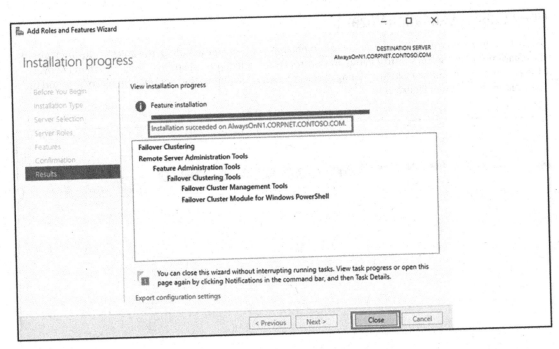

Figure 7-9. Results screen for installing the Failover Clustering feature

After you install the Failover Clustering feature, the Failover Cluster Manager interface is available in the Tools menu of the Server Manager interface. Alternately, you can also open Failover Cluster Manager by opening Control Panel then selecting Administrative Tools and Failover Cluster Manager.

■ **Note** Repeat the above steps to add the Failover Clustering feature to all the servers that you want to include in the Windows Server 2016 Failover Cluster. Without installing the Failover Clustering feature on a server, you cannot include it in a failover cluster.

Step 2: Validate Failover Cluster

After installing the Failover Clustering feature on all the servers that you want to include in the cluster, the next step is to run the *cluster validation wizard* to ensure that failover clustering will be supported on the entire configured solution (servers, network, storage). The cluster validation wizard tests the underlying hardware and software and tells us if anything is missing or configured improperly. It also simulates common cluster operations to obtain an accurate assessment of how well failover clustering can be installed and supported.

A Windows Server 2016 Failover Cluster is considered to be officially supported by Microsoft Customer Support Services (CSS) if they meet the below criteria:

- All the hardware and software components are "Certified for Windows Server 2016" and

- The fully configured solution (servers, network and storage) must pass *all tests* in the cluster validation wizard.

In this step, we will show how to run the cluster validation wizard using Failover Cluster Manager.

Open Cluster Validation Wizard

Using the setup account, log on to one of the servers that you want to include in the failover cluster. Right-click Start menu and select Control Panel. In Control Panel, select Administrative Tools and then Failover Cluster Manager. In Failover Cluster Manager, select Validate Configuration action, which can be found in three places as shown in Figure 7-10.

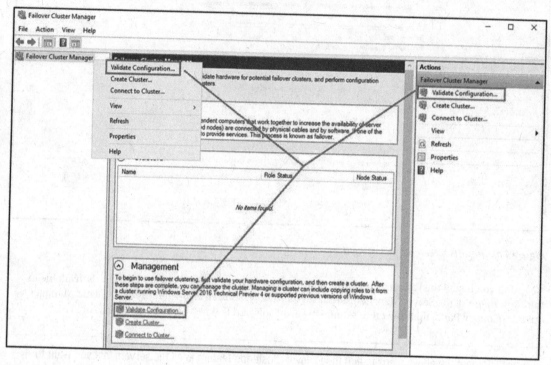

Figure 7-10. *Invoking the Cluster Validation Wizard using Failover Cluster Manager*

This will invoke the Validate a Configuration Wizard (also referred to as the Cluster Validation wizard) as shown in Figure 7-11. Review the Before You Begin screen and click Next to start the validation process.

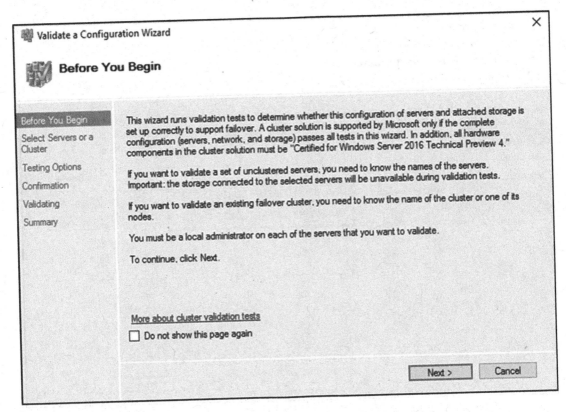

Figure 7-11. Reviewing the Before you begin screen of the Cluster Validation Wizard

Select Servers or a Cluster

In the Select Servers or a Cluster screen, enter the names of all the servers that will be part of the failover cluster separated by a semicolon and click Add. Figure 7-12 shows the screen for our environment with the three server names AlwaysOnN1, AlwaysOnN2, and AlwaysOnN3. Click Next to continue.

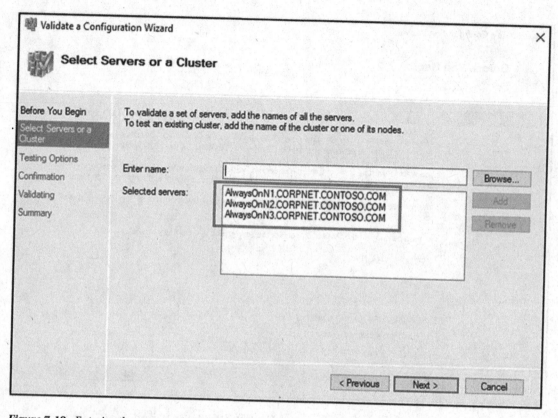

Figure 7-12. Entering the servers names that you want to include in the cluster

Select Testing Options

In the Testing Options screen, select Run all tests (recommended) as shown in Figure 7-13. As mentioned earlier, Microsoft supports a cluster solution only if the complete configuration can pass all the tests in the wizard. Click Next to continue.

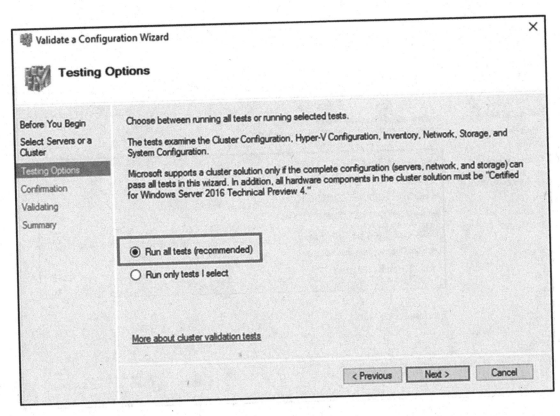

Figure 7-13. *Selecting Run all tests in the Testing Options screen*

The cluster validation wizard is a very powerful tool and is not only used for initial cluster validation, but it is often used to troubleshoot an existing failover cluster. While troubleshooting an existing cluster, you may not want to run all the tests and run only the tests that are affecting the issue. For such scenarios, select the second testing option Run only tests I select. A common scenario is to uncheck some or all the storage tests when you are not troubleshooting storage. If storage tests are selected, the disks assigned to cluster roles will be taken offline during the tests, making them unavailable during the tests.

Confirm Selections

In the Confirmation screen as shown in Figure 7-14, review the settings and confirm that you want to run the selected validation tests. Click Next to start the validation process.

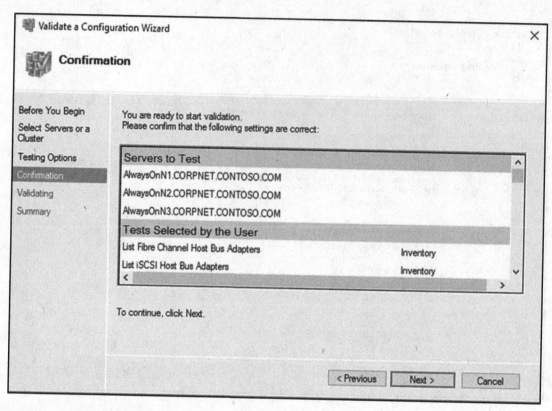

Figure 7-14. *Confirming the selections for Cluster Validation*

Review Report

In the Summary screen, ensure that the tests completed successfully and the configuration is suitable for clustering. A sample Summary screen is shown in Figure 7-15.

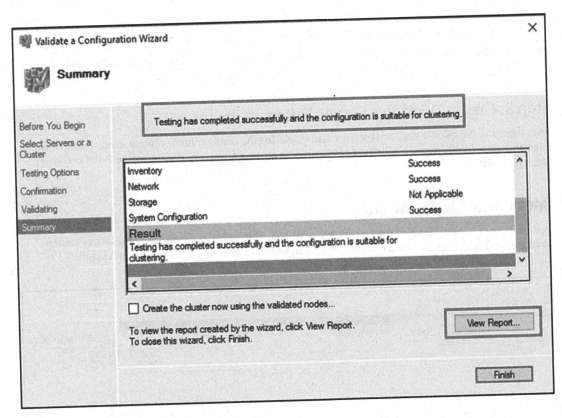

Figure 7-15. Reviewing Cluster Validation Summary Screen

Click View Report to review the validation report. A sample validation report is shown in Figure 7-16. Click Finish to close the wizard. The validation report is stored on the C:\Windows\Cluster\Reports folder for future review.

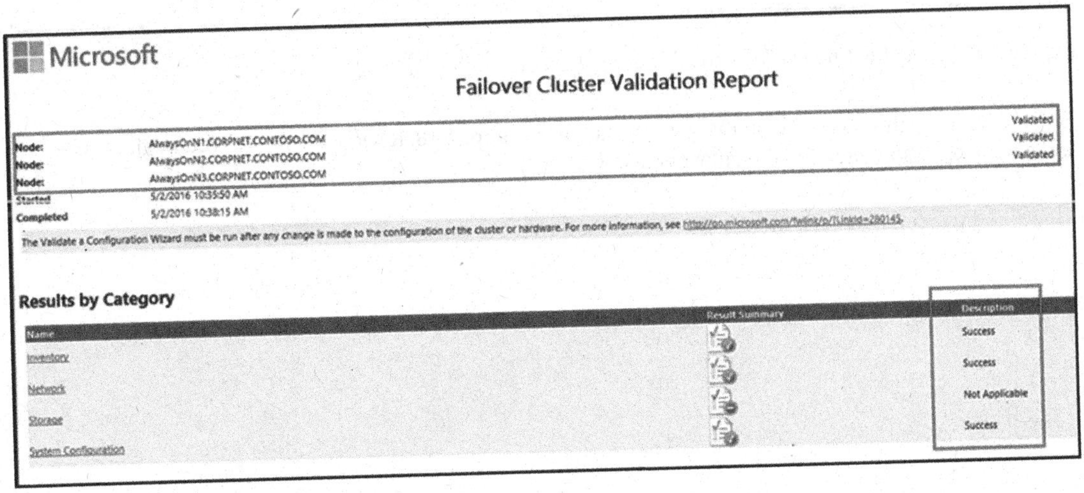

Figure 7-16. Sample Validation Report

■ **Note** If any tests fail, Microsoft does not consider the configuration to be supported. The problem must be corrected and the cluster validation wizard rerun to confirm that the configuration passes all the tests.

Step 3: Create Windows Server Failover Cluster

After installing the failover clustering feature and validating the configuration, you are ready to create a new failover cluster. In this step, we will demonstrate how to create a failover cluster using the Failover Cluster Manager interface.

Open Create Cluster Wizard

Open Failover Cluster Manager (Start menu ➤ Control Panel ➤ Administrative Tools ➤ Failover Cluster Manager) and select Create Cluster action, which can be found in three places as shown in Figure 7-17.

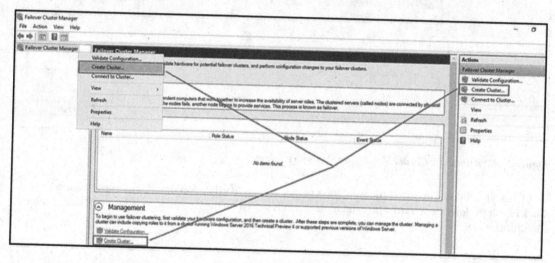

Figure 7-17. *Invoking Create Cluster action in the Failover Cluster Manager*

This invokes the Create Cluster Wizard as shown in Figure 7-18. Review the Before You Begin screen and click Next to start creating the failover cluster.

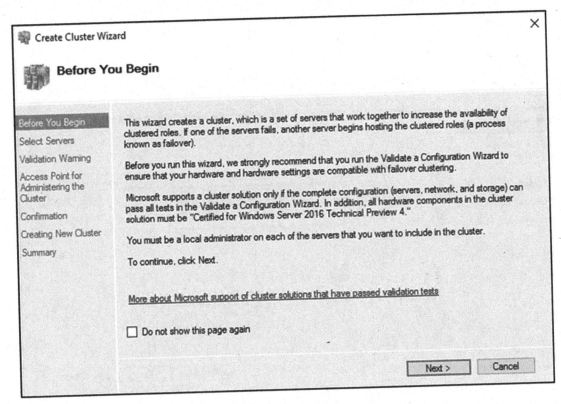

Figure 7-18. Reviewing the Before You Begin screen of the Create Cluster Wizard

Select Servers

In the Select Servers screen, enter the names of all the servers that will be part of the failover cluster separated by a semicolon and click Add. Figure 7-19 shows the screen for our environment with the three server names AlwaysOnN1, AlwaysOn2, and AlwaysOnN3. Click Next to continue.

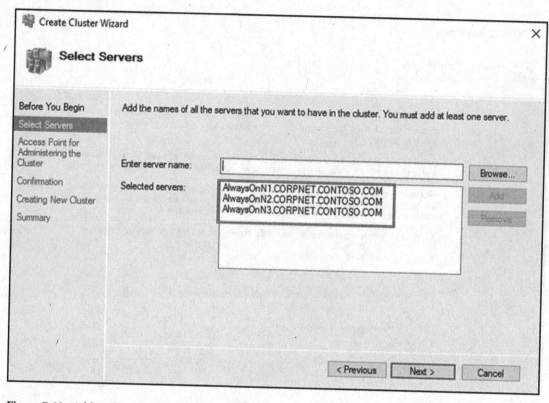

Figure 7-19. *Adding the servers that you want to include in the cluster*

Type Access Point for Administering the Cluster

In the Access Point for Administering the Cluster screen, type the name for the failover cluster. This cluster name is also the name that can be used to connect to manage it. During the cluster creation, the cluster name is registered as the *cluster name object (CNO)* in the Active Directory domain. By default, the CNO gets created in the same organization unit (OU) where the computer objects for the cluster nodes reside.

For increased flexibility, if you wish to create the CNO in a different OU location, you can do so by specifying the fully distinguished name. The distinguished name includes the path to the OU under which you would like the computer object created. For example, if you want to create a cluster name object named AlwaysOnCluster and want to place it in an OU called AlwaysOnOU in the Corpnet.Contoso.Com domain, the fully distinguished name will be CN=AlwaysOnCluster,OU=AlwaysOnOU,DC=Corpnet,DC=Contoso,DC=Com

The cluster name account (CNO) is very important, because through this account, other accounts also referred to as Virtual Computer Objects (VCOs) are automatically created as you configure new highly available roles in the cluster. This would include roles such as availability group, SQL Server failover clustering instance (FCI), etc.

■ **Note** The cluster name object (CNO) needs to have *Create Computer Objects* privilege on the organization unit (OU) it currently resides in to be able to create Virtual Computer Objects (VCOs). If the cluster name account is deleted or permissions are removed, other accounts cannot be created until the cluster name account is restored or the correct permissions are reinstated.

Also, in the Access Point for Administering the Cluster screen, select the networks you want to be used and type the cluster IP address as shown in Figure 7-20. In this figure, we have two cluster IP addresses as we have two subnets (one in primary datacenter and the other in the disaster datacenter) in our environment. Click Next to continue.

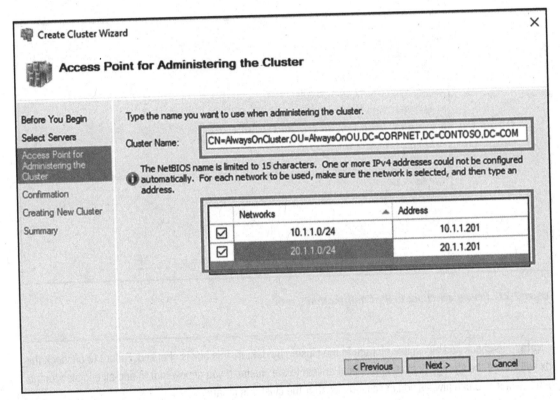

Figure 7-20. Entering the cluster name and network address to access the failover cluster

■ **Note** If you are using a specific organizational unit (OU) like we have done in our setup environment, ensure that the setup account is given the *Create Computer Objects* and *Read all Properties* on the OU.

Confirm Selections

Confirm the selections in the Confirmation screen as shown in Figure 7-21. Click Next to continue.

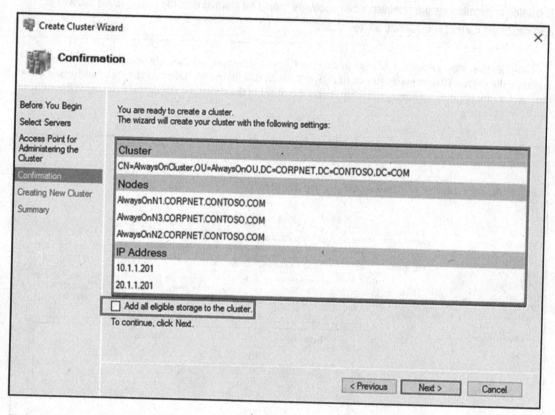

Figure 7-21. *Review selections in the Confirmation screen*

■ **Note** Uncheck Add all eligible storage to the cluster. By default, this box is checked. Failure to uncheck this box will add all the storage (including the local drives) to the cluster. If you choose not to add all eligible storage to the cluster, you can always add specific disks after the cluster is created.

Review Report

Review the Summary screen to ensure that the cluster is successfully created as shown in Figure 7-22.

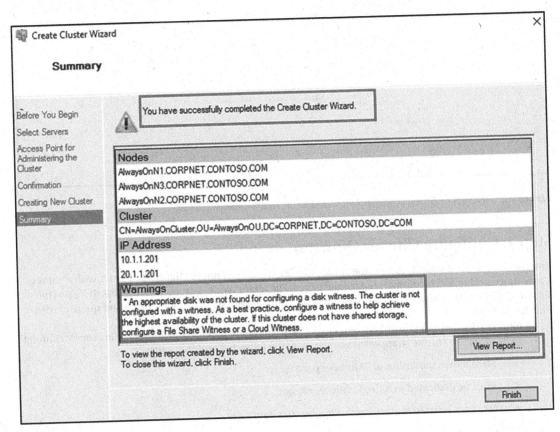

Figure 7-22. Reviewing the Create Cluster Summary

Review any warnings that may be displayed. For example, the following warning is displayed in the Summary screen for our setup:

An appropriate disk was not found for configuring a disk witness. The cluster is not configured with a witness. As a best practice, configure a witness to help achieve the highest availability of the cluster. If this cluster does not have shared storage, configure a File Share Witness or a Cloud Witness.

This warning is expected in our environment as we do not have any shared disk in the environment. Click the View Report to review the report created by the wizard. This report is stored on the C:\Windows\ Cluster\Reports folder for future review. Click Finish to close the wizard. The Failover Cluster Manager interface will automatically connect to the cluster when the wizard closes as shown in Figure 7-23.

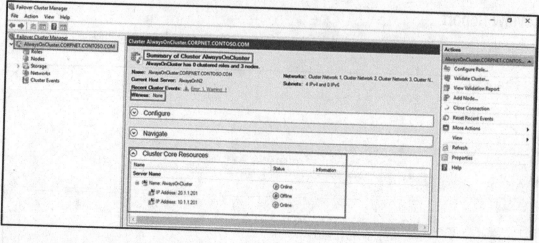

Figure 7-23. *Failover Cluster Manager connected to the newly created cluster*

Step 4: Configure Cluster Quorum

Since we did not have shared storage, the Create Cluster Wizard did not configure the cluster with a witness. It gave us a warning and recommended to configure a File Share Witness or a Cloud Witness to help achieve high availability of the cluster. In this step, we will demonstrate the steps to configure cluster quorum with a File Share Witness.

A file share witness is a Server Message Block (SMB) file share that is configured on a file server running on a Windows Server. The file share witness must meet the following requirements:

- Must have a minimum of 5MB free space

- Must be dedicated to a single failover cluster

- Must not be used to store user or application data

- Cluster name object (CNO) must have write permissions on the file share witness

Below are some considerations for the file server that hosts the file share witness:

- If you need the file server to be highly available, you can configure the file server on a separate failover cluster

- A single file server can be configured with multiple file share witnesses for multiple clusters

- For multisite clusters, consider having the file server on a different site to allow equal opportunity for any cluster site to survive if site-to-site networking has problems.

Open Configure Cluster Quorum Wizard

Open Failover Cluster Manager, right-click cluster name, select More Actions, and then select Configure Cluster Quorum Settings as shown in Figure 7-24.

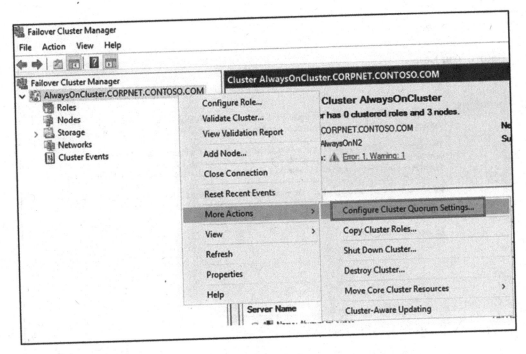

Figure 7-24. *Invoking Configure Cluster Quorum Wizard*

This will open the Configure Cluster Quorum Wizard as shown in Figure 7-25. Review the Before You Begin screen and click Next to continue.

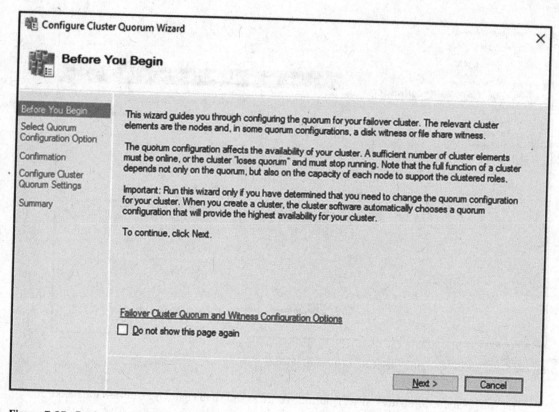

Figure 7-25. *Reviewing the Before You Begin Screen of Configure Cluster Quorum Wizard*

Select Quorum Configuration Option

On the Select Quorum Configuration Option screen, choose Select the quorum witness option as shown in Figure 7-26. Click Next to continue.

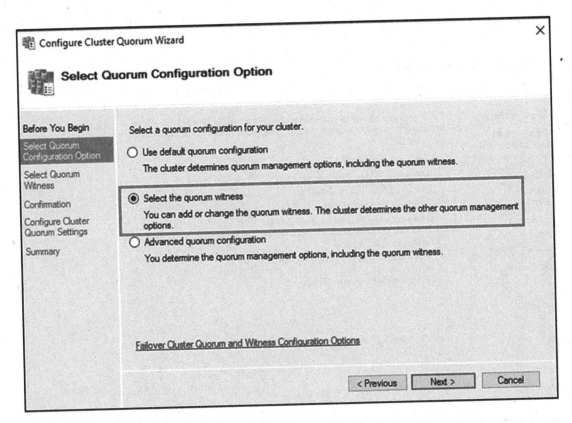

Figure 7-26. *Selecting a quorum configuration*

Select Quorum Witness

On the Select Quorum Witness screen, choose Configure a file share witness as shown in Figure 7-27. Click Next to continue.

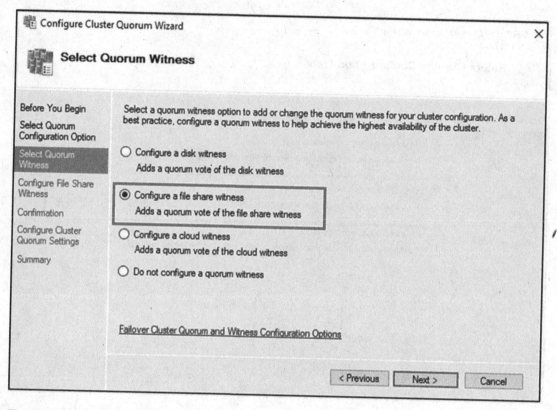

Figure 7-27. *Selecting a quorum witness option*

Starting with Windows Server 2016 Technical Preview, failover cluster introduces the *cloud witness* quorum type. The cloud witness quorum takes advantage of the Microsoft Azure public cloud as the witness for the failover cluster. This can be very useful for multisite clusters that do not have a third site to place a file share witness. The cloud witness acts the same as a file share witness, gets a vote, and can participate in quorum calculations.

■ **Note**   To configure a cloud witness quorum, you need a valid Microsoft Azure Storage Account Name and Access Key corresponding to the Storage Account. This information is entered in the Configure cloud witness screen that is invoked by selecting the option Configure a cloud witness in the Select Quorum Witness screen shown in Figure 7-27.

Configure File Share Witness

On the Configure File Share Witness screen, type or browse the file share that will be used as the file share witness as shown in Figure 7-28 and then click Next to continue.

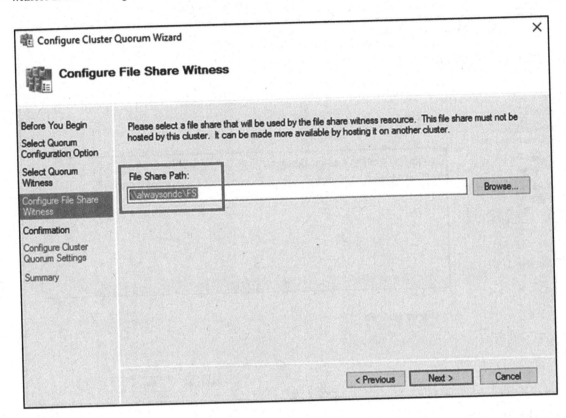

Figure 7-28. *Configuring file share witness*

Confirm Selections

Confirm the quorum settings on the Confirmation screen as shown in Figure 7-29 and then click Next to start the quorum configuration.

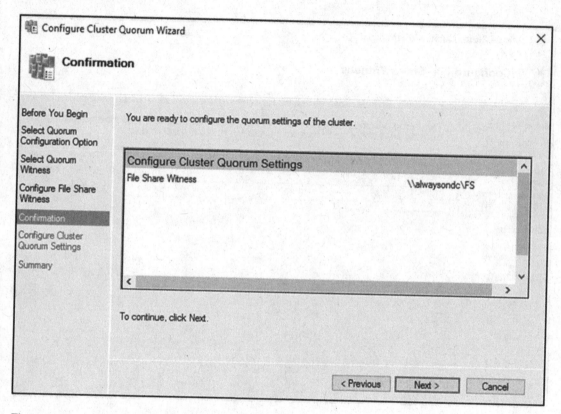

Figure 7-29. *Confirming cluster quorum settings*

Review Report

Review the Summary screen to ensure that the quorum is configured successfully as shown in Figure 7-30.

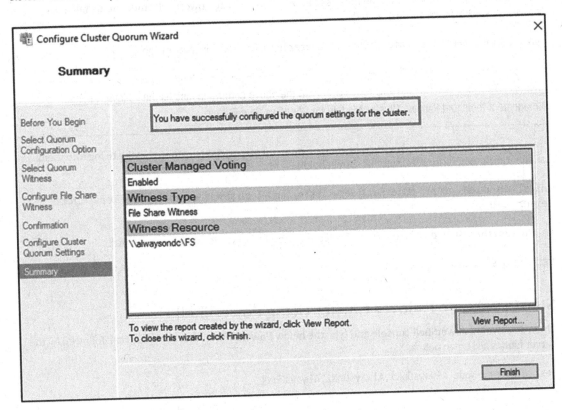

Figure 7-30. *Reviewing the Cluster Quorum Settings Summary*

Click the View Report to review the report created by the wizard. This report is stored on the C:\Windows\Cluster\Reports folder for future review. Click Finish to close the wizard.

Create a Windows Server Failover Cluster Using PowerShell

Earlier in this chapter, we demonstrated the steps to create a three-node Windows Server 2016 Failover Cluster using the Graphical User Interface Server Manager and Failover Cluster Manager. In this section, we will demonstrate the steps to create the failover cluster using Windows PowerShell cmdlets.

■ **Note**   To run the PowerShell cmdlets, open the PowerShell console with elevated privileges by right-clicking the PowerShell app and selecting *Run as administrator*.

Step 1: Install Failover Clustering Feature Using PowerShell

Log on to the server that you want to include in the failover cluster using your setup account. Open an elevated PowerShell console and type the Install-WindowsFeature PowerShell cmdlet to install the Failover Clustering feature as shown below:

```
Install-WindowsFeature -Name Failover-Clustering -IncludeManagementTools
```

■ **Note**   The -IncludeManagementTools switch in the above command installs the Failover Cluster Management tools and Failover Cluster Module for Windows PowerShell.

If you want to install the Failover Clustering feature on other servers without having to log into them, use the -ComputerName parameter as shown below:

```
Install-WindowsFeature -Name Failover-Clustering -IncludeManagementTools -ComputerName
server_name
```

To view the installed Failover Clustering feature, run the below PowerShell command:

```
Get-WindowsFeature *clus*
```

Step 2: Validate Failover Cluster Using PowerShell

Open an elevated PowerShell console and type the below PowerShell cmdlet Test-Cluster followed by the server names as shown below:

```
Test-Cluster -Node AlwaysOnN1,AlwaysOnN2,AlwaysOnN3
```

Step 3: Create Windows Server Failover Cluster Using PowerShell

Open an elevated PowerShell console and type the PowerShell New-Cluster cmdlet to create a new cluster and have the cluster name object (CNO) AlwaysOnCluster placed in the OU named AlwaysOnOU in the Corpnet.Contoso.com domain as shown below:

```
New-Cluster -Name "CN=AlwaysOnCluster,OU=AlwaysOnOU,DC=CORPNET,DC=CONTOSO,DC=COM" -Node
AlwaysOnN1,AlwaysOnN2,AlwaysOnN3 -StaticAddress 10.1.1.201,20.1.1.201 -NoStorage
```

■ **Note**   The -NoStorage parameter is specified to not add all eligible storage to the cluster.

Step 4: Configure Cluster Quorum Using PowerShell

To configure the cluster quorum to use file share witness using PowerShell, use the Set-ClusterQuorum cmdlet as shown below:

```
Set-ClusterQuorum -NodeAndFileShareMajority "\\File Share Path"
```

Workgroup and Multi-Domain Clusters

As we discussed in chapter 5, Windows Server 2016 Failover Clusters no longer require the cluster nodes to be part of the same domain or live in any domain at all. Now you can create a failover cluster using servers that are in workgroups. You can now create failover clusters without Active Directory (AD) dependencies.

SQL Server 2016 Always On Availability Groups are supported on workgroup and multi-domain clusters. You can now deploy SQL Server 2016 Always On Availability Groups not only on single-domain clusters which a majority of our customers use but also on workgroup and multi-domain clusters that caters to the needs of a select set of customers.

■ **Note**   The ability to create failover clusters without domains and support availability groups opens up a number of new scenarios for our customers, and removes previous blocks that prevented migration from the deprecated Database Mirroring technology to Always On Availability Groups.

In this section, we will demonstrate the steps to create a workgroup and/or multi-domain cluster. The below prerequisites for single-domain clusters still apply for workgroup and multi-domain clusters:

- All the hardware and software components must be "Certified for Windows Server 2016."
- The fully configured solution (servers, network and storage) must pass all cluster validation tests.

■ **Note**   Similar to creating traditional single-domain failover clusters, Failover Cluster Manager interface and Windows PowerShell can be used to create workgroup or multi-domain clusters.

In addition to the prerequisites of single-domain clusters, the below steps are needed to create a workgroup and multi-domain cluster.

Step 1: Create a Local User Account on Each Cluster Node

In an environment without AD security, you need to do the following on all the nodes of the cluster:

- Create a local user account
- The user name and password of the account must be the same on all nodes
- The account must be a member of the local *Administrators* group
- If you are using a non-built-in local administrator account to create the cluster, open an elevated PowerShell console and set the `LocalAccountTokenFilterPolicy` registry policy to 1 as follows:

```
new-itemproperty -path HKLM:\SOFTWARE\Microsoft\Windows\CurrentVersion\Policies\System -Name
LocalAccountTokenFilterPolicy -Value 1
```

■ **Caution** Without setting the `LocalAccountTokenFilterPolicy` registry policy will result in *Requested registry access is not allowed* error while trying to create a cluster using non-built-in administrator accounts.

Step 2: Ensure All Nodes Have Primary DNS Suffix

One of the many things that happen when a server is joined to a domain is that the primary DNS suffix is automatically configured, which matches the name of the AD DNS domain name and is identical to the DNS zone name. However, workgroup servers normally do not have a primary DNS suffix. Before you can create a workgroup cluster, you will need to manually configure the primary DNS suffix on all the servers that you want to include in the failover cluster.

Step 3: Create Workgroup or Multi-Domain Cluster

Workgroup and multi-domain clusters needs to be created as an Active Directory-Detached Cluster without any associated computer objects. Therefore, the cluster needs to have a cluster network name (also referred to as the administrative access point) of type DNS. Open an elevated PowerShell console, and type the below New-Cluster cmdlet to create the workgroup or multi-domain cluster

```
New-Cluster –Name <Cluster Name> -Node <Nodes to Cluster> -AdministrativeAccessPoint DNS
```

Step 4: Configure Quorum

The recommended cluster witness type for workgroup or multi-domain clusters is a cloud witness or disk witness. File share witness is not supported with a workgroup or multi-domain cluster. To configure cloud witness quorum, open an elevated PowerShell command and type the Set-ClusterQuorum cmdlet as shown below:

```
Set-ClusterQuorum –CloudWitness –AccountName <StorageAccountName> -AccessKey
<StorageAccountAccessKey>
```

Summary

In this chapter, we created Windows Server 2016 Failover Cluster, one of the key requirements for availability groups, using Graphical User Interface (Server Manager and Failover Cluster Manager) and Windows PowerShell. We also discussed the workgroup and multi-domain cluster deployment that is introduced in Windows Server 2016. In the next chapter, we will create the Always On Availability Groups.

CHAPTER 8

■ ■ ■

Create Availability Groups

In chapter 7 you created a Windows Server Failover Cluster (WSFC), one of the key requirements for Always On Availability Groups. In this chapter, we will look at how to create and configure availability groups.

The setup environment used for this chapter was introduced in the previous chapter. Just to recap, the environment consists of five servers:

- 1 DC (AlwaysOnDC)
- 2 Nodes in the Primary datacenter (AlwaysOnN1 and AlwaysOnN2)
- 1 Node in the secondary datacenter (AlwaysOnN3)
- 1 Client machine (AlwaysOnClient)

A Windows Server 2016 Cluster (AlwaysOnCluster) was created on three nodes: AlwaysOnN1, AlwaysOnN2, and AlwaysOnN3 in chapter 7.

This chapter assumes a stand-alone SQL Server 2016 Enterprise Edition installation has already been performed on all machines that are going to be the replicas in the Always On Availability Group. The SQL instances, AlwaysOnN1, AlwaysOnN2, and AlwaysOnN3 will be the replicas for the availability groups.

Review chapter 6 for a detailed list of prerequisites before attempting to create an availability group.

Step 1: Enable the Always On Availability Groups Feature

The next step is to ensure that the Always On Availability Group feature is enabled for each SQL Server instance To do this, open up SQL Configuration Manager ➤ select SQL Server Services ➤ Right-click the SQL Server Service and click on Properties.

Figure 8-1 shows the SQL Configuration Manager window to select the SQL Server Service Properties.

© Uttam Parui and Vivek Sanil 2016
U. Parui and V. Sanil, *Pro SQL Server Always On Availability Groups*, DOI 10.1007/978-1-4842-2071-9_8

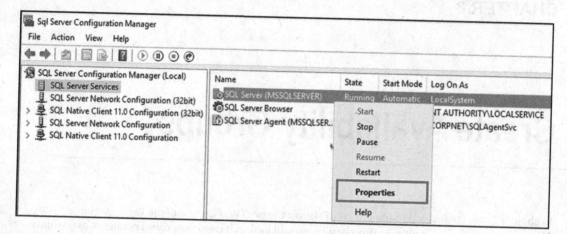

Figure 8-1. *SQL Server Service properties option in the SQL Server Configuration Manager*

Figure 8-2 shows the SQL Server service properties box and Always On Availability Group tab with the option to enable the Always On Availability Groups feature.

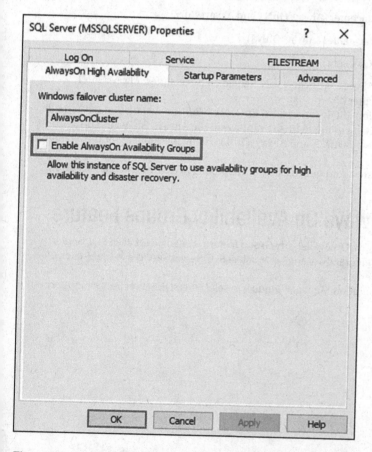

Figure 8-2. *Enable Always On Availability Group Feature*

After the Properties window opens up, select the Always On High Availability tab and then check the Enable Always On Availability Groups check box and click Apply. As soon as you click apply, you will see a dialog box warning that the changes will not take effect until the service is restarted. Click ok on the dialog box.

You might have noticed in the above figure that Windows Failover Cluster Name (AlwaysOnCluster) shows up under the Always On High Availability tab. This is the Windows Cluster you created in chapter 7.

While you are in the SQL Server Service Properties window, also review the Log On Service account being used for the SQL instance by clicking on the **Log On** tab. Figure 8-3 shows the Log On tab in the SQL Server Service properties window.

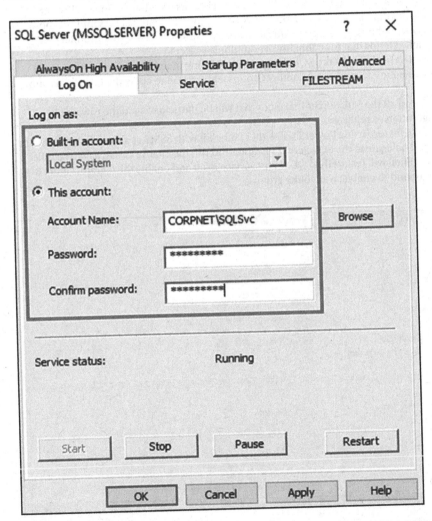

Figure 8-3. Change SQL Service Log On account

The SQL Service Log On account should have access to the replica instances. To keep things simple, you can also use the same Service Log On account on all the replica instances.

■ **Note**   *Group managed service accounts* (gMSA) are now supported in SQL Server 2016. It is recommended to use gMSA for Always On SQL Server instances. If gMSA cannot be used, then it is recommended to use the same domain account as the logon account for all the replica SQL server instances.

MSAs are recommended when resources external to the SQL Server computer are needed, or else Virtual Accounts are recommended on servers that are Windows Server 2008 R2 and higher. MMSAs are managed domain accounts that provide automatic password management and simplified SPN management, including delegation of management to other administrators within the domain. They are much more secure than regular domain accounts. However, MSAs cannot be shared across multiple hosts; hence they could not be used on the SQL servers hosting availability groups. *gMSAs* were introduced in Windows Server 2012, which extends that functionality over multiple servers.

After clicking OK, go ahead and restart the SQL Server service during maintenance window to avoid service interruption, to enable the Always On Availability Groups feature, and to apply the Log On account change.

Repeat the above steps on all the SQL Server Instances that will be participating in the Always On Availability Groups configuration as replicas.

To enable the Always On feature using PowerShell, either launch it with SSMS as shown in Figure 8-4 or launch it from Windows and navigate to the SQL Server instance and run the Enable-SQLAlwaysOn cmdlet to enable the feature. PowerShell will restart the SQL Server service itself and enable the feature. Figure 8-4 shows the PowerShell command to enable availability groups.

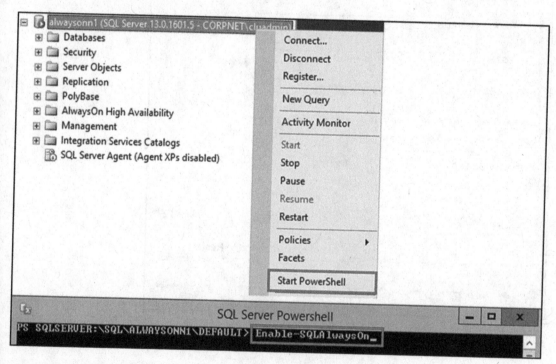

Figure 8-4. *Enabling Always On Availability Groups feature using PowerShell*

Step 2: Invoke Availability Group Wizard

Now that the SQL Server services have been enabled for the Always On Availability Groups feature, the next step is to create an availability group. We will be initializing the availability group creation from AlwaysOnN1 SQL instance. The AlwaysOnN1 instance already has two databases: AdventureWorks2016 and AdventureWorksDW2016 that will be participating in the availability group.

Figure 8-5 shows the databases that will be participating in the availability group.

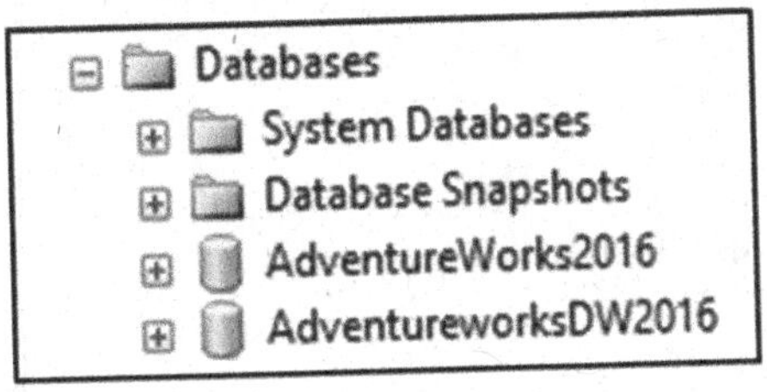

Figure 8-5. Databases for the availability group

■ **Note** A new sample database (WideWorldImporters) has been released for SQL Server 2016. It is supposed to be an upgrade over the old AdventureWorks database that has been around since SQL Server 2005. The new sample database can be downloaded from here: `https://msdn.microsoft.com/library/mt734199(v=sql.1).aspx`

We have used AdventureWorks2016 database for our book as it will still be around. It can be downloaded from here: `https://www.microsoft.com/en-us/download/details.aspx?id=49502`

We will be using the availability group Wizard to create an availability group. To invoke this wizard, right-click either on the Always On High Availability node or availability groups node in SSMS.

Figure 8-6 shows the location in SSMS from where the New Availability Group Wizard can be launched.

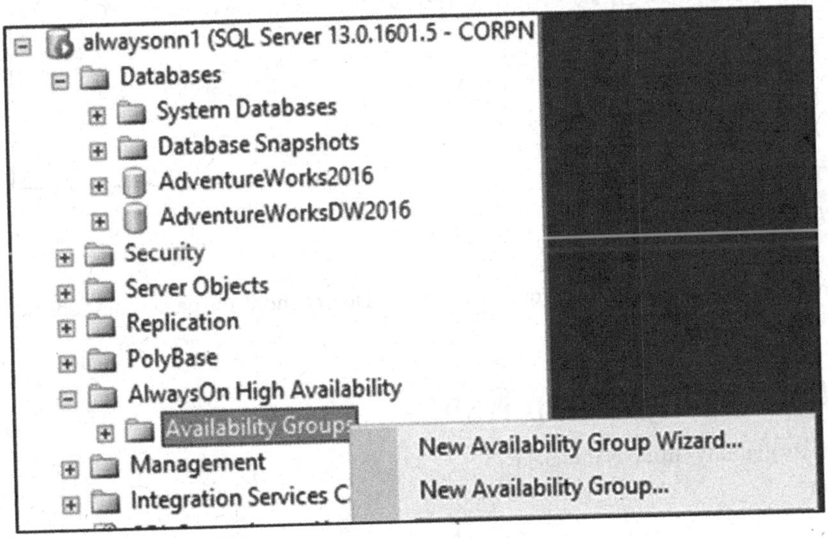

Figure 8-6. Launching New Availability Group Wizard

An Introduction page appears the first time you run this wizard. Figure 8-7 shows the introduction page.

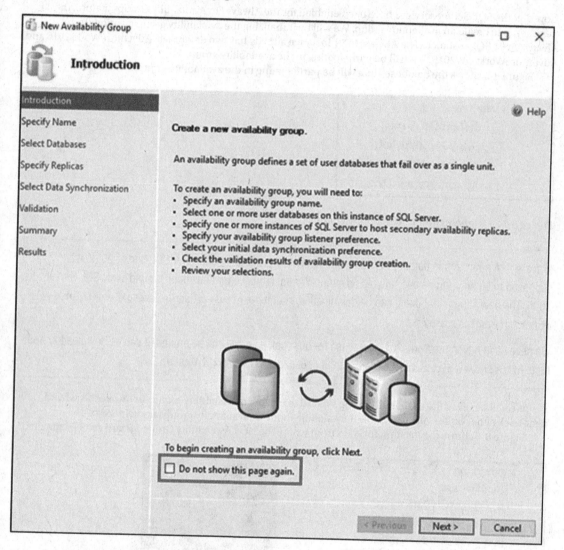

Figure 8-7. New availability group Wizard

To avoid this page from showing up in the future, you can click the "Do not show this page again" check box and then click Next.

Step 3: Select Availability Group Name

Figure 8-8 shows the Specify Availability Group Name page.

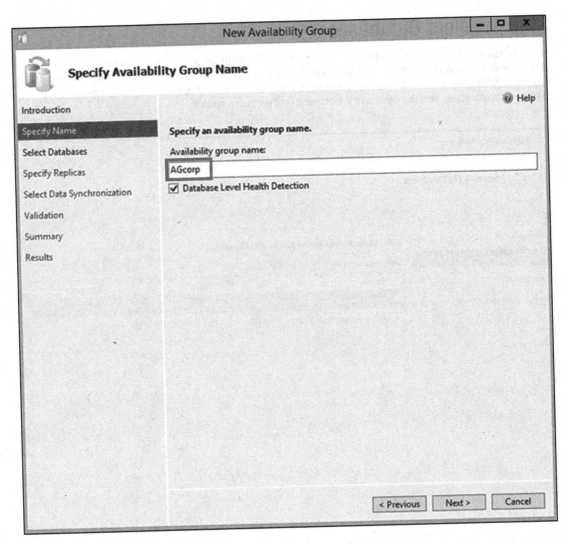

Figure 8-8. *Specify availability group Name*

On the Specify Availability Group Name page, enter the name of the new availability group. This name is only to identify the availability group. The clients will not be connecting to this name as they will be connecting to the listener, which we will be configuring later.

Prior to SQL Server 2016, availability group health only monitored the health of the instance. A database can be offline or corrupt, but as long as the instance itself is healthy, a failover won't be triggered. SQL Server 2016 introduces database level health detection that allows you to optionally change the health monitoring to also consider the health of the databases in the AG.

After choosing the Database Level Health Detection option, click Next.

Step 4: Select Databases

Figure 8-9 shows the Select user databases for the availability group page. Here you can select the database to include in the availability group. Pay special attention to the Status column. If the database does not fulfill any prerequisite, then it would show up in the Status column: for example, if a Full backup has not been taken for the database or if the database is not using Full recovery model.

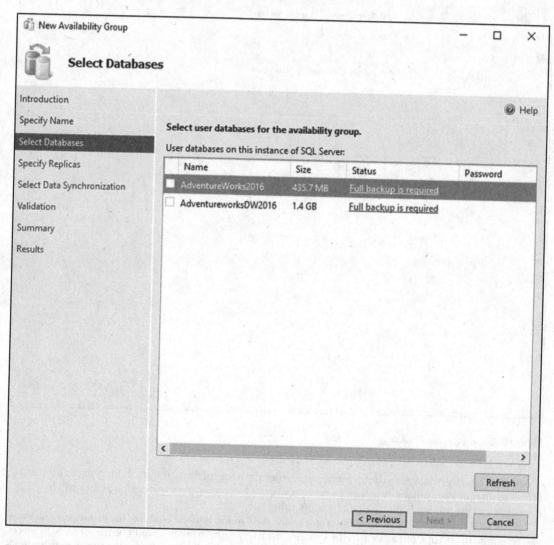

Figure 8-9. *Select user database cannot proceed to next screen*

As can be seen in the Status column, one of the database prerequisites for availability groups has not been met. In this case, full backup has not been taken. The check box to select the database will be grayed out, and you won't be able to proceed to the next screen unless a full backup is taken.

■ **Note** For a complete list of all the prerequisites for availability groups, please refer to chapter 6.

Perform the full backup and on the select user database page, click Refresh. The status should now say Meets prerequisites.

Figure 8-10 shows the Select user databases for the availability group page where the prerequisites have been met.

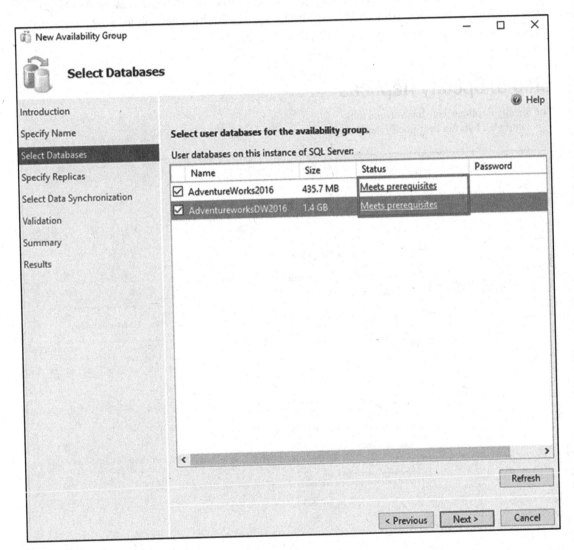

Figure 8-10. *Select user databases for the availability group*

Click Next.

■ **Note** In SQL Server 2012 and 2014, encrypted databases could be added to an availability group, but they could not be added using the availability group wizard. Additionally, the encrypted databases could not be accessed in the event of a failover. SQL Server 2016 adds support to the availability group wizard for adding encrypted databases and simplifies database access following a failover. In SQL Server 2016, if you select an encrypted database in the Select Databases page, the wizard detects that the databases is defined with a database master key and prompts the administrator for the database master key password. After adding the database, the wizard will verify the password during the validation phase. After you enter all the information and click Finish (Figure 8-24), the wizard creates the credentials on each replica using the password of the database master key.

Step 5: Specify Replicas

The Specify Replicas page has various tabs.

Figure 8-11 shows the Specify Replicas page.

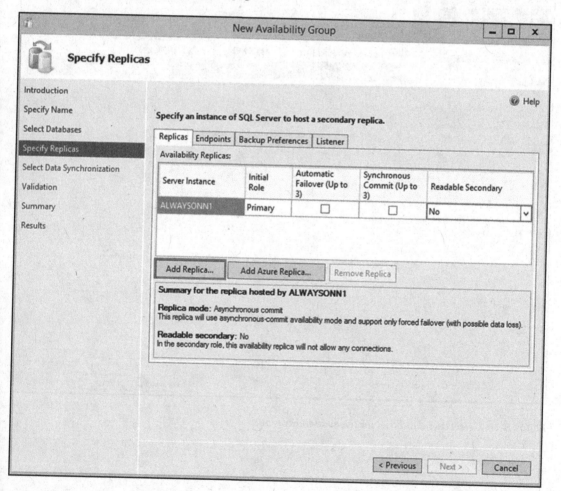

Figure 8-11. Specify Replicas page

In the first tab Replicas, add the replicas that will be participating in the availability group. In this case, AlwaysOnN2 and AlwaysOnN3 instances. Click the Add Replicas button to add new Replicas.

■ **Note** We will be covering the Add Azure Replica option later in chapter 18.

Figure 8-12 shows the Connect to Server window.

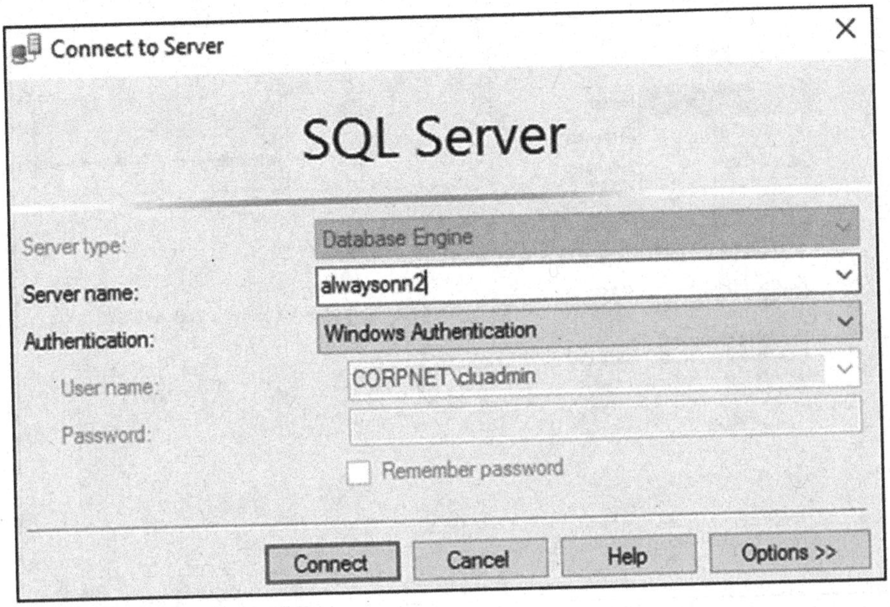

Figure 8-12. Connect to Server

In the Connect to Server window, provide the SQL instance name that you want to configure as a replica for the availability group. Click Connect and repeat the Add Replica step for other replica instances in the availability group. In this case, that would be the AlwaysOnN3 instance.

Figure 8-13 shows the Specify Replicas page with all the replicas added.

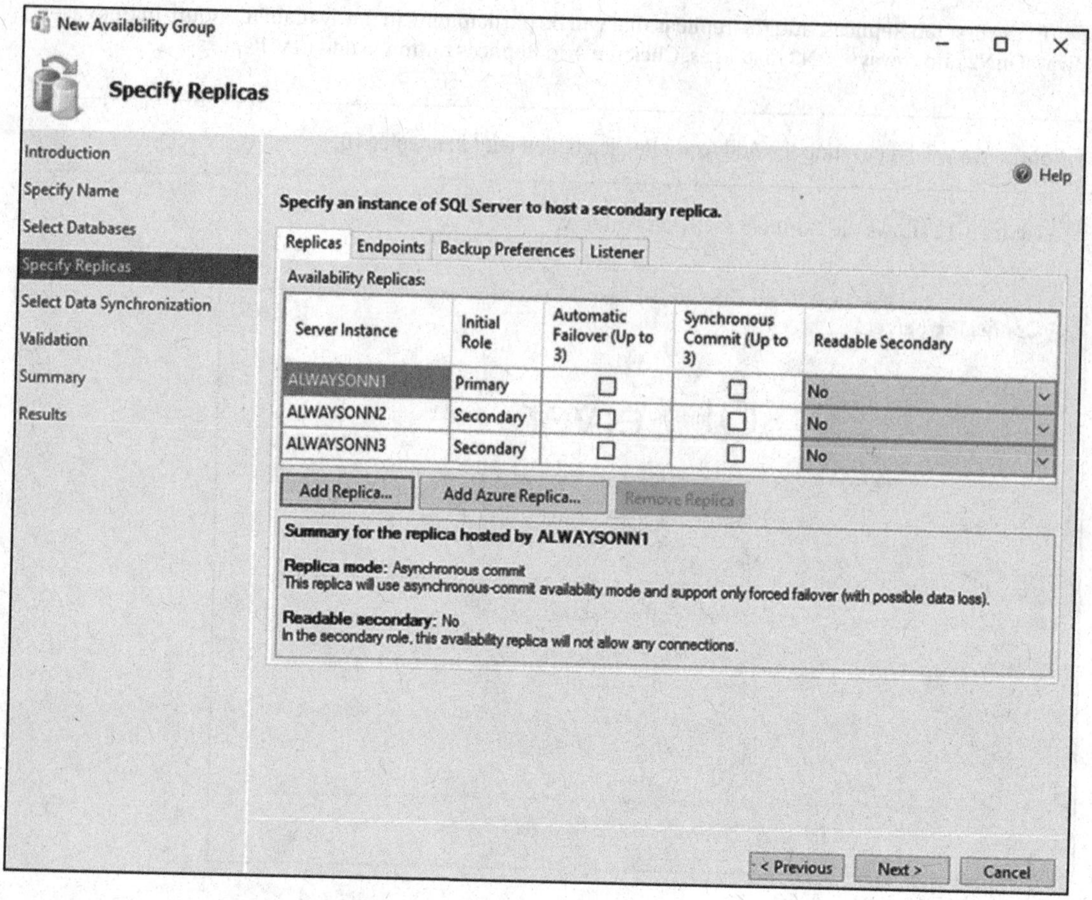

Figure 8-13. *Specify Replicas page with all the replicas added*

- Automatic Failover option

    If you want the availability replica to be an automatic failover partner, then select this
    check box. Select this option for the initial primary replica and for one secondary
    replica. The replicas selected for automatic failover will use the synchronous-commit
    availability mode.

■ **Note** In SQL Server 2016 you can have three replicas configured for Automatic Failover.

- Synchronous-Commit option

    Select this checkbox to configure the replica to use synchronous-commit or leave it
    blank to use asynchronous-commit mode. We discussed the data synchronization
    modes in detail in chapter 4, the one about Data Synchronization Internals.

■ **Note** Only three replicas can use synchronous-commit mode.

- Readable Secondary

  The Readable Secondary drop-down has three options:

  - No (Default Setting) – Secondary databases of this replica are not available for read access and direct connections are not allowed to secondary databases of this replica.

  - Read-intent only – The secondary databases are available for read access only if the connection string has the application intent property set to read only.

  - Yes – Read only access is available to the secondary databases for all connections.

Figure 8-14 shows the Specify Replicas page with the options selected in the Replicas tab.

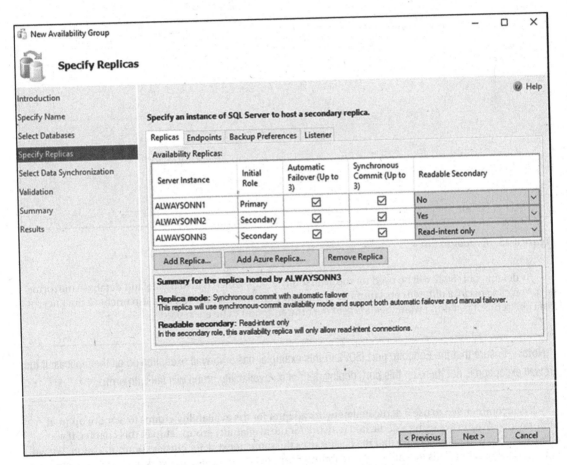

Figure 8-14. Specify Replicas page with the options selected in the Replicas tab

Step 6: Configure Endpoint

Click on the Endpoints tab to review the values.

Figure 8-15 shows the Specify Replicas page with the Endpoints tab.

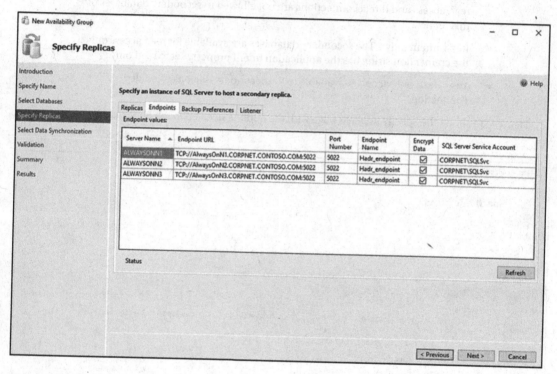

Figure 8-15. *Endpoints tab*

By default, port 5022 will be used for the availability group, which is also the default database mirroring port. You can specify a different port number in the port number column. You can also uncheck the Encrypt Data check box if you don't want the data sent over the endpoint to be encrypted.

■ **Note**   Ensure that the Endpoint port (5022 in this example) has a firewall exception on all the replicas. If the firewall exception is not there on this port, deployment of an availability group will fail with error.

It is recommended to use a dedicated network adapter for the availability groups to achieve optimal performance. We are not using a dedicated network for the availability group setup in this chapter. If you choose to do this, then make sure that the cluster uses the same network for cluster communication. We will cover the TSQL commands to configure availability groups over a dedicated network in the TSQL section later in this chapter.

Step 7: Configure Backup Preferences

Click the Backup Preferences tab to review the values.

Figure 8-16 shows the Specify Replicas page with the Backup Preferences tab. The options on this lets you specify your backup preference for the availability group and your backup priorities for the individual availability replicas.

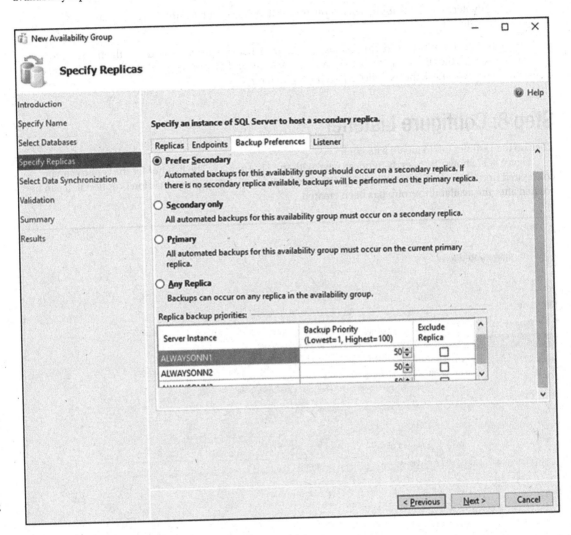

Figure 8-16. Backup Preferences tab

The options here only matter for automated backups. They do not apply for manual backups. Database maintenance plan and log shipping are aware of this setting and can leverage the preferences selected here. For custom maintenance jobs, the script will have to contain the logic to use the preferences selected here. We will be discussing the script and logic to use in detail later in chapter 11.

- Prefer Secondary (Default) - Backups occur on a secondary replica except when the primary replica is the only replica online.

- Secondary only - Backups always occur on the secondary. Backups will not occur if the primary is the only replica online.

- Primary - Backups always occur on the primary replica. You might want to choose this option if differential backups are to be taken. Differential backups are not supported on secondary replicas.

- Any Replica – Backups can occur on any replica; however backup priority will still be applicable.

To set the backup priorities, set the values in the replica backup priorities grid. For the backup priority, you can select any other integer between 1 and 100. One is the lowest priority, and 100 is the highest priority. To exclude a replica, check the exclude replica box for that replica.

Step 8: Configure Listener

Click on the Listener tab to create a listener.

Figure 8-17 shows the Specify Replicas page with the Listener tab. The listener for the replica can be configured from this tab. The creation of the listener during availability group creation is optional. It can be created after the availability group has been created.

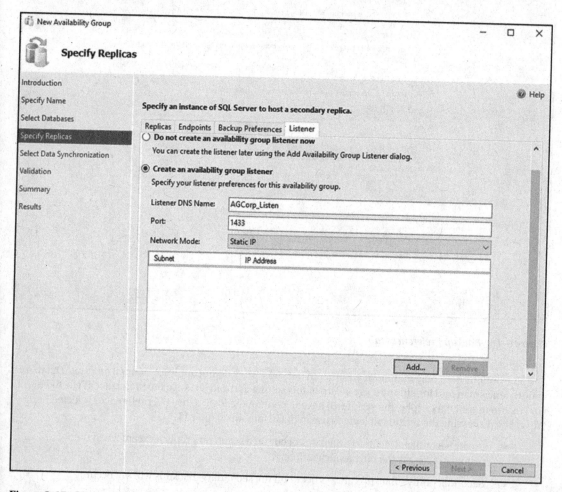

Figure 8-17. Listener tab

Choose the "Do not create an availability group listener now option" if you do not wish to create the listener along with the availability group.

■ **Note** Ensure that the cluster name object (AlwaysOnCluster in our setup) has *Create Computer Objects* and *Read All Properties* privileges on the organization unit (AlwaysOnOU in our setup) it currently resides in to be able to create Virtual Computer Objects (AGCorp_Listen in our setup).

To create it along with an availability group, select the "Create an availability group listener" option.

Specify the network name in the Listener DNS name box and the port number in the Port box. Listener Name must be unique in the domain. It can be alphanumeric and 15 characters long.

■ **Note** If you choose to use port 1433, you do not need to provide a port number in a connection string. If you choose a port other than 1433 for your listener port, you will also need to explicitly specify a target port in your connection string. Also ensure that no other services on the cluster node are using this port; otherwise this would cause a port conflict. If one of the instances of SQL Server is listening on TCP port 1433 and there are no other services (including additional instances of SQL Server) on the computer listening on port 1433, this will not cause a port conflict with the availability group listener. An availability group listener can share the same TCP port inside the same service process. Multiple instances of SQL Server should not be configured to listen on the same port.

Click on the Network mode drop-down list to select the network mode to be used by this listener. Select DHCP if you want dynamic IPv4 address assigned by a server running Dynamic Host Configuration Protocol (DHCP). DHCP is limited to a single subnet. DHCP is not recommended for production environments. If you want the listener to listen on more than one subnet, use the static IP network mode option. In this chapter we will be setting up a multi-subnet availability group, hence static IP was selected.

Next click on the Add button.

Figure 8-18 shows the IP Address window.

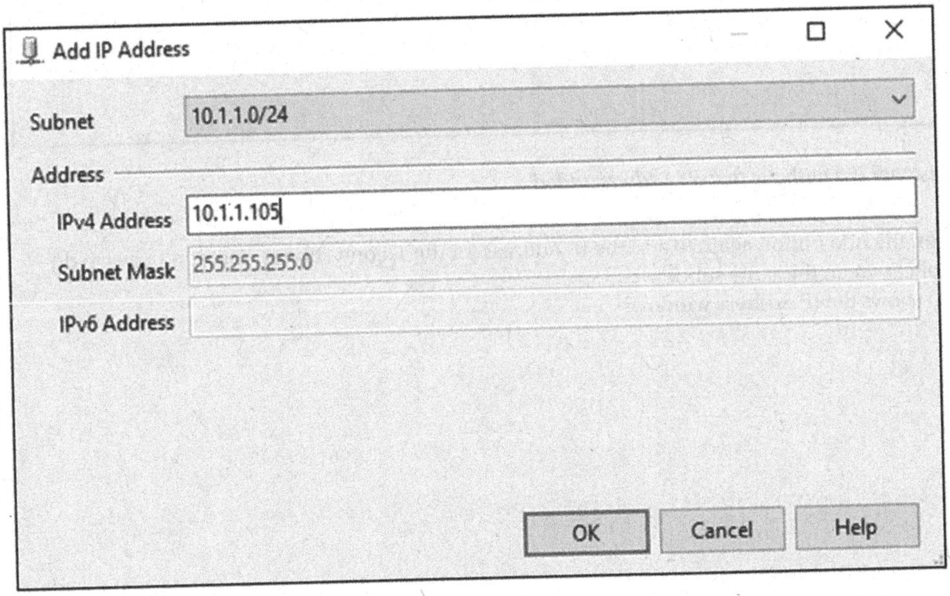

Figure 8-18. *Add IP Address*

In the Subnet drop-down, select the first subnet and provide a new IPv4 address and click OK. Figure 8-19 shows the Specify Replicas page with the IP Address added for the first subnet.

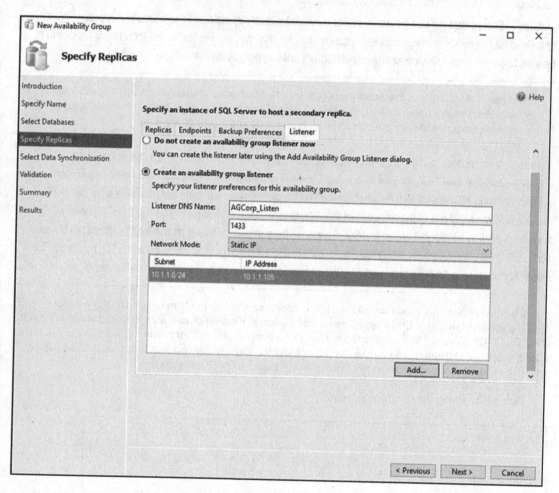

Figure 8-19. *Listener tab with the first IP Address added*

Next click on the Add button again to add the IP Address for the second subnet. You don't have to do this if all the replicas are in the same subnet.

Figure 8-20 shows the IP Address window.

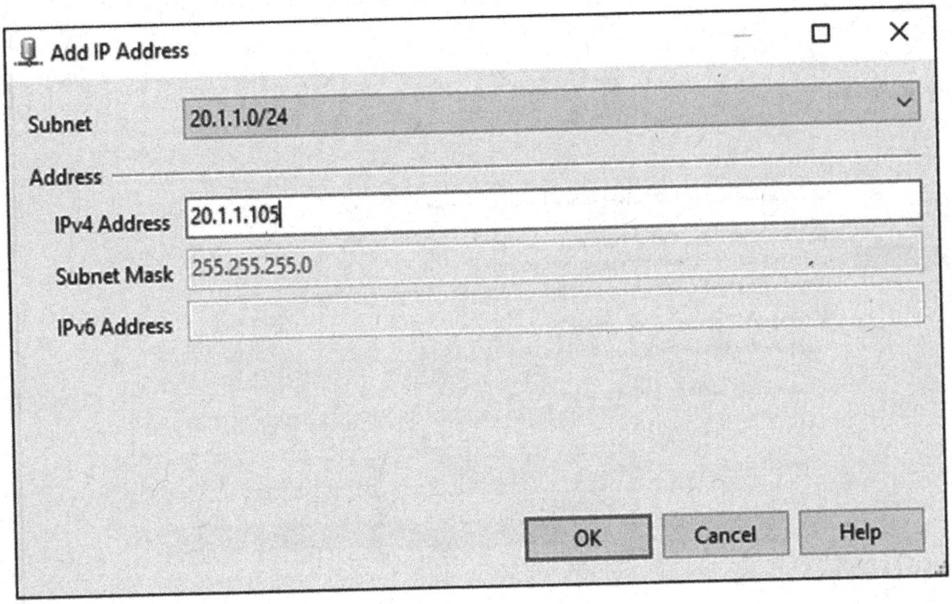

Figure 8-20. *Add IP Address*

This time select the second subnet in the Subnet drop-down and provide a new IPv4 Address and click OK. Figure 8-21 shows the Specify Replicas page with both of the IP Addresses for the listener.

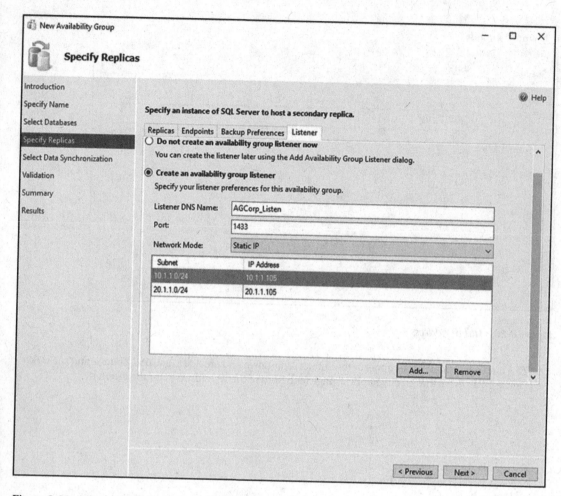

Figure 8-21. *Listener tab with the second IP Address added*

Click on Next to proceed to the Data Synchronization screen.

Step 9: Select Initial Data Synchronization

Figure 8-22 shows the Select Initial Data Synchronization page.

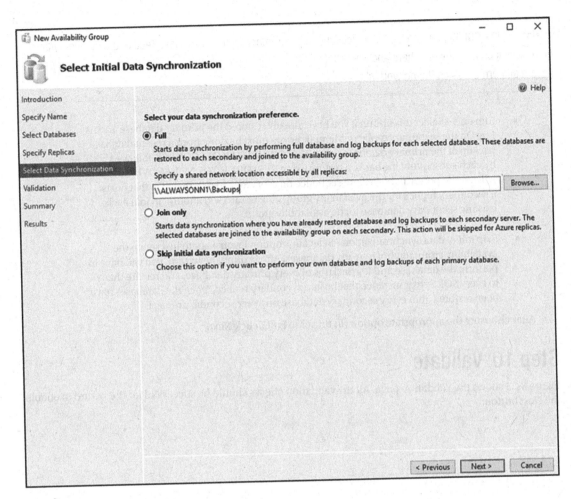

Figure 8-22. Select Initial Data Synchronization

Select your preference for initial data synchronization of new secondary databases on this page. The options you have is Full, Join only, and Skip initial data synchronization.

- Full – If you choose the full option, the wizard will create a full and log backup of the primary database, create the corresponding secondary databases by restoring these backups on every server instance that is hosting a secondary replica, and join each secondary database to an availability group in one workflow. You will need to specify a network share for the wizard to create and access backups.

■ **Note**   The SQL Server service logon account on the primary replica must have read and write file-system permissions on the network share and the SQL Server service logon account on the secondary replica must have read permission on the network share.

- Join only - Select this option if you have already restored the primary database and its Log On the secondary replicas. Manual restore must be done from a recent database backup of the primary database using RESTORE WITH NORECOVERY, followed by each subsequent log backup restore using RESTORE WITH NORECOVERY. You will have to perform this restore sequence on every SQL Server instance that hosts a secondary replica for the availability group. The wizard will attempt to join each existing secondary database to the availability group.

- Skip initial data synchronization - Select this option if you want to just set up the availability group but not join any databases. After exiting the wizard, you will have to perform the database and log backups of every primary database, and restore them to every SQL Server instance that hosts a secondary replica. Once the databases have been restored, join every secondary database on every secondary replica.

After choosing the appropriate option (in this case Full), click Next.

Step 10: Validate

Figure 8-23 shows the Validation page. All the validation checks should be successful for the wizard to enable the Next button.

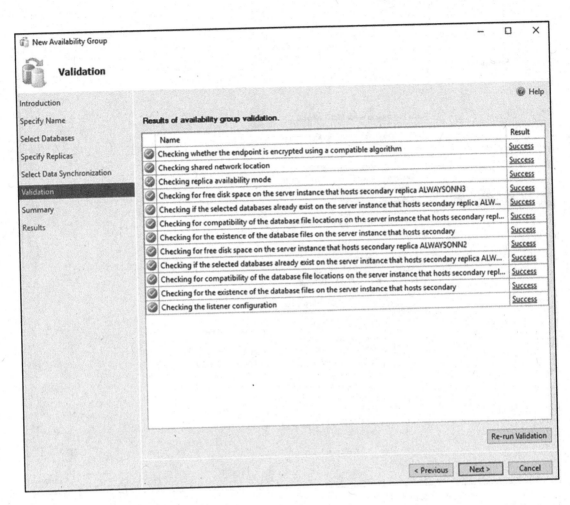

Figure 8-23. Availability group validation

After reviewing the validation results, click Next.

Figure 8-24 shows Part 1 of the Summary page with values provided for the availability group creation.

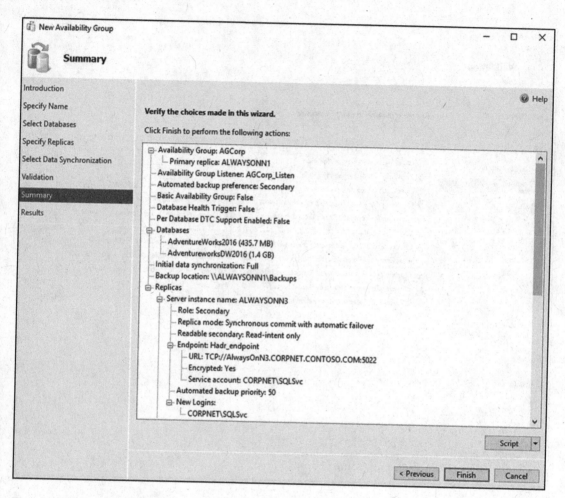

Figure 8-24. *Summary Part 1*

Figure 8-25 shows Part 2 of the Summary page with values provided for the availability group creation.

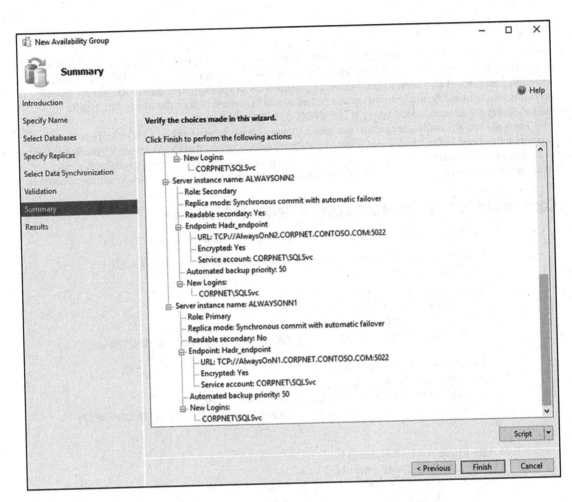

Figure 8-25. *Summary Part 2*

After reviewing the summary page, click Finish.

Other Ways to Create an Availability Group

In this chapter we covered creating availability groups using the availability group wizard. This is the most common method and the easiest one to create an availability group. Following are some of the other methods that are available to you:

Availability group dialog box

You can invoke the availability group dialog box from SSMS by expanding Always On High Availability node and right-clicking on the availability groups node. You can enter the name of the availability group, add Databases and Availability Replicas, modify roles, availability and failover modes, and configure backup preferences from this dialog box. Unlike the wizard, you cannot create a listener from this dialog box.

T-SQL

You can also use the CREATE AVAILABILITY GROUP T-SQL commands to create and configure availability group. You need to first create a database mirroring endpoint manually using CREATE ENDPOINT T-SQL command. You would also need to grant CONNECT permissions to appropriate logins if SQL Server service accounts runs under different domain accounts. You would also need to start the AlwaysOn_Health extended event session manually using ALTER EVENT SESSION command.

There are certain availability group operations that can be performed only via TSQL as there is no GUI support at this time. For example, configuring availability groups over a dedicated network, creating a Basic Availability Group (BAG), enabling DTC support, enabling automatic seeding on the availability group, creating a distributed availability group, and configuring an Always On Availability Group without Domains.

Configuring Availability Groups over a Dedicated Network

1. Create the endpoints manually or modify them later to use the dedicated NIC IPs.

   Following is the TSQL script for creating endpoints manually (where 10.1.1.x is the dedicated network):

   ```
   -- On AlwaysOnN1 (Replica 1)
   CREATE ENDPOINT [Hadr_endpoint]
       AS TCP (LISTENER_PORT = 5022, LISTENER_IP = (10.1.1.1))
       FOR DATA_MIRRORING (ROLE = ALL, ENCRYPTION = REQUIRED ALGORITHM AES);
   GO
   -- On AlwaysOnN2 (Replica 2)
   CREATE ENDPOINT [Hadr_endpoint]
       AS TCP (LISTENER_PORT = 5022, LISTENER_IP = (10.1.1.2))
       FOR DATA_MIRRORING (ROLE = ALL, ENCRYPTION = REQUIRED ALGORITHM AES);
   GO


   -- On AlwaysOnN3 (Replica 3)
   CREATE ENDPOINT [Hadr_endpoint]
       AS TCP (LISTENER_PORT = 5022, LISTENER_IP = (10.1.1.3))
       FOR DATA_MIRRORING (ROLE = ALL, ENCRYPTION = REQUIRED ALGORITHM AES);
   GO
   ```

2. Provide the dedicated network IP in the endpoint URL, while creating an availability group.

```
CREATE AVAILABILITY GROUP AGCorp
WITH (AUTOMATED_BACKUP_PREFERENCE = SECONDARY)
FOR DATABASE [AdventureWorks2016]
REPLICA
ON N'AlwaysOnN1' WITH (ENDPOINT_URL = N'TCP://10.1.1.1:5022', FAILOVER_MODE = AUTOMATIC,
AVAILABILITY_MODE = SYNCHRONOUS_COMMIT, BACKUP_PRIORITY = 50, SECONDARY_ROLE(ALLOW_
CONNECTIONS = NO)),
   N'AlwaysOnN2' WITH (ENDPOINT_URL = N'TCP://10.1.1.2:5022', FAILOVER_MODE = AUTOMATIC,
   AVAILABILITY_MODE = SYNCHRONOUS_COMMIT, BACKUP_PRIORITY = 50, SECONDARY_ROLE(ALLOW_
   CONNECTIONS = NO)),
   N'AlwaysOnN3' WITH (ENDPOINT_URL = N'TCP://10.1.1.2:5022', FAILOVER_MODE = AUTOMATIC,
   AVAILABILITY_MODE = SYNCHRONOUS_COMMIT, BACKUP_PRIORITY = 50, SECONDARY_ROLE(ALLOW_
   CONNECTIONS = NO)),
;
```

Basic Availability Group (BAG)

BAG replaces the deprecated Database Mirroring feature for SQL Server 2016 Standard Edition. It is a high availability solution for SQL Server 2016 Standard Edition or higher.

Following are some of the limitations of BAG:

- It is limited to two replicas (primary and secondary).

- There is no read access on the secondary replica.

- You cannot perform backups on the secondary replica.

- You cannot add or remove a replica to an existing basic availability group.

- Only one availability database is supported in a BAG.

- They cannot be upgraded to advanced availability groups.

- The group must be dropped and re-added to a group that contains servers running the SQL Server 2016 Enterprise Edition.

To create a basic availability group, you will have to use the CREATE AVAILABILITY GROUP command along with the WITH BASIC option. If WITH BASIC option is not provided during the availability group creation, then an advanced availability group is created by default.

The following is the sample code for creating a basic availability group:

```
CREATE AVAILABILITY GROUP AGCorp
WITH (BASIC)
FOR DATABASE AdventureWorks2016
REPLICA ON
 N'AlwaysOnN1' WITH (ENDPOINT_URL = N'TCP://AlwaysOnN1.Contoso.COM:5022', FAILOVER_MODE =
AUTOMATIC, AVAILABILITY_MODE = SYNCHRONOUS_COMMIT),
 N'AlwaysOnN2' WITH (ENDPOINT_URL = N'TCP://AlwaysOnN2.Contoso.COM:5022', FAILOVER_MODE =
AUTOMATIC, AVAILABILITY_MODE = SYNCHRONOUS_COMMIT);
```

- Per Database DTC Support

  Prior to SQL Server 2016, distributed transactions on databases in an availability group were not allowed. In SQL Server 2016, this is now supported. SQL Server 2016 registers a Resource Manager per availability database, which then works with the DTC service to keep track of the distributed transactions. This allows guaranteed integrity of a distributed transaction.

  DTC with availability groups is only available on Windows Server 2012 R2 (with KB3090973) and above. Also the availability group must have been created with the WITH DTC_SUPPORT = PER_DB clause in the CREATE AVAILABILITY GROUP command.

  The following is the sample code for enabling DTC support on the availability group:

```
CREATE AVAILABILITY GROUP AGCorp
WITH (DTC_SUPPORT = PER_DB)
FOR DATABASE AdventureWorks2016
REPLICA ON
 N'AlwaysOnN1' WITH (ENDPOINT_URL = N'TCP://AlwaysOnN1.Contoso.COM:5022', FAILOVER_MODE =
AUTOMATIC, AVAILABILITY_MODE = SYNCHRONOUS_COMMIT),
 N'AlwaysOnN2' WITH (ENDPOINT_URL = N'TCP://AlwaysOnN2.Contoso.COM:5022', FAILOVER_MODE =
AUTOMATIC, AVAILABILITY_MODE = SYNCHRONOUS_COMMIT),
 N'AlwaysOnN3' WITH (ENDPOINT_URL = N'TCP://AlwaysOnN3.Contoso.COM:5022', FAILOVER_MODE =
MANUAL, AVAILABILITY_MODE = ASYNCHRONOUS_COMMIT);
```

■ **Note** SQL Server 2016 RTM only supports distributed transactions where no two databases are hosted by the same instance. Also an existing availability group cannot be altered.

Automatic Seeding

When automatic seeding is enabled for an availability group, SQL Server automatically creates the secondary databases for every replica in the group. That means you no longer have to manually back up and restore secondary replicas.

If you want to enable automatic seeding for an existing availability group, then you can run the ALTER AVAILABILITY GROUP command.

```
ALTER AVAILABILITY GROUP AGCorp
MODIFY REPLICA ON 'AlwaysOnN1' WITH (SEEDING_MODE = AUTOMATIC)

GO
```

If you are creating a new availability group, then do the following:

1. You will have to create an endpoint on each SQL Server instance participating in the availability group. The following script creates endpoints for TCP port 5022 for the listener.

    ```
    CREATE ENDPOINT HADR_Endpoint
    STATE=STARTED
    AS TCP (LISTENER_PORT = 5022, LISTENER_IP = ALL)
            FOR DATA_MIRRORING (ROLE = ALL, AUTHENTICATION = WINDOWS
            NEGOTIATE, ENCRYPTION = REQUIRED ALGORITHM AES)
    GO
    ```

■ **Note** Open inbound firewall rules to the mirroring endpoint port on each server as automatic seeding communicates over the mirroring endpoint.

2. Next create the availability group with seeding_mode set to automatic.

    ```
    CREATE AVAILABILITY GROUP AGCorp
    FOR DATABASE db1
    REPLICA ON'AlwaysOnN1'
    WITH (ENDPOINT_URL = N'TCP://AlwaysOnN1.contoso.com:5022',
    FAILOVER_MODE = AUTOMATIC,
    AVAILABILITY_MODE = SYNCHRONOUS_COMMIT,
    BACKUP_PRIORITY = 50,
    SECONDARY_ROLE(ALLOW_CONNECTIONS = NO),
    SEEDING_MODE = AUTOMATIC),
    ON N'AlwaysOnN2'WITH (ENDPOINT_URL = N'TCP://AlwaysOnN2.contoso.
    com:5022',
    FAILOVER_MODE = AUTOMATIC,
    ```

```
AVAILABILITY_MODE = SYNCHRONOUS_COMMIT,
BACKUP_PRIORITY = 50,
SECONDARY_ROLE(ALLOW_CONNECTIONS = NO),
SEEDING MODE = AUTOMATIC),
ON N'AlwaysOnN3'WITH (ENDPOINT_URL = N'TCP://AlwaysOnN3.contoso.
com:5022',
FAILOVER_MODE = AUTOMATIC,
AVAILABILITY_MODE = SYNCHRONOUS_COMMIT,
BACKUP_PRIORITY = 50,
SECONDARY_ROLE(ALLOW_CONNECTIONS = NO),
SEEDING_MODE = AUTOMATIC);
GO
```

■ **Note**   Data and log file paths should be the same on every SQL Server instance participating in the availability group. This is a requirement for automatic seeding to work. Also the database should be in full recovery model and should have a current full and transaction log backup.

---

3. Next join the secondary server to the availability group and grant availability group permission to create databases.

    ```
    ALTER AVAILABILITY GROUP AGCorp JOIN
    GO
    ALTER AVAILABILITY GROUP AGCorp GRANT CREATE ANY DATABASE
    GO
    ```

You can also prevent automatic seeding on the secondary replicas by denying secondary replica availability group permission to create databases.

```
ALTER AVAILABILITY GROUP AGCorp DENY CREATE ANY DATABASE
GO
```

There might be scenarios where you might want to stop the automatic seeding. Run the following command on the primary replica to switch the seeding mode to manual.

```
ALTER AVAILABILITY GROUP AGCorp
    MODIFY REPLICA ON 'AlwaysOnN1'
    WITH (SEEDING_MODE = MANUAL)
GO
```

Be careful while using automatic seeding with very large databases (VLDBs). If it is added during business hours, then the network load caused by automatic seeding could potentially impact data synchronization performance. You might want to consider temporarily turning off automatic seeding while VLDBs are being added to the availability group.

Distributed Availability Group

Distributed Availability Groups enable you to associate two availability groups residing on different Windows Server Failover Clusters (*WSFC*). In chapter 3, we looked at the distributed availability group topology and how it differs from an availability group on the same WSFC. Here we will look at how to create a distributed availability group.

1. To create a distributed availability group, create an availability group and listener on each WSFC and join the replicas to their availability group. For example, create availability group AGCorp1 with AGCorp1-listen as the listener name on the first cluster and create availability group AGCorp2 with AGCorp2-listen as the listener name on the second cluster.

2. Create the distributed availability group on the first cluster.

   Use the CREATE AVAILABILITY GROUP command with the DISTRIBUTED option.

   ```
   CREATE AVAILABILITY GROUP [distributedAGCorp]
       WITH (DISTRIBUTED)
       AVAILABILITY GROUP ON
         'AGCorp1' WITH
         (
            LISTENER_URL = 'tcp://AGCorp1_listen.contoso.com:5022',
            AVAILABILITY_MODE = ASYNCHRONOUS_COMMIT,
            FAILOVER_MODE = MANUAL,
            SEEDING_MODE = AUTOMATIC
         ),
         'AGCorp2' WITH
         (
            LISTENER_URL = 'tcp://AGCorp2_listen.contoso.com:5022',
            AVAILABILITY_MODE = ASYNCHRONOUS_COMMIT,
            FAILOVER_MODE = MANUAL,
            SEEDING_MODE = AUTOMATIC
         );
   GO
   ```

   The AVAILABILITY GROUP ON clause specifies the member availability groups of the distributed availability. In this case, they are AGCorp1 and AGCorp2.

■ **Note** The LISTENER_URL option specifies the listener for each availability group along with the database mirroring endpoint of the availability group. Hence the port number 5022 in the example is the mirroring port.

---

3. On the second cluster, join the distributed availability group.

   ```
   ALTER AVAILABILITY GROUP [distributedAGCorp]
       JOIN
       AVAILABILITY GROUP ON
         'AGCorp1' WITH
         (
            LISTENER_URL = 'tcp://AGCorp1_listen.contoso.com:5022',
   ```

```
            AVAILABILITY_MODE = ASYNCHRONOUS_COMMIT,
            FAILOVER_MODE = MANUAL,
            SEEDING_MODE = AUTOMATIC
        ),
        'AGCorp2' WITH
        (
            LISTENER_URL = 'tcp://AGCorp2_listen.contoso.com:5022',
            AVAILABILITY_MODE = ASYNCHRONOUS_COMMIT,
            FAILOVER_MODE = MANUAL,
            SEEDING_MODE = AUTOMATIC
        );
    GO
```

Following is the command to failover to the secondary availability group:ALTER AVAILABILITY GROUP [distributedAGCorp] FORCE_FAILOVER_ALLOW_DATA_LOSS

■ **Note** Only manual failover is supported at this time.

Following is the command to drop a distributed availability group:

```
DROP AVAILABILITY GROUP [distributedAGCorp]
```

■ **Note** As distributed availability groups associates two availability groups that have their own listeners, you could use the old database mirroring connection string syntax for transparent client redirection after failover.

For example: "Server=AGCorp1_listen; Failover_Partner=AGCorp2_listen; Database=Adventure Works2016"

Configuring an Always On Availability Group without Domains

Starting with Windows Server 2016, WSFC will no longer require that all nodes in a cluster reside in the same domain or in any domain. Due to this change, SQL Server 2016 is now able to deploy Always On Availability Groups in multi-domain or domain-less environments. Let me warn you that this is a cumbersome process right now as there is no GUI support and it involves a number of steps to get it configured.

1. In order to set up an availability group in a multi-domain or domain-less environment, you will have to first set up a multi-domain or domain-less Windows Server 2016 Failover Cluster. Please refer to chapter 7 for information on the WSFC setup steps.

2. It is recommended to configure the SQL Server service to run as a user account with the same user name and password on all the nodes. This account does not need to be an administrator on the nodes. However, this account will need to have read/write access on the certificate network share that will be used later.

3. Create an endpoint on each node:

    a. Create a certificate (master key will need to be created if it does not exist).

    b. Create a database mirroring endpoint authenticated by the certificate.

    c. Back up the certificate to a common network share that is accessible by all the nodes for import into the other nodes.

4. Install the certificates on each node:

    a. Create a login and a user for each remote machine.

    b. Create a certificate from the certificate backup file for each remote machine and grant authorization to the login created in step a.

    c. Grant connect permission to the remote computer login created in step a to the endpoint.

■ **Note** To help simplify the implementation, the Always On feature Program Manager created and published two stored procedures (CreateEndpointCert and InstallEndpointCert) in a blog article. Consider using these two stored procedures if you need to configure a multi-domain or a domain-less availability group. The stored procedures can be found here: `https://blogs.technet.microsoft.com/dataplatforminsider/2015/12/15/enhanced-always-on-availability-groups-in-sql-server-2016/`

PowerShell

PowerShell cmdlets such as `New-SqlAvailabilityReplica`, `New-SqlAvailabilityGroup`, `Join-SqlAvailabilityGroup`, and `Add-SqlAvailabilityDatabase` can be used for creating availability groups. Just like in case of T-SQL, a database mirroring endpoint needs to be created (using `New-SqlHadrEndPoint`) on each replica and an AlwaysOn_Health extended event session also needs to be started manually.

Summary

In this chapter we saw how to successfully configure and deploy availability groups using the availability group wizard. In the next chapter we will take a look at the post-installation/deployment tasks.

■ ■ ■

CHAPTER 9

Post-Installation Tasks

After creating Always On Availability Groups in chapter 8, you are now ready to review the resources that were created by the availability group deployment and discuss the important post-installation tasks. In this chapter, you will review the newly created availability group, learn about different ways to connect to the availability group, observe the current health of the availability group, review and modify the availability group configuration, and replicate the logins and jobs to the secondary replicas.

Reviewing the Availability Group

In this section, you will use SQL Server Management Studio (SSMS) and Failover Cluster Manager to review the availability group that you created in chapter 8. You will also learn about the built-in Always On Dashboard tool to review the availability group details.

Using Object Explorer

Open SSMS, type the availability group listener name in the Connect to Server dialog box as shown in Figure 9-1, and click Connect.

© Uttam Parui and Vivek Sanil 2016
U. Parui and V. Sanil, *Pro SQL Server Always On Availability Groups*, DOI 10.1007/978-1-4842-2071-9_9

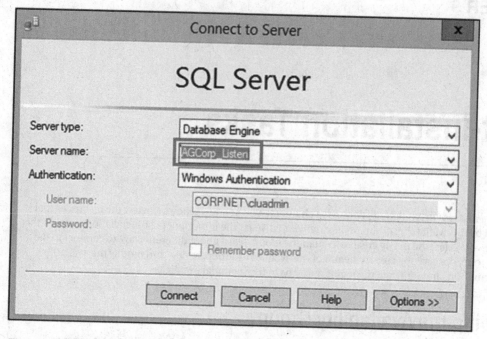

Figure 9-1. *Using availability group listener to connect to primary replica*

■ **Note** An availability group listener allows us to connect to primary replica for read-write access without needing to know the name of the SQL Server instance that it is connecting to. Also, when a primary replica goes offline and a secondary replica takes the role of the primary replica, the availability group listener enables the new connections to automatically connect to the new primary replica. The existing connections are disconnected and the client must establish a new connection in order to work with the same database.

You will be connected to the primary replica for the availability group. To verify this, open a query window, execute the command `select @@servername`, and verify that the results displayed the name of the SQL Server instance hosting the primary replica.

If your application is using ADO.NET or SQL Native Client driver to connect to an availability database, specify the availability group listener name followed by the availability group listener port in your application's connection string as shown here:

```
Server=tcp: AGCorp_Listen,1433;Database=AdventureWorks2016;IntegratedSecurity=SSPI
```

It is recommended to use the `MultiSubnetFailover` connection option (if supported by your client libraries) in the connection string for both single and multi-subnet connections to availability groups listeners as shown below:

```
Server=tcp: AGCorp_Listen,1433;Database=AdventureWorks2016;IntegratedSecurity=SSPI;MultiSub
netFailover=True
```

■ **Note**   By default, starting from .NET Framework 4.6.1, `MultiSubnetFailover` property is set to true.

Although the `MultiSubnetFailover` connection option is not required, it provides faster subnet failover because the client driver attempts to open up a TCP socket for each IP address associated with availability group in parallel. The client driver waits for the first IP to respond with success and uses it for connection. Using the `MultiSubnetFailover` connection option in a single subnet configuration allows you to preconfigure new clients to support future spanning of subnets without any need for future client connections string changes.

■ **Note**   In a multi-subnet cluster setup, if your application is using a legacy client that does not support the `MultiSubnetFailover` property, then consider setting the listener's `RegisterAllProvidersIP` value to 0 to avoid intermittent timeout issues.

Viewing Availability Groups

After getting connected to the availability group listener in Object Explorer, expand Always On High Availability and then expand Availability Groups as shown in Figure 9-2.

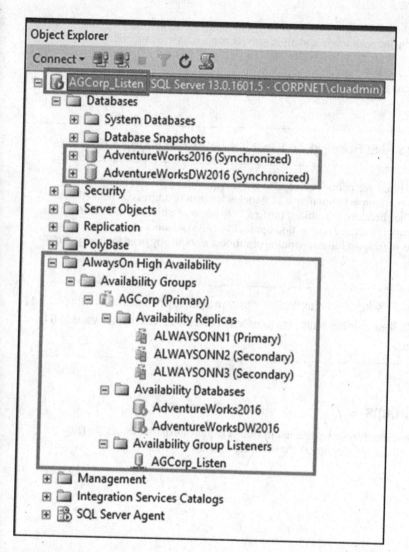

Figure 9-2. Reviewing availability groups using Object Explorer

You will see all the availability groups running on this SQL Server instance. Figure 9-2 shows only one availability group named AGCorp (Primary) as you created only one availability group in chapter 8. Notice it has the availability replica role in parentheses after the availability group name. Expand the availability group to see availability replicas, availability databases, and availability group listeners. Expand Availability Replicas to see all the SQL Server instances participating in the availability group. In Figure 9-2, there are three availability replicas: AlwaysOnN1 is the current primary replica, and AlwaysOnN2 and AlwaysOnN3 are the secondary replicas. Expand Availability Databases, and you will see the availability databases that are being replicated to the replicas. Figure 9-2 shows two availability databases AdventureWorks2014 and AdventureWorksDW2014. These are the two databases that you selected while creating availability groups in chapter 8. Expand Availability Group Listeners to see the availability group listener. Also, if you expand the Databases node you will see the two availability databases along with their synchronization state.

A client connection can use the SQL Server instance name directly instead of using the availability group listener name. SQL Server instance does not care if a client connects using the availability group listener name or another instance endpoint. SQL Server instance verifies the state of the targeted database and either allows or disallows connections based on the availability group configuration. Here is a sample connection string to connect directly using the SQL Server instance name (AlwaysOnN1):

```
Server=tcp: AlwaysOnN1,1433;Database=AdventureWorks2016;IntegratedSecurity=SSPI
```

■ **Note** If you choose to connect directly using the SQL Server instance name and not the availability group listener name, you will lose the benefit of new connections being directed automatically to the current primary replica. Also, you will lose the benefit of read-only routing, which we will discuss in chapter 10.

Viewing Availability Group Properties

To review the properties of an availability group, expand Always On High Availability, expand Availability Groups, and then right-click the availability group and select Properties. This will show the availability group properties as shown in Figure 9-3.

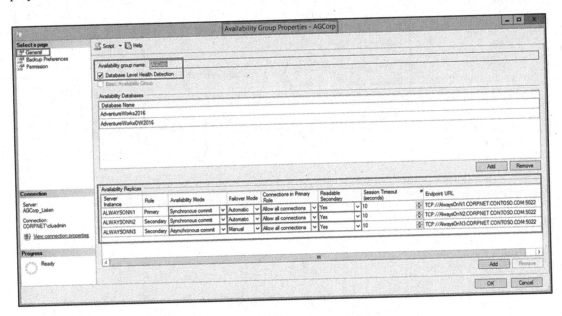

Figure 9-3. Reviewing availability group properties

■ **Note** If you open the availability group properties from a secondary replica, you will only be able to review the properties and will not be able to modify them.

In the availability group properties window, most of the columns are self-explanatory. Notice the column called *Session Timeout (seconds)*. The session timeout (default value is 10 seconds) controls how long an availability replica waits for a ping response from a connected replica before considering the connection to have failed. If a replica receives a ping within the session timeout period, then it means

129

that the connection is still active and the replicas are still communicating. If no ping is received within the session timeout period, the replica times out. Its connection is closed and the timed-out replica enters the *DISCONNECTED* state. This replica property applies only to the connection between a given secondary replica and the primary replica of the availability group.

■ **Note**   The default session timeout period of 10 seconds works well for most of the environment. It is recommended to set this value to 10 seconds or greater. If you set this value to less than 10 seconds, you have a possibility of declaring a false failure when the replica is busy.

Viewing Availability Group Listener Properties

To review the properties of an availability group listener as shown in Figure 9-4, right-click the availability group listener and select Properties.

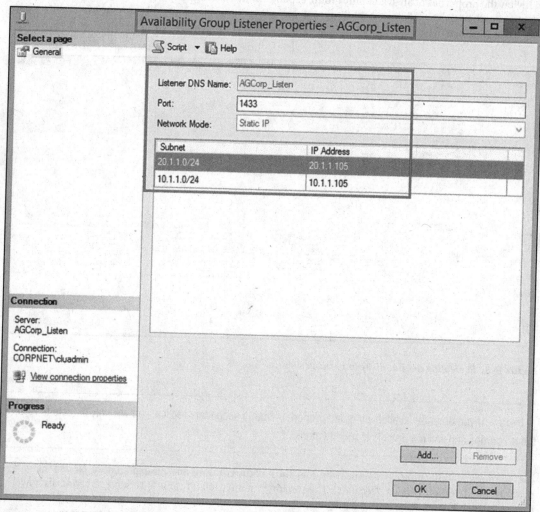

Figure 9-4. *Reviewing availability group listener properties*

130

Using Always On Availability Groups Dashboard

In this section, you will learn about a very powerful tool called Always On Availability Group Dashboard or simply Always On Dashboard. Always On Dashboard is a Graphical User Interface (GUI) that, similar to your automobile's dashboard, organizes and presents the information about availability groups in a way that is easy to interpret. Always On Dashboard is available after you deploy availability groups. Some of the typical uses of the Always On Dashboard are the following:

- Monitoring the health of availability groups, availability replicas, and availability databases. For example, you can use the dashboard to monitor the status of the data synchronization as it is happening. Or you can use it to estimate the data loss if you lose your primary replica and perform a forced failover.

- Administering the availability group. For example, you can use the dashboard to manually failover the availability group from one replica to another.

- Troubleshooting the availability group if there is an issue.

Invoking Always On Dashboard

1. Open SQL Server Management Studio and connect to the SQL Server instance on which you want to run the Always On Dashboard.

2. Expand the Always On High Availability node, right-click Availability Groups node, and then click Show Dashboard as shown in Figure 9-5.

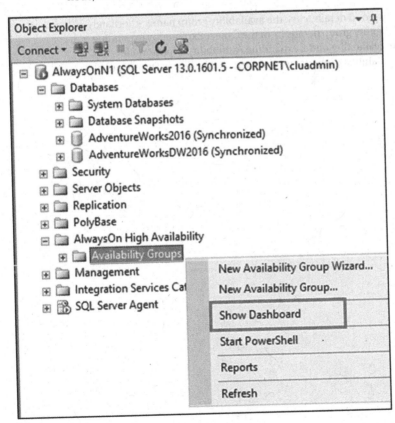

Figure 9-5. *Opening the Always On Dashboard*

3. This will open the Always On Dashboard on the SQL Server instance. The dashboard will show you the name of all the availability groups configured on the SQL Server instance, the primary instance name, the failover mode, and issues (if any) as shown in Figure 9-6. Figure 9-2 displays one availability group named AGCorp hosted on primary instance AlwaysOnN1 and configured with "Automatic" failover mode. This is the availability group that you created in chapter 8. If you had multiple availability groups on this instance, then you would have seen them over here too.

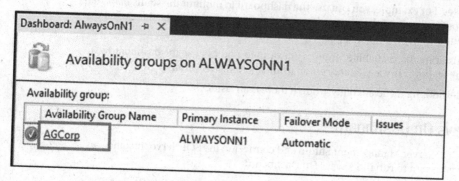

Figure 9-6. *Sample Always On dashboard*

4. To see the availability group details, click the availability group name. Alternately, you can see the availability group details from the Object Explorer by expanding the Always On High Availability node, expanding Availability Groups node, right-clicking the availability group name, and then clicking Show Dashboard as shown in Figure 9-7.

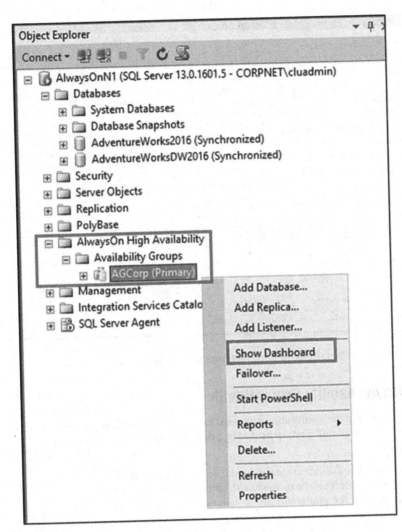

Figure 9-7. *Opening availability group details dashboard*

5. This will open the availability group details dashboard as shown in Figure 9-8.

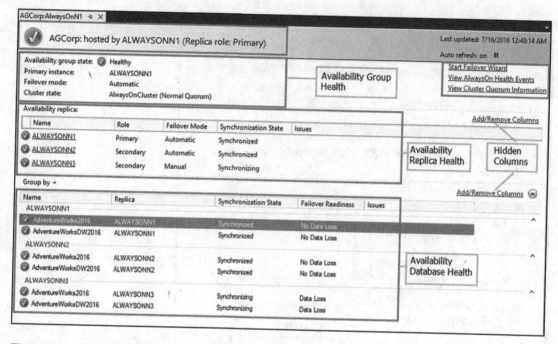

Figure 9-8. *Sample availability group details dashboard launched from the primary replica*

Reviewing the Always On Availability Group Health

The Always On Dashboard displays most of the information you need to monitor an availability group. Figure 9-8 shows the details for AGCorp availability group hosted by primary replica AlwaysOnN1. The dashboard has three main sections:

- *Availability Group Health* – The availability group health section displays the health of the availability group. This section tells us the health of the availability group, the current primary replica for the availability group, failover mode (automatic or manual), and the cluster state.

- *Availability Replica Health* – The availability replica health section displays the health of the availability replica. By default, this section shows us the availability group replicas, their current role (primary or secondary), their failover mode (automatic or manual), synchronization state (synchronized, synchronizing or not synchronized), and issues (if any).

- *Availability Database Health* – The availability database health section displays the health of the availability databases. By default, this section is grouped by replicas. For each replica, it displays the availability databases in the replica, their synchronization state, failover readiness and issues (if any).

■ **Note**   You can group the availability group information by clicking Group by and selecting one of the following: Availability replicas, Availability databases, Synchronization state, Failover readiness, Issues or None.

Apart from the above three main sections, the dashboard has three links on the top right-hand corner:

- *Start Failover Wizard* – As the name suggests, this link invokes the *Failover Availability Group Wizard*. This wizard allows us to perform a planned failover. It allows us to failover the availability group to a new secondary replica, making it the new primary replica.

- *View Always On Health Events* – This link allows us to view the Extended Events captured via the *AlwaysOn_Health* session. A sample Always On Health Events screen is shown in Figure 9-9. In this screen, you can view the recent availability group activity and state changes and events. You can add columns by right-clicking the column headers and then selecting what you need. Also, when you click a specific row, you can see the details of the rows below.

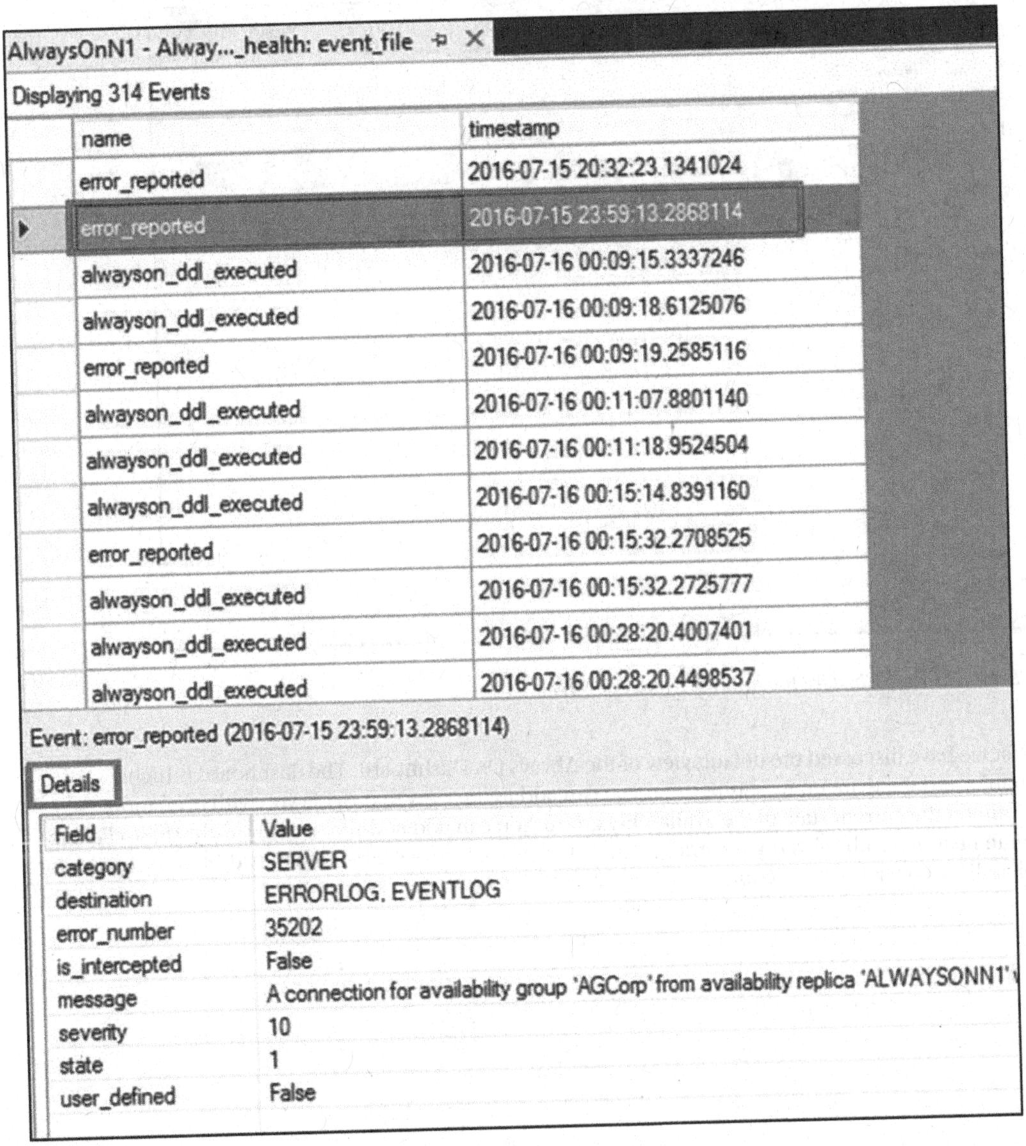

AlwaysOnN1 - Alway..._health: event_file ⊹ ✕

Displaying 314 Events

name	timestamp
error_reported	2016-07-15 20:32:23.1341024
error_reported	2016-07-15 23:59:13.2868114
alwayson_ddl_executed	2016-07-16 00:09:15.3337246
alwayson_ddl_executed	2016-07-16 00:09:18.6125076
error_reported	2016-07-16 00:09:19.2585116
alwayson_ddl_executed	2016-07-16 00:11:07.8801140
alwayson_ddl_executed	2016-07-16 00:11:18.9524504
alwayson_ddl_executed	2016-07-16 00:15:14.8391160
error_reported	2016-07-16 00:15:32.2708525
alwayson_ddl_executed	2016-07-16 00:15:32.2725777
alwayson_ddl_executed	2016-07-16 00:28:20.4007401
alwayson_ddl_executed	2016-07-16 00:28:20.4498537

Event: error_reported (2016-07-15 23:59:13.2868114)

Details

Field	Value
category	SERVER
destination	ERRORLOG, EVENTLOG
error_number	35202
is_intercepted	False
message	A connection for availability group 'AGCorp' from availability replica 'ALWAYSONN1'
severity	10
state	1
user_defined	False

Figure 9-9. Sample Always On Health Events screen

- *View Cluster Quorum Information* – This link displays the Windows Cluster Quorum information as shown in Figure 9-10. This screen tells us the Windows Server Failover Cluster (WSFC) name, Quorum model, member name, member type, member state, and vote count. By default, all cluster members can vote and have a vote count of 1. Administrators can change the vote functionality in the quorum model by configuring a node to have 0 votes. For example, say you have a node in a disaster recovery datacenter and you have poor network connectivity to that datacenter. To ensure the node in the DR datacenter does not participate in the quorum voting, you can configure its vote to 0 using the Failover Cluster Manager or PowerShell.

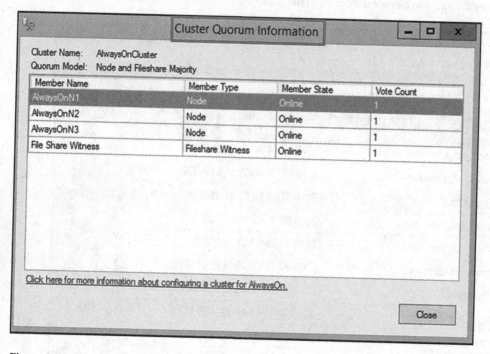

Figure 9-10. Sample Cluster Quorum Information screen

So far we have discussed the default view of the Always On Dashboard. The dashboard is highly configurable, and there are many settings that you can add to the view to provide you with even more information on the current state of the availability group. You can add additional columns by right-clicking the column headings or by clicking the Add/Remove Columns. Figure 9-11 shows the additional column for the Availability Replica Health section.

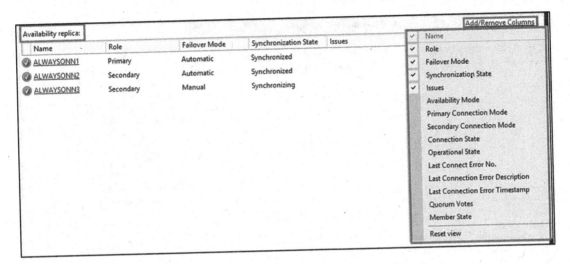

Figure 9-11. *Additional columns to monitor availability replicas*

For example, one column that you may want to add is the Availability mode column. This tells us if the availability mode is synchronous-commit or asynchronous-commit mode. Or you may want to add the Secondary Connection Mode column. This tells us if the secondary is connected or not.

■ **Note** The dashboard remembers the columns that you add/remove manually from the Add/Remove Columns list. Check it out by adding some columns manually and then close and reopen the dashboard. You should see all the columns that you had added manually. If you want to revert back to the default columns, then select Reset view.

Figure 9-12 shows the additional column for the Availability Database Health section.

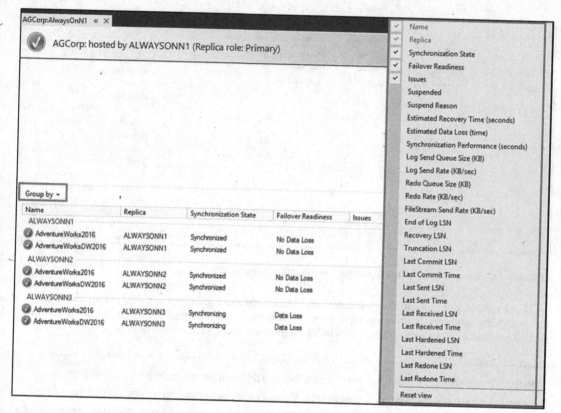

Figure 9-12. *Additional columns to monitor availability databases*

Say your boss comes up to you and asks you, "If we lose our primary replica or databases, how much data will we lose and how much time will it take us to recover?" Or maybe, you are asked, "If the primary replica goes down, how many seconds or minutes' worth of data will we lose at this time?" Or if the primary replica goes down and automatic failover happens, how much time will the secondary replica take to finish the recovery and make the databases available for use? Without writing a single line of code and almost instantly you can find the answer and impress your boss, by opening the availability group dashboard and manually adding the Estimated Recovery Time (seconds) and Estimated Data Loss (time) columns. You will be able to see this information for every individual availability database for every replica. So you can quickly provide the information to your boss. Most of the columns are self-explanatory but do not worry too much if you are not familiar with them. We will cover the most important columns in chapter 15.

It is important to note that the dashboard shows a different view based on where you launch it. The dashboard shown in Figure 9-8 was launched from the primary replica. From this view, you can monitor the health of the whole availability group. If you launch the dashboard from a secondary replica, then the view only shows the health of that secondary replica. Figure 9-13 shows the dashboard when launched from the secondary replica AlwaysOnN2. As can be seen in Figure 9-13, you are only getting the information from the perspective of the secondary replica AlwaysOnN2. Even if you open the dashboard from a secondary replica, the dashboard does show which SQL Server instance is our primary instance. For example, Figure 9-13 shows that AlwaysOnN1 is the primary instance. If you click AlwaysOnN1 on the dashboard, it will show you the full dashboard as in Figure 9-8.

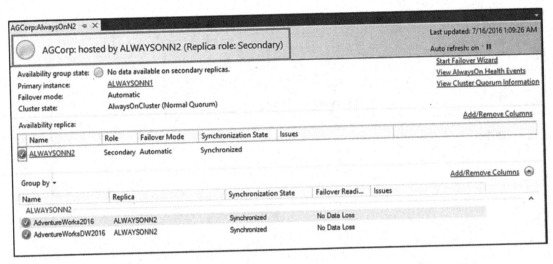

Figure 9-13. *Sample availability group details dashboard launched from the secondary replica*

■ **Tip** To ensure that you launch the dashboard from the primary replica, connect to SQL Server Management Studio using the availability group listener name instead and then invoke the dashboard.

Changing Always On Dashboard Options

As you have seen, the dashboard provides us with a lot of useful information. You might wonder how often the information displayed on the dashboard is refreshed and if you can change the dashboard options. You can change the Always On Dashboard options from SQL Server Management Studio as follows:

1. Click the Tools menu and select Options. This will invoke the Options screen as shown in Figure 9-14.

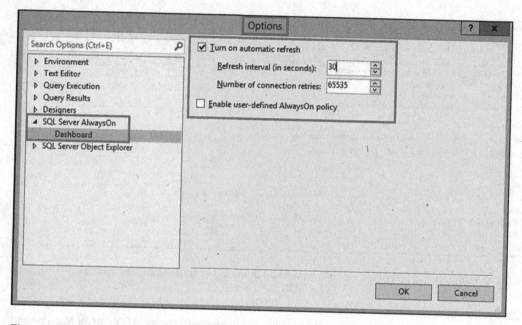

Figure 9-14. *Changing Always On Dashboard Options*

2. In the left-hand pane of the Options screen, expand SQL Server Always On, and then expand Dashboard.

3. As can be seen in Figure 9-14, by default Turn on automatic refresh is selected and the default refresh interval is 30 seconds. To change the default settings, enter the new refresh interval in seconds and optionally change the number of times you want to retry the connection. Typically, I change the refresh interval from 30 seconds to 10 seconds or lower when I am monitoring the availability groups. If you want to enable user-defined Always On policy, select Enable user-defined Always On policy. Click OK to apply the changes.

■ **Note**   The Dashboard options are client-specific configuration options and will only apply to the current user's SQL Server Management Studio.

Using Windows Server Failover Cluster Manager

While it's true that a SQL DBA will typically spend most of the time reviewing the availability group in SSMS, there are sometimes when you may need to use the Failover Cluster Manager. In this section, you will review the availability group using the Failover Cluster Manager tool. After creating an availability group, a new role for the availability group is created in Failover Cluster Manager. Open Failover Cluster Manager, expand cluster name, and click Roles. Within that role you will find the SQL Server Availability Group resource, availability group listener resource and its associated IP address resource(s) as shown in Figure 9-15.

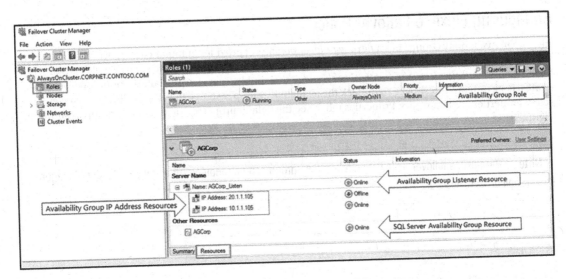

Figure 9-15. *Availability group role in Failover Cluster Manager*

Notice that the name AGCorp_Listen that you typed while creating availability group listener in chapter 8 has been added to the AGCorp role as a cluster resource. Expand AGCorp_Listen resource to see the dependent IP address resources that you had specified during the availability group listener creation. Notice that the IP address 20.1.1.105 is offline and 10.1.1.105 is online because at any point of time only one of the IP address resources can be online. Currently, AGCorp is owned by AlwaysOnN1 node residing in the primary datacenter and hence the IP address 10.1.1.105 is online. If AGCorp had failed over to the disaster recovery datacenter and was owned by AlwaysOnN3, then the IP address 20.1.1.105 will become online and 10.1.1.105 will become offline. In case all the replicas are in the same subnet, only one IP Address resource will exist and will be online all the time.

Right-click the SQL Server Availability Group Resource AGCorp, select More Actions, and then select Show Dependency Report to see the dependency report for the availability group as shown in Figure 9-16.

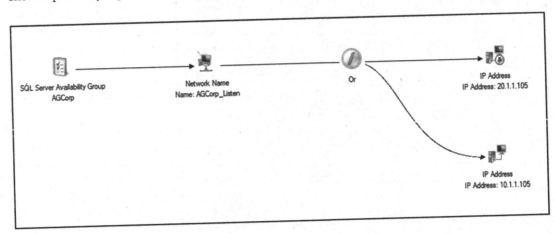

Figure 9-16. *Availability group dependency report in Failover Cluster Manager*

Configuring Flexible Failover Policy

Always On Availability Groups has a *flexible failover policy* that provides granular control over the conditions that need to be met to cause automatic failover for an availability groups. Flexible failover policy is defined by the *failure condition level* and *heath-check timeout* thresholds. To review the failure condition level and heath-check timeout thresholds, right-click the availability group resource in Failover Cluster Manager, select Properties, and then click Properties tab to see the default properties of availability group as shown in Figure 9-17.

■ **Note**   The flexible failover policy of an availability group can be modified from Failover Cluster Manager or PowerShell or Transact-SQL.

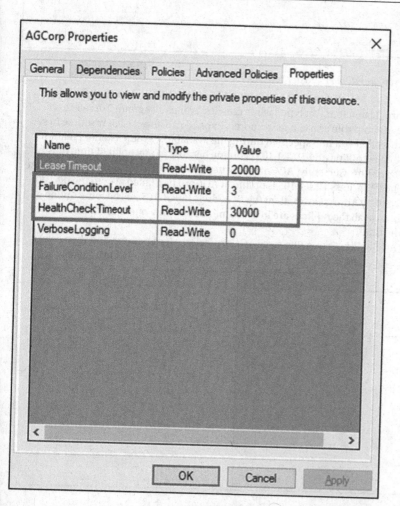

Figure 9-17.   Reviewing availability group properties in Failover Cluster Manager

The availability group resource DLL performs a health check of the primary replica by calling the sp_server_diagnostics stored procedure with a repeat interval. It captures diagnostic data and health information of the primary replica and returns results at an interval that equals one-third of the HealthCheck Timeout period. The sp_server_diagnostics stored procedure collects the data on the following five components: system, resource, query_processing, io_subsystem, and events. It also provides the health state of each component as clean, warning, error, or unknown. Additionally, on the primary replica, sp_server_diagnostics displays the availability group name and whether the lease is valid or not for each availability group. Table 9-1 has the description of the five components:

Table 9-1. Component Level Description

Components	Description
system	Collects data from a systems perspective on spinlocks, severe processing conditions, non-yielding tasks, page faults, and CPU usage.
resource	Collects data from a resource perspective on physical and virtual memory, buffer pools, pages, cache, and other memory objects.
query_processing	Collects data from a query-processing perspective on the worker threads, tasks, wait types, CPU intensive sessions, and blocking tasks.
io_subsystem	Collects data on IO subsystem.
events	Collects data on the errors and event of interest recorded by the server, including details about out of memory, scheduler monitor, buffer pool spinlocks, security, connectivity, ring buffer exceptions, and ring buffer events about memory broker.

■ **Note** Even though sp_server_diagnostics stored procedure collects data for five components, only the data for system, resource and query_processing are currently being used for failure detection whereas io_subsystem and events data are available for diagnostic purposes only.

Based on the issues reported in the result sets of the sp_server_diagnostics stored procedure and FailureConditionLevel, the resource DLL decides whether the primary replica is healthy or not. The availability group resource DLL responds back to the WSFC cluster. The WSFC cluster then initiates an automatic failover to the secondary replica.

When an availability group failover occurs, existing connections to the primary replica are terminated, and the client applications must establish a new connection in order to continue working. While a failover is occurring, connectivity to the availability group databases will fail, forcing the client applications to retry connecting until the primary is fully online and ready to accept connections. If the availability group comes back online during the client's connection attempt but before the connection timeout period, the client may successfully connect during one of the retry attempts and no error will be reported to the application.

As seen in Figure 9-17, the default HealthCheck Timeout is 30 seconds. Hence, the sp_server_diagnostics stored procedure returns results at a 10-second interval. If the primary replica is unresponsive and not a single result set has been received by the resource DLL during the 30 second period, the server is considered to be hung.

The FailureConditionLevel determines whether the diagnostic information returned by sp_server_diagnostics warrants an automatic failover. The FailureConditionLevel specifies what failures trigger an automatic failure. There are five failure conditions level 1 through 5. The checks are accumulative with 1 being the least restrictive and 5 being the most restrictive. The checks that are done in level 5 are all checks of the lower levels plus the checks of level 5. Table 9-2 shows the FailureConditionLevel and its description,

Table 9-2. *Failure Condition Level*

Failure Condition Level	Description
1 (least restrictive)	Level 1 checks if SQL Server is down. An automatic failover is initiated if any one of the following occurs: • The SQL Server service is down. • Lease of the availability group for connecting to the Windows Server Failover Cluster expires.
2	Level 2 checks if the server is unresponsive. An automatic failover is initiated if any one of the following occurs: • Any condition of lower level is satisfied. • The SQL Server instance does not connect to the cluster, and the HealthCheck Timeout is exceeded. • The availability replica is in a failed state.
3 (Default level)	Level 3 checks for critical server errors. An automatic failover is initiated if any one of the following occurs: • Any condition of lower level is satisfied • Critical SQL Server internal errors like orphaned spinlocks, serious write-access violations, or too many dumps occur.
4	Level 4 checks for moderate server errors. An automatic failover is initiated if any one of the following occurs: • Any condition of lower level is satisfied • Moderate SQL Serve internal errors like out-of-memory conditions occurs.
5 (most restrictive)	Level 5 checks for qualified failure conditions. An automatic failover is initiated if any one of the following occurs: • Any condition of a lower level is satisfied • Any qualified failure conditions like exhaustion of SQL Server engine worker-threads, detection of an unsolvable deadlock occurs.

The default failover condition level is 3, which means that it checks if the SQL Server service is up, whether the `sp_server_diagnostics` stored procedure responds within the health check timeout, and whether there are critical server errors reported in the result set.

■ **Note**　The failure condition level and sp_server_diagnostics only monitors the health of the SQL Server instance and not the health of the database. However, starting from SQL Server 2016, if you selected Database Level Heath Detection while creating the availability group (or added the detection after the creation of availability group), then an automatic failover is initiated when the database status on the primary replica is anything other than ONLINE. If you did not select Database Level Heath Detection, then only the health of the instance is used to trigger automatic failover.

Figure 9-17 has another property called the *Lease Timeout*. The Lease Timeout is set to a default value of 20,000 ms or 20 secs. The Lease Timeout is used to avoid *split brain scenarios* in availability group. A split brain scenario occurs if more than one availability replica considers itself to be the primary replica, tries to bring the availability group online and thereby accepting queries and responding to queries. This typically happens when the cluster nodes are disconnected. To understand this better, let's consider a scenario where in the SQL Server instance running the primary replica of an availability group is detected unresponsive and a failover is initiated. However, the resource DLL is not able to connect to the unresponsive SQL Server instance anymore. Therefore, the SQL Server instance would think that it is still the primary replica and will accept queries and respond to queries. To avoid such a scenario, the SQL Server instance running the primary replica needs to get a lease from the resource DLL before the lease timeout threshold hits. If the lease is not renewed within that threshold, the primary replica is removed from the primary and a failover to a secondary is initiated.

Viewing Availability Group Failover Properties

While testing availability group failure, oftentimes I have seen our customers complaining that the availability group failover worked fine for first one or two times but now it has stopped working. This typically happens when the availability group exceeds it WSFC *failure threshold*. The WSFC *failure threshold* is defined as the maximum number of failures supported for the availability group in a specified period. To check the WSFC failure threshold, right-click availability group role in Failover Cluster Manager, select Properties, and then click the Failover tab as shown in Figure 9-18.

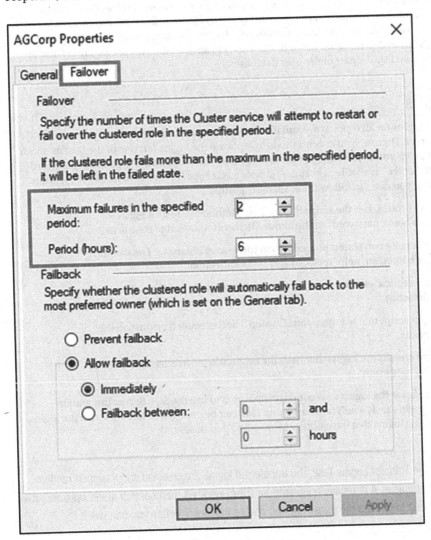

Figure 9-18. *Reviewing availability group WSFC failure threshold*

The default time period is 6 hours, and the maximum failures supported is N-1, where N is the number of cluster nodes. Since we have a 3-node WSFC, maximum failures allowed is (3 - 1) = 2 in 6 hours. This means that if you are testing automatic failover on our 3-node cluster, you will be able to perform automatic failover only twice in 6 hours. The third time, the availability group will remain in a failed state until a cluster administrator manually brings the failed availability group resource online or a DBA performs a manual failover of the availability group.

Replicating Logins and Jobs

In chapter 6, you learned that availability groups provide user database level protection because system databases are not allowed to participate in availability groups. This means that any objects that are stored in the system databases on the primary replica are not being replicated to the secondary replicas. We know that logins are stored in the master database and jobs are stored in the msdb database. Even if the user databases are available on the secondary replicas, if we are unable to log in to the secondary replicas then the data on the secondary replicas is unusable. Similarly, if the availability group fails over from the primary replica to the secondary replica, you would like the jobs to be running on the new primary replica (i.e., old secondary replica). For this reason, you need to replicate the logins and jobs to all availability replicas. This is true for linked servers or anything that is not a part of the user databases.

Replicating Logins

The steps to replicate the logins on all replicas are still the same as you used to transfer logins from one SQL Server to another SQL Server. There are various methods to replicate the logins but one of the best methods is to use the T-SQL script in Microsoft Knowledge Base article titled "How to transfer logins and passwords between instances of SQL Server" available at https://support.microsoft.com/en-us/kb/918992. Here are the high-level steps that you need to follow for availability groups:

1. On the primary replica, run the script in step 2 of "Method 3: Create a log in script that has a blank password" in the above Microsoft Knowledge Base article.

2. This script will create two stored procedures in the master database. The stored procedures are named sp_help_revlogin and sp_hexadecimal.

3. On the primary replica, execute the stored procedure sp_help_revlogin. This will create the login script.

4. Review the login script that was generated in step 3 and execute it against all the secondary replicas.

5. The login script creates the logins that have the original Security Identifier (SID) and the original password.

Another method to replicate the logins to secondary replicas is to use the SQL Server Integration Services (SSIS) – Transfer Logins Task. The Transfer Logins Task can be configured to transfer all the logins, only specified logins, or all the logins that have access to specified databases only.

■ **Note** If you are using the Transfer Logins Task, the transferred logins are disabled and assigned random passwords at the secondary replicas. A database administrator (DBA) who has membership in the sysadmin role on the secondary replicas need to change the password and enable the logins before you can use it.

If you only have few logins, you could create the logins on the secondary replicas using the T-SQL CREATE LOGIN command.

Using Contained Database with Availability Groups

SQL Server 2016 supports partially contained databases. A partially contained database allows us to create contained users that authenticate at the database level making the database more independent from the SQL Server instance. Creating contained users allows the users to directly connect to the partially contained database without creating logins on the instance hosting the database. This feature can be very useful for availability groups. If the availability database is a partially contained database with contained users and a failover occurs, clients can connect to the secondary replica without creating the logins on the secondary replica.

■ **Note** Partially contained databases do not store the jobs. So you still need to replicate the jobs to all the secondary replicas.

Replicating SQL Agent Jobs and SSIS Packages

To ensure that you have all the jobs and SSIS packages on the secondary replicas, you need to manually copy them from the primary replica to all the secondary replicas. Before copying them, you need to modify them by adding some logic. For example, you may need to run the job only if the local replica is the primary replica. Or you may need to run the backup job on the preferred replica.

We have two functions that we can use:

- sys.fn_hadr_backup_is_preferred_replica ('dbname') – This function is used in backup jobs to find out if the local replica is the preferred replica for backups, according to the backup preferences that you learned in chapter 8. If the availability replica that is hosted by the current SQL Server instance is the preferred replica for backups, this function returns 1. If not, the function returns 0. Below is a sample code to use this function in backup jobs

```
If sys.fn_hadr_backup_is_preferred_replica( @dbname ) <> 1
BEGIN
-- If this is not the preferred backup replica, exit
END
-- If this is the preferred replica, continue to do the backup.
```

■ **Note** Backup jobs created using the built-in Maintenance Plan Wizard and Log Shipping Wizard automatically calls and checks the sys.fn_hadr_backup_is_preferred_replica function.

- sys.fn_hadr_is_primary_replica ('dbname') – This function is used to determine if the current replica is the primary replica for the specified availability database. If the availability database on the current SQL Server instance is the primary replica, this function returns 1. If not, the function returns 0. This function is typically used for non-backup jobs. Below is some sample code to use this function.

```
If sys.fn_hadr_is_primary_replica ( @dbname ) <> 1
BEGIN
-- If this is not the primary replica, exit.
END
-- If this is the primary replica, continue to do the job.
```

■ **Note**   SQL Server Integration Services (SSIS) – Transfer Jobs Task can also be used to transfer one or more SQL Server Agent jobs between the SQL Server instances.

Summary

In this chapter, we covered the post-installation tasks and ensured that everything was configured properly. Now you are ready to explore the benefits of availability groups. In the next chapter, we will discuss about Always On Availability Groups Readable Secondary feature that allows read-only access to all the secondary databases. We will learn the benefits, configuration, limitations and performance considerations of using readable secondaries.

Active Secondary Replicas

CHAPTER 10

■ ■ ■

Readable Secondary Replicas

Now that we have created an Availability Group and made sure it's configured correctly, let's take a look at how to fully leverage the features provided by this technology within SQL Server. The secondary replicas participating in the Availability Group maintain redundant copies of the production data on the primary replica. Wouldn't it be nice to leverage the redundant copies and the processing power on the secondary replicas to offload some of the production workload? The readable secondary feature within Always On Availability Groups allows you to do that.

It allows you to leverage the investment in highly available hardware by offloading read workload such as reporting to one or more secondary replicas. Offloading reporting workload to secondary replicas frees up resources on the primary replica to achieve higher throughput, at the same time allowing resources on secondary replicas for reporting workload to deliver higher performance.

Whenever we are overloaded with work, we usually wish we could clone ourselves and offload some of our work to our clones. We would be more effective and would be able to focus on the important tasks rather than trying to do everything ourselves. But this is just wishful thinking.

The world is becoming a 24/7 global marketplace. Sharing same servers/databases for the primary and reporting workloads takes CPU cycles and IO bandwidth away from the main workload. Sharing of workloads can also cause contention, impacting the overall performance and availability of the applications. In addition, server and database maintenance is critical for maintaining the health of the database servers and to protect the data from unexpected failures. But due to the 24/7 global marketplace, maintenance windows are shrinking day-by-day, making it difficult for administrators to perform maintenance without impacting performance and availability.

Offloading Reporting Workload

Offloading the reporting workloads to a secondary copy of the database on a different server will free up the resources on the primary for the OLTP workload to achieve higher throughput. It also allows you to leverage the existing resources on the secondary replica to provide higher performance for the reporting workloads. Before we proceed, let's quickly take a look at the options available prior to SQL Server 2012 for offloading reporting workloads. This will help us better understand what Always On Availability Groups bring to the table.

Solutions Prior to SQL Server 2012

Figure 10-1 shows the options in SQL Server for offloading reporting workloads prior to SQL Server 2012.

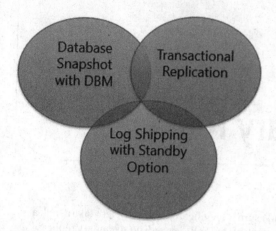

Figure 10-1. *Offload reporting workload options prior to SQL Server 2012*

- Database Snapshot with Database Mirroring

  You can create a point-in-time copy of your database called database snapshot on the mirror database and use it for reporting. But it will be a static copy with data as it existed at the moment of snapshot creation. Hence, it is not useful if you need near real-time data for your reporting. Also, the database must be in a synchronized mirroring state for the snapshot to be created.

- Log Shipping with Standby option

  You can also configure log shipping with the secondary database in *Standby* mode. This places the secondary database in read-only mode, which can be used for limited reporting functionality. But the database will not be available for read-only access while applying transactional log backups, which limits reporting functionality. Also the data is as current as the frequency of the transactional log restores.

- Transactional Replication

  The subscription database of a transactional replication can be used for offloading reporting workloads. However, being configured at the individual object level, all the data from the primary database may not be available at the subscription database, leading to reporting inaccuracies. Also, Replication is relatively complex to configure and manage compared to other synchronizing technologies. There are specific scenarios where Transactional replication might be a more viable reporting solution than Availability Group Active Secondary.

Offloading Reporting Workload Using Always On Availability Groups Secondary Replicas

Figure 10-2 shows a stand-alone SQL Server instance at the primary datacenter, configured as a primary replica of an availability group with three secondary replicas configured as readable secondary. Two replicas have been configured as synchronous replicas, whereas one is configured as an asynchronous replica.

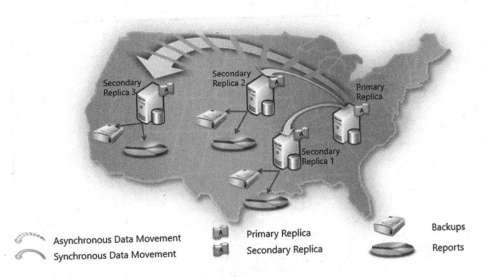

Figure 10-2. *Readable secondary architecture*

■ **Note** SQL Server 2012 supports one primary replica and up to four secondary replicas. SQL Server 2014 and 2016 support one primary replica and up to eight secondary replicas.

As shown in Figure 10-2, you can configure multiple secondary replicas, each of which can be used for read-only workload and/or backups and/or DBCC integrity checks. The secondary can be either in synchronous-commit mode or asynchronous-commit mode for using it as an Active Secondary.

■ **Note** We cover the Secondary Replica on Microsoft Azure later in chapter 18.

How to Configure Readable Secondary

You can configure connection access on a Secondary Replica of an Availability Group in SQL Server by using SQL Server Management Studio, Transact-SQL, or PowerShell. The settings can be selected during Availability Group creation itself or after by altering the Availability Group.

Using SQL Server Management Studio

In SSMS, you can configure connectivity to the secondary replica during the creation of Availability Groups by using the Availability Group Wizard. In Object Explorer, connect to the server instance that hosts the primary replica, and expand the server tree. Then expand the Always On High Availability node and the Availability Groups node ➤ Right-click the availability replica, and click on Properties.

Figure 10-3 shows the Availability Group properties dialog box.

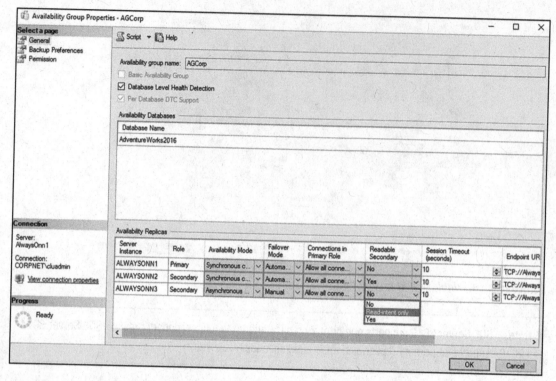

Figure 10-3. *Availability Group properties*

You can change the connection access for the secondary role by selecting Yes, No, or Read-intent only options, as shown in the diagram. We had discussed these options in detail in the chapter 8 earlier.

Using Transact-SQL

You can also configure the connection access for the secondary role by using CREATE/ALTER AVAILABILITY GROUP commands. The SECONDARY_ROLE option in the ADD/MODIFY REPLICA clause will take NO, ALL, or READ_ONLY options, which equates to No, Yes, or Read-intent only options respectively.

Figure 10-4 shows the TSQL command to configure connection access for the secondary role.

```
ALTER AVAILABILITY GROUP [AGCorp]
MODIFY REPLICA ON
N'ALWAYSONN2' WITH
(SECONDARY_ROLE (ALLOW_CONNECTIONS = READ_ONLY));
```

Figure 10-4. *Configure connection access using TSQL*

Using PowerShell

If creating a new replica, use the New-SqlAvailabilityReplica cmdet or when modifying an existing replica use the Set-SqlAvailabilityReplica cmdlet. To configure connection access for the secondary role, specify the ConnectionModeInSecondaryRole secondary_role_keyword parameter, where secondary_role_keyword equals one of the following values:

AllowNoConnections, AllowReadIntentConnectionsOnly, or AllowAllConnections

Figure 10-5 shows the PowerShell command to configure connection access for the secondary role.

Figure 10-5. Configure connection access using PowerShell

Configure Client Connectivity

Applications can specify the purpose of the connection through a property of the connection string called Application Intent. This property specifies whether the connection is directed to a read-write or a read-only version of the availability group database. Not all client drivers support this property in the connection string. SQL Native Client (SNAC), SQL OLEDB, ADO.net, JDBC, and new versions of ODBC currently support this property.

The following is an example of a connection string using the Application Intent property:

Server=AGCorp,1433;Database=AdventureWorks2016;IntegratedSecurity=SSPI;**ApplicationIntent=Read Only**

The Application Intent options are ReadOnly and ReadWrite (default).

Clients can connect either directly to the SQL Server instance name hosting the read-only database or by using the Availability Group listener name.

Using the availability group listener name allows for *read-only routing* to an available readable secondary replica. Read-only routing refers to the ability of SQL Server to route incoming connections to an availability group listener to a secondary replica that allows read-only workloads.

Configure Read-Only Routing

Read-only routing refers to the ability of SQL Server to route incoming connections to a secondary replica that is configured to allow read-only workloads. An availability group listener must be specified in order to use read-only routing, and the following should be true:

- Application Intent is set to READONLY for the incoming connections.

- Allow connections property of the secondary replica is set to READ_ONLY or ALL.

- The READ_ONLY_ROUTING_URL for each replica is set. This option must be set before configuring the read-only routing list.

- The READ_ONLY_ROUTING_LIST option must be set for each replica.

Execute the following query to check if a routing list has been configured for your Availability Group:

```
SELECT ag.name, ar.replica_server_name as primary_server_role,
(SELECT replica_server_name from sys.availability_replicas as b WHERE
b.replica_id = a.read_only_replica_id) as secondary_route_reader_server,
```

155

```
a. routing_priority, ar.availability_mode_desc, ar.failover_mode_desc,
ar.secondary_role_allow_connections_desc
FROM sys.availability_read_only_routing_lists as a
RIGHT JOIN sys.availability_replicas as ar
ON a.replica_id = ar.replica_id
INNER JOIN sys.availability_groups as ag
ON ar.group_id = ag.group_id
```

Figure 10-6 shows the output from the preceding query. As you see, there is no read-only routing currently set up for any of the replicas.

	name	primary_server_role	secondary_route_reader_server	routing_priority	availability_mode_desc	failover_mode_desc	secondary_role_allow_connections_desc
1	AGCorp	ALWAYSONN1	NULL		SYNCHRONOUS_COMMIT	AUTOMATIC	ALL
2	AGCorp	ALWAYSONN2	NULL	NULL	SYNCHRONOUS_COMMIT	AUTOMATIC	ALL
3	AGCorp	ALWAYSONN3	NULL	NULL	ASYNCHRONOUS_COMMIT	MANUAL	READ_ONLY

Figure 10-6. Is read-only routing configured?

Next we will configure the read-only routing list.

■ **Note** There is no GUI available in SSMS to accomplish this task; it can only be accomplished through ALTER AVAILABILITY GROUP DDL scripts.

The first step is to configure the *read-only routing URL* for each replica. Read-only routing URL is used for routing read-intent connection requests to a specific readable secondary replica. A routing URL consists of a system address for the replica and the port number that is used by the database engine of that instance. For example, the routing URL for AlwaysOnN1 would be tcp://alwaysonn1:1433. Note that since we are specifying the port number used by the database engine, we do not specify the name of the SQL Server instance, only the server name. Usually, every readable secondary replica is assigned a read-only routing URL. To configure read-only routing URL, connect to the primary replica in the script window and execute the following code. In the below example we are configuring the routing URL for all the replicas in the availability group.

```
USE MASTER
GO

ALTER AVAILABILITY GROUP AGCorp
MODIFY REPLICA ON 'AlwaysOnN1' WITH
(secondary_role(read_only_routing_url='tcp://AlwaysOnN1:1433'))

ALTER AVAILABILITY GROUP AGCorp
MODIFY REPLICA ON 'AlwaysOnN2' WITH
(secondary_role(read_only_routing_url='tcp://AlwaysOnN2:1433'))

ALTER AVAILABILITY GROUP AGCorp
MODIFY REPLICA ON 'AlwaysOnN3' WITH
(secondary_role(read_only_routing_url='tcp://AlwaysOnN3:1433'))
```

■ **Note** You must set the read-only routing URL before configuring the read-only routing list.

Next configure the routing list:

```
USE MASTER
GO

ALTER AVAILABILITY GROUP AGCorp
MODIFY REPLICA ON 'AlwaysOnN1' WITH
(primary_role(read_only_routing_list=('AlwaysOnN2','AlwaysOnN3','AlwaysOnN1')))

ALTER AVAILABILITY GROUP AGCorp
MODIFY REPLICA ON 'AlwaysOnN2' WITH
(primary_role(read_only_routing_list=('AlwaysOnN3','AlwaysOnN1','AlwaysOnN2')))

ALTER AVAILABILITY GROUP AGCorp
MODIFY REPLICA ON 'AlwaysOnN3' WITH
(primary_role(read_only_routing_list=('AlwaysOnN1','AlwaysOnN2','AlwaysOnN3')))
```

■ **Note**   Prior to SQL Server 2016, read-only routing always directed traffic to the first available replica in the routing list, unless it was not accessible, and then it would direct the connection to the next replica in the routing list. It wasn't possible to spread out the load across replicas, even when you had multiple secondaries.

Configure Load Balancing Across Replicas

Starting SQL Server 2016, you can now configure load balancing across a set of read-only replicas. Use one level of nested parentheses around the READ_ONLY_ROUTING_LIST to achieve this:

```
USE MASTER
GO
-- Configure routing list on current primary replica
ALTER AVAILABILITY GROUP AGCorp
MODIFY REPLICA ON 'AlwaysOnN1' WITH
(primary_role(read_only_routing_list=(('AlwaysOnN2','AlwaysOnN3'),'AlwaysOnN1')))
```

The nested parentheses that surround the servers identify the load-balanced set.
Basically there are two lists in the preceding example:
List 1: AlwaysOnN2 and AlwaysOnN3
List 2: AlwaysOn1

Routing logic

The read-only connections will be routed to the replicas in the first list AlwaysOnN2 and AlwaysOnN3. There will be a round-robin distribution of read-only connections between the two replicas in the first list. In the preceding example, the first incoming read-only connection will be routed to AlwaysOnN2, the second read-only connection will be routed to AlwaysOnN3, the third read-only connection will be routed to AlwaysOnN2, the fourth read-only connection will be routed to AlwaysOnN3, and so on.

If a replica becomes unavailable, routing will continue with remaining replicas in the first list. In the preceding example, if AlwaysOnN2 becomes unavailable, then the read-only connections will only be routed to AlwaysOnN3.No read-only connections will be routed to the primary (AlwaysOnN1), if there is at least one readable secondary replica is accessible in the routing list. If all replicas in the first list are unavailable, then the read-only connections are routed to the replicas in the next list. In the preceding example, the read-only connections will be routed to AlwaysOnN1, If AlwaysOnN2 and AlwaysOnN3 become unavailable.

If any replicas in the first list become available again, a read-only connection once again will start routing to those replicas as they have higher priority.

Make sure you configure the routing list on all the replicas, as they would assume the primary role after failover.

```
USE MASTER
GO


ALTER AVAILABILITY GROUP AGCorp
MODIFY REPLICA ON 'AlwaysOnN2' WITH
(primary_role(read_only_routing_list=(('AlwaysOnN3','AlwaysOnN1'),'AlwaysOnN2')))

ALTER AVAILABILITY GROUP AGCorp
MODIFY REPLICA ON 'AlwaysOnN3' WITH
(primary_role(read_only_routing_list=(('AlwaysOnN1','AlwaysOnN2'),'AlwaysOnN3')))
```

Now execute the following query again to check if a routing list has been configured correctly for your Availability Group:

```
SELECT ag.name, ar.replica_server_name as primary_server_role,
(SELECT replica_server_name from sys.availability_replicas as b WHERE
b.replica_id = a.read_only_replica_id) as secondary_route_reader_server,
a. routing_priority, ar.availability_mode_desc, ar.failover_mode_desc,
ar.secondary_role_allow_connections_desc
FROM sys.availability_read_only_routing_lists as a
RIGHT JOIN sys.availability_replicas as ar
ON a.replica_id = ar.replica_id
INNER JOIN sys.availability_groups as ag
ON ar.group_id = ag.group_id
```

Figure 10-7 shows the output from the preceding query. Review the secondary_route_reader_server and routing_priority column values.

	name	primary_server_role	secondary_route_reader_server	routing_priority	availability_mode_desc	failover_mode_desc	secondary_role_allow_connections_desc
1	AGCorp	ALWAYSONN1	ALWAYSONN2	1	SYNCHRONOUS_COMMIT	AUTOMATIC	ALL
2	AGCorp	ALWAYSONN1	ALWAYSONN3	1	SYNCHRONOUS_COMMIT	AUTOMATIC	ALL
3	AGCorp	ALWAYSONN1	ALWAYSONN1	2	SYNCHRONOUS_COMMIT	AUTOMATIC	ALL
4	AGCorp	ALWAYSONN2	ALWAYSONN3	1	SYNCHRONOUS_COMMIT	AUTOMATIC	ALL
5	AGCorp	ALWAYSONN2	ALWAYSONN1	1	SYNCHRONOUS_COMMIT	AUTOMATIC	ALL
6	AGCorp	ALWAYSONN2	ALWAYSONN2	2	SYNCHRONOUS_COMMIT	AUTOMATIC	ALL
7	AGCorp	ALWAYSONN3	ALWAYSONN1	1	ASYNCHRONOUS_COMMIT	MANUAL	READ_ONLY
8	AGCorp	ALWAYSONN3	ALWAYSONN2	1	ASYNCHRONOUS_COMMIT	MANUAL	READ_ONLY
9	AGCorp	ALWAYSONN3	ALWAYSONN3	2	ASYNCHRONOUS_COMMIT	MANUAL	READ_ONLY

Figure 10-7. Review routing list

Considerations, Limitations, and Best Practices

Now that we have looked at how to configure a replica as a readable secondary, it's also important to understand some of the considerations.

Impact of Read Workload

Read or reporting workloads that run on the secondary replica need system resources and so does the REDO thread. REDO thread is the one that is applying transactions from the transaction log to keep the database in sync. The REDO thread needs I/O to read the transaction log and to fetch the page from disk to apply the change, and it requires CPU to apply the change. Significant resource contention is possible between REDO and Read workloads as they have to share resources. This can cause blocking and even deadlock scenarios. SQL Server never chooses REDO thread as the victim in deadlock scenarios. Any increase in latency on the Secondary Replica can impact the Recovery Time Objective (RTO) of your application.

Figure 10-8 shows the REDO thread operation and the possibility of resource contention due to the reporting workloads.

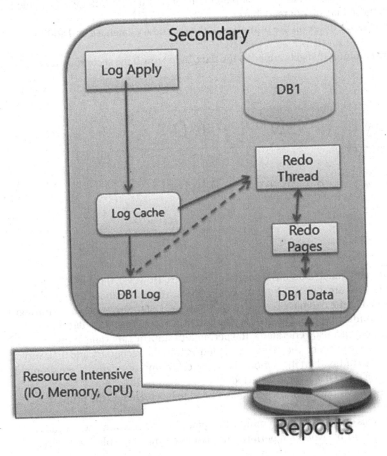

Figure 10-8. *REDO thread operation and reporting workload*

The read operations do not take shared locks because of row versioning; however they do take schema stability (Sch-S) locks. Redo operations applying DDL changes can get blocked due to this. Hence monitor your secondary replica for resource contention issues and provision adequate resources on the secondary replica. Extended events can be used to monitor REDO thread blocking, sqlserver.lock_redo_blocked event will be raised if the REDO thread is blocked. Ensure that you are using best practices while building the reporting queries to minimize resource consumption. Also consider running or scheduling the resource intensive queries during low-latency periods.

The Role of Row Versioning

All reporting workloads will internally use the snapshot isolation level to avoid blocking between REDO and the read workloads. Snapshot isolation level means that row versions will be created and used. As shared locks are not taken on rows by the reporting workload, the redo thread will not be blocked when it wants to update that row. However, the row version has an overhead. TempDB will require more space for the row versions. Also, the row version requires a 14-byte pointer added to each data/index row on the primary on deleted, modified, or inserted data rows as they cannot be directly added on the Secondary Replica. When this 14-byte pointer is added to the primary database it is carried over to the secondary database. Increase in page size can cause frequent page splits, which impacts performance. This all happens internally without having snapshot isolation enabled on the primary. The 14-byte pointer will be added as soon as at least one secondary's readable secondary option is set to either yes or read intent only and the pointer will be copied over to all the secondaries (even those that are not readable).

Hence plan for the additional space usage on the primary and the secondary database and additional TempDB usage on the secondary.

Figure 10-9 shows the 14-byte pointer that gets added to the data/index row if the secondary replica is made readable.

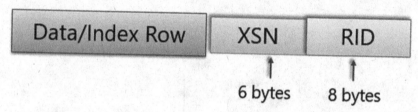

Figure 10-9. 14-byte pointer

Query Performance

Statistics on the primary databases are available on the secondary databases. However, if the read-only secondary database needs statistics that are different from the ones on the primary database then those statistics cannot be manually created as the database is read-only. In this case, SQL Server creates temporary statistics in the TempDB on the secondary replica. These temporary statistics have readonly_database_ statistic appended to its name. They are also generated if the permanent statistics are stale. If the permanent statistics are updated on the primary, then they are copied over to the secondary and SQL Server uses the updated permanent statistics rather than the temporary statistics. Temporary statistics are dropped if the availability group fails over or if the SQL Server is restarted.

Indexes required for the read-only workload on the secondary need to be created on the primary database.

Keep these indexing and statistics considerations in mind while planning the read-only workload or when you are troubleshooting any read-only workload performance issues on the Readable Secondary.

Data Latency

When the log records are sent from the primary replica to the secondary replicas, a dedicated REDO thread applies those log records on each secondary database. If you query the secondary database, the committed data is only available once the REDO thread has applied the logs to the database. In this case, the Always On dashboard would show zero data loss under the estimated data loss column, which is an accurate representation as the data is committed. However, a common misconception is that the data on the secondary replica when queried will be up-to-date if the dashboard shows zero data loss. This is not the case. Hence offloading your reporting workloads to the Readable Secondary is only useful if the application can tolerate some amount of data latency. If not, then it might be better to run the reporting queries against the primary replica. The latency is usually only a matter of seconds, between the primary and secondary replicas. In some cases, if there is resource contention then the latency can increase.

In the case of In-Memory OLTP tables, when accessing these tables on secondary replica, a `safe timestamp` is used to return rows from transactions that have committed earlier than a safe timestamp. Garbage collection uses this as the oldest timestamp hint to garbage collect the rows on the primary replica. If transactional activity on the primary replica stops before the internal threshold for the safe-timestamp update is reached, the changes made since the last update to the `safe timestamp` will not be visible on the secondary replica. You may need to run a few DML transactions on a dummy durable memory-optimized table on the primary replica to work around this issue. Or run a manual checkpoint to force shipping of a safe timestamp, although this is not recommended.

Blocking on Existing Transactions

Secondary databases can start accepting connections as soon as it is enabled for read. However, the row versions will not be fully available on the secondary database if there are active transactions existing on a primary database. The active transactions on the primary when the secondary replica was configured must commit or roll back. Until this happens, the transaction isolation level mapping on the secondary database is not complete and queries are temporarily blocked.

The same is true for memory-optimized tables. Even though row versions are always generated for memory-optimized tables, queries are blocked until all existing transactions are completed.

No Support for Change Tracking and Change Data Capture

Both Change tracking and change data capture are not supported on Readable Secondary databases. Change Tracking is disabled on Secondary databases. However, Change Data Capture can be enabled, but not supported.

Ghost Record Cleanup

When rows are deleted from an index leaf page, they are logically removed by marking them for deletion as *ghost records*. SQL Server has a background thread that periodically checks B-trees for ghosted records and asynchronously removes them from the leaf level of the index. The cleanup of ghost records on the primary replica can be blocked by transactions on the secondary replicas. You may need to kill a long-running query on a Secondary for the Ghost record cleanup on the Primary to continue in some cases. In-Memory OLTP tables do not have this problem, as the row versions are kept in memory and are independent of the row versions on the primary replica. DBCC SHRINKFILE also gets impacted by this and it might fail on the primary replica if the file contains ghost records that are still in use on a secondary replica.

Read-Only Routing Does Not Work if Primary Is Down

Read-only routing does not work if the primary is down, because the availability group listener is offline as well. Clients would have to connect directly to the read-only secondary replicas for read-only workloads. Prior to SQL 2014, you could not read from a secondary replica database if it was in a disconnected or not synchronized state. Hence the direct connection to read from the secondary is only available from SQL Server 2014 onwards.

Support for In-Memory OLTP

Querying In-Memory OLTP tables is supported on the secondary replica. In-Memory OLTP tables in an availability group can be setup using the same steps that you would use for any other disk-based tables database. One main difference is, unlike disk-based tables, there is no need to map the connections to Snapshot Isolation level. This is because the access to memory-optimized tables is done using optimistic concurrency by default. There are, however, certain restrictions on the usage of isolation levels and hints on both Primary and Secondary Replicas.

Following are some best practices to use if you are considering read-only workloads on your secondary databases.

Resource Governance

To manage the CPU, Memory, and I/O resources used by connections from Reporting Workload, use the Resource Governor feature. This will ensure that enough resources are available for the REDO thread and hence reduce contention between the REDO thread and Reporting Workload.

Multiple Secondary Replicas

Distribute the Reporting Workload using multiple secondary replicas. As explained earlier in the chapter, with the introduction of load balancing for read-only routing, this is much easier with SQL 2016. This will ensure that a single Secondary replica is not overloaded. Also, having multiple Secondary replicas gives the flexibility to reserve one or more Secondary Replicas purely for failover, hence removing the possibility of RTO (Recovery Time Objective) getting impacted by reporting workload. Also, when you have multiple Secondary replicas, prefer replicas in Asynchronous-Commit availability mode for reporting workload.

Monitor REDO Activity

Always monitor REDO activity, such as redo queue size, redo rate, and redo blocked events on the Secondary. Set certain thresholds on these counters based on your RTO requirements and take necessary actions when REDO activity exceeds your thresholds.

Summary

In this chapter we saw how to successfully configure Readable Secondary and some considerations and limitations of using a Readable Secondary. In the next chapter we will take a look at the database maintenance operations using Readable Secondary.

CHAPTER 11

■ ■ ■

Database Maintenance Using Secondary Replicas

Now that you have deployed your high availability and disaster recovery (HADR) solution using Always On Availability Groups, it's important to ensure that you are maximizing the investment made in the solution by fully utilizing all the replicas. Unfortunately, we still find database administrators (DBAs) using the primary replica for almost everything and rarely using the secondary replicas for production, reporting and/or database maintenance workloads. It's very common to see DBAs using the secondary replicas only for DR just like they did with older HADR solutions. Most of the older solutions did not allow use of the secondary replicas for anything except for DR and one of the asks from customers was the ability to fully utilize the secondaries.

In chapter 10, you saw how you can leverage the investment in the hardware by offloading reporting workload to one or more secondary replicas thereby freeing up resources on the primary replica to achieve higher throughput. In this chapter you will see how you can further free up resources on the primary replica by offloading resource intensive jobs like database backup and integrity check to the secondary replicas.

Offloading Database Backups

We all know how important it is to take database backups and most DBAs do it religiously. Also, to minimize the work-loss exposure and to keep the transaction log size in check, it is very common to take transaction log backups every 15 minutes to 30 minutes. We know that running backup jobs on the SQL Server is a very I/O intensive operation that may affect the production workload. Backup operations can also be CPU intensive if we are using the backup compression feature. Also, production workload may affect the backup speed. Wouldn't it be nice if we could perform backups without affecting the production workload? Also, wouldn't it be nice if the production load did not affect the backup operations? In an availability group environment, can we take backups on the secondary replicas since it has a copy of the availability databases? These are some of the features customers have been asking Microsoft for a long time with previous HADR solutions.

Always On Availability Groups allow us to run backups (with some restrictions) on the secondary replicas. Taking backups on the secondary replicas significantly increases the performance of the mission-critical workload on the primary replica by reducing the I/O and CPU contention usually caused by backups. This may increase the speed of the backups too if there is no significant reporting workload running on the secondary replica.

© Uttam Parui and Vivek Sanil 2016
U. Parui and V. Sanil, *Pro SQL Server Always On Availability Groups*, DOI 10.1007/978-1-4842-2071-9_11

Backup Types Supported on Secondary Replica

Secondary replica supports the following backup types:

- BACKUP DATABASE – supports only *copy-only* full backups of databases, files, or filegroups.

■ **Note**   A copy-only full backup is an SQL Server backup that is independent of the sequence of regular SQL Server backups. They do not impact the log chain or clear the differential bitmap. Copy-only full backups cannot be used as a base for differential backups. However, copy-only full backup can still be used as a base for subsequent transaction log backups.

- BACKUP LOG – supports only regular transaction log backups.

Secondary replicas do not support the following backup types:

- Differential backups and
- Copy-only transaction log backups.

If your backup strategy uses differential backups, then you need to take regular full backups and differential backups on the primary replica. You can still offload the transaction log backups on the secondary replica.

In order for the backups to work on the secondary replica, the secondary replica needs to be communicating with the primary replica. The secondary replica needs to be in synchronized or synchronizing state for backups to work on secondary replica. The replica state cannot be in 'not synchronizing,' 'disconnected,' or 'resolving' state.

■ **Note**   Secondary replica can be in synchronous or asynchronous availability mode. Even if an asynchronous replica has significant latency, you can still take backups from it. If the secondary replica is lagging behind the primary replica, then the backup on the secondary replica will not have all the data that the primary replica has at that point.

Role of Primary in Backups

Regardless of the type of backup that you take on the secondary replica, the primary replica plays a major role in coordinating the backups between replicas. Figure 11-1 shows the communication between the primary and secondary replicas.

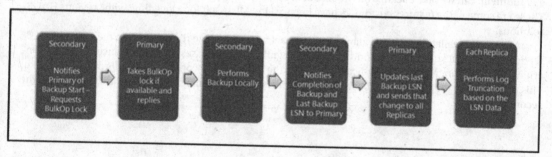

Figure 11-1. *Primary playing a major role in backups*

When a secondary replica starts a backup, it notifies the primary replica that it wants to start a backup. The primary replica will attempt to take a BulkOp lock for that database. The BulkOp lock prevents two replicas to take backup at the same time. Assuming no other replica is taking a backup, primary replica will get the BulkOp lock on the database on behalf of the secondary replica and notify the secondary replica. The secondary replica will start performing the backup locally. It is going to copy data out of the secondary database or transaction log depending upon the type of backup to the backup media. There is no interaction for backup purposes with the primary replica during this stage.

After the secondary replica completes the backup, it notifies the primary replica and gives it the last log sequence number (LSN) that was active in the log at the point it stopped copying data from the transaction log. The primary replica updates the last LSN in its copy of the database, which is the updatable copy, and that's the one that is used for the next backup. The update of the last backup LSN now gets replicated to all the secondary replicas. At this point, the primary replica also releases the BulkOp lock so other backup operations can take place. Also, now each replica can perform log truncation based on this last backup LSN.

How Transaction Log Backups Work

You may already know this but as a refresher, a series of ordered transaction log backups is called a log chain. When the log chain is intact, you can restore the database from the full database backup followed by subsequent log backups. Always On Availability Groups guarantee a consistent log chain of log backups taken across replicas (primary or secondary configured with synchronous- or asynchronous-commit availability mode). Regardless of which replica that the transaction log backup is taken, there will be no overlap of the contents between these backups. Figure 11-2 shows the three replicas AlwaysOnN1, AlwaysOnN2, and AlwaysOnN3 that you configured using availability groups in chapter 8.

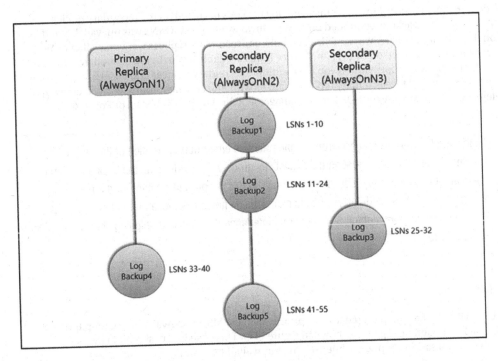

Figure 11-2. *Taking transaction log backups on all replicas*

Let's assume that currently AlwaysOnN1 is the primary replica and AlwaysOnN2 and AlwaysOnN3 are the secondary replicas. AlwaysOnN1 and AlwaysOnN2 are configured with synchronous availability mode whereas AlwaysOnN3 is configured as asynchronous availability mode. To minimize the impact of the backups on the primary, you want to take backups on the secondary replica preferably AlwaysOnN2 as it is in the same datacenter and is in synchronous availability mode.

The first transaction log backup is taken on secondary replica AlwaysOnN2. Let's assume that this log backup (Log Backup1) includes transactions with log sequence numbers (LSNs) from 1 to 10. The next transaction log backup (Log Backup2) occurs on AlwaysOnN2. This backup will include any transactions with LSN after the last LSN from Log Backup1 taken on AlwaysOnN2. Let's assume this second log backup includes transactions with LSNs 11 to 24.

Let's assume that AlwaysOnN2 is down for some reason and the next log backup (Log Backup3) is taken on our secondary replica AlwaysOnN3 that is located in the DR datacenter. Log Backup3 will have LSNs from 25 onwards. Let's assume the third log backup includes transactions with LSNs 25 to 32. Now say, AlwaysOnN3 also goes down and you take the next transaction log backup (Log Backup 4) on the primary replica AlwaysOnN1, this backup will have LSNs from 33 onwards. Let's say it has LSNs 33 to 40.

By this time, let's assume AlwaysOnN2 and AlwaysOnN3 are back online. And you resume taking transaction log backup on AlwaysOnN2. The fifth log backup will include transactions from 41 onwards. As you may have noticed, there are no overlaps of LSNs between the log backups. If you need to recover the database using the backups, you will need to restore a full backup (or a copy-only full backup) followed by all the transaction log backups taken from all the replicas and restored in order as if they were all taken from a single SQL Server.

Configuring Backup Preference and Priority

In the preceding section, you saw how the transaction log backups occurred on the secondary replica AlwaysOnN2 and how the backups continued on AlwaysOnN3 when AlwaysOnN2 was unavailable and later continued on the primary replica AlwaysOnN1 when both our secondary replicas were unavailable. Also, you saw the log backups resumed on AlwaysOnN2 once it was available again. In this section, we will show you how to configure backup priority when you have multiple secondary replicas and ensure that backups still continue to occur even if the secondary replica/s fail. As with most configurations, you can configure backup preferences and priority using SQL Server Management Studio (SSMS), TSQL, or PowerShell.

■ **Note**　You can configure the backup preferences and priorities either during creation of the availability group as you saw in chapter 8 or after creating the availability group. After configuring the backup preferences and priorities, you need to script backup jobs (discussed later in this chapter) to account for them as there is no automatic enforcement of these settings. Ad-hoc backup jobs do not check these preferences by default. However, backup jobs created using default SQL Server maintenance plan and Log Shipping checks the backup settings that you configure.

Using SSMS

To configure or review the backup preferences and priority using SSMS, open Availability Group Properties and select the Backup Preferences page as shown in Figure 11-3. This page is very similar to the Backup Preferences tab that you saw in chapter 8 while creating the availability group.

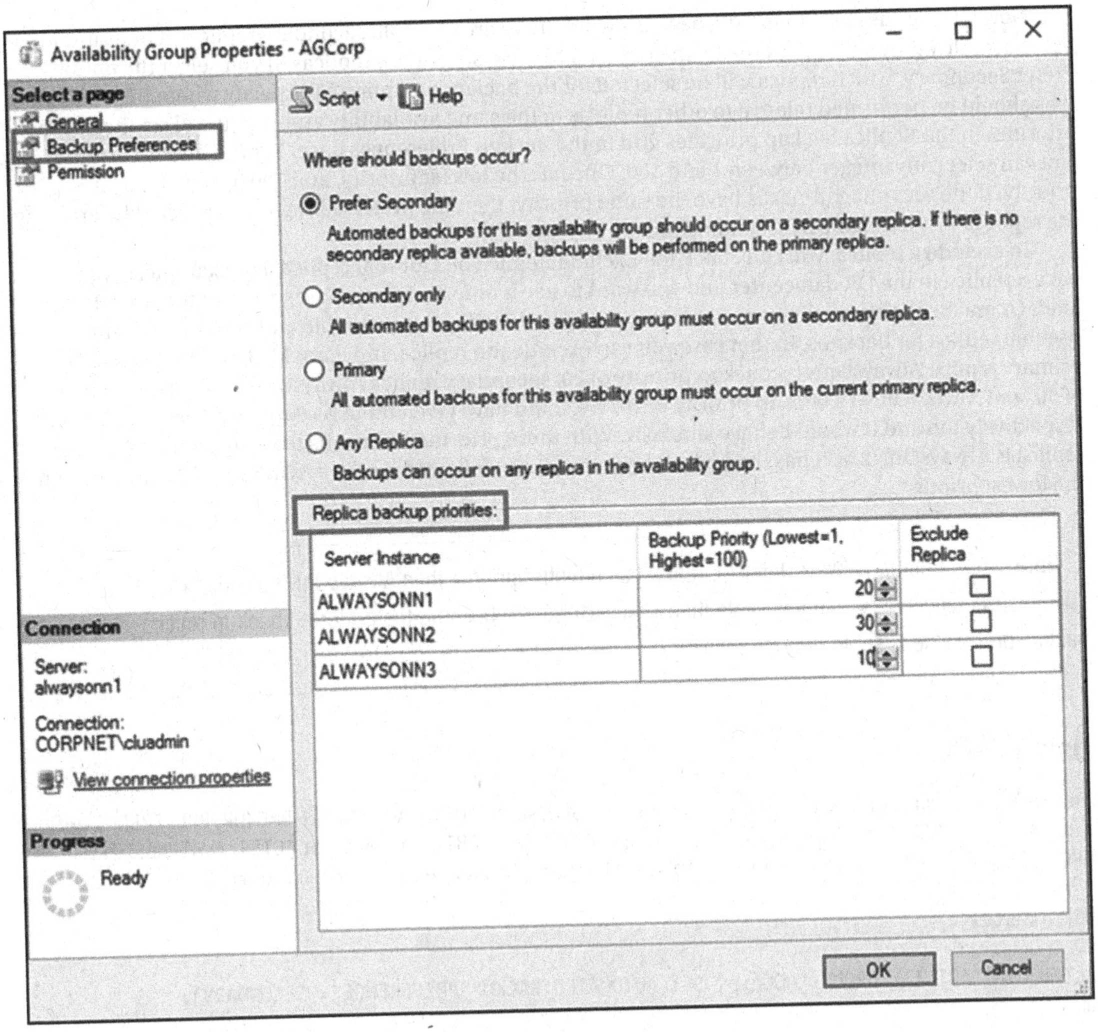

Figure 11-3. *Configuring backup preferences and priorities using SSMS*

As shown in Figure 11-3, you have the following options for backup preference

- *Prefer Secondary* – This is the default backup preference. As the name suggests, when this option is selected, backups will occur on a secondary replica except when the primary replica is the only replica online. When there are multiple secondary replicas available, backup priority defines the secondary with highest priority for backups.

- *Secondary only* – If you do not want backups to occur on the primary replica then select this option. When this option is selected, backups always occur on the secondary and will not occur if primary is the only replica online.

- *Primary* – As the name suggests, when this option is selected, backups always occur on the primary replica. You want to choose this option if differential backups are to be taken as differential backups are not supported on secondary replicas.

- *Any Replica* – When this option is selected, backups can occur on any replica; however backup priority will still be applicable.

Now let's discuss how to handle backups when there are multiple secondary replicas. For example, the availability group that you created in chapter 8 has two secondary replicas. If you select the option Prefer Secondary, which replica will be selected for the backup operation? To specify where the backup jobs should be performed relative to other replicas in the same availability group, you will set the backup priorities in the Replica backup priorities grid in the Backup Preferences page. For the backup priority, you can select any integer between 1 and 100. One has the lowest priority, and 100 has the highest priority. If the secondary replicas have the same priority, then the preferred replica is selected by ordering the replicas by their name in ascending order.

To exclude a replica, you can check the Exclude Replica box for that replica. For example, say you have a replica in the DR datacenter and you want to use it only for DR purposes and not for any other load. Or maybe the network connectivity to a secondary replica is not reliable and you do not want to use that replica for backups. In that case you can exclude the replica. In Figure 11-3, we have given the primary replica AlwaysOnN1 a backup priority of 20, secondary replica AlwaysOnN2 a backup priority of 30, and AlwaysOnN3 a backup priority of 10. We could have given them backup priorities of 2, 3, and 1 respectively too and it would behave similarly. With these priorities, it means that our preferred backup replica is AlwaysOnN2 as it has the highest backup priority followed by AlwaysOnN1 and AlwaysOnN3 has the lowest priority.

■ **Note**   Even though AlwaysOnN1 (primary) has a higher priority than AlwaysOnN3 (secondary), if AlwaysOnN2 (secondary) is unavailable then AlwaysOnN3 will become the preferred backup replica as the backup preference is set to Prefer Secondary.

Using TSQL

To configure backup preference and priority using TSQL set the WITH AUTOMATED_BACKUP_PREFERENCE option and BACKUP_PRIORITY option respectively of the CREATE AVAILABILITY GROUP or ALTER AVAILABILITY GROUP TSQL. Below is a sample code to configure backup preference to prefer secondary.

```
USE [master]
GO
ALTER AVAILABILITY GROUP [AGCorp] SET(AUTOMATED_BACKUP_PREFERENCE = SECONDARY);
GO
```

The following is a sample code to configure backup priority of 20 for AlwaysOnN1 replica, 30 for AlwaysOnN2 replica and 10 for AlwaysOnN3 replica:

```
ALTER AVAILABILITY GROUP [AGCorp]
MODIFY REPLICA ON N'ALWAYSONN1' WITH (BACKUP_PRIORITY = 20)
GO
ALTER AVAILABILITY GROUP [AGCorp]
MODIFY REPLICA ON N'ALWAYSONN2' WITH (BACKUP_PRIORITY = 30)
GO
ALTER AVAILABILITY GROUP [AGCorp]
MODIFY REPLICA ON N'ALWAYSONN3' WITH (BACKUP_PRIORITY = 10)
GO
```

Using PowerShell

To configure backup preference and priority using PowerShell, use the `AutomatedBackupPreference` option and `BackupPriority` options respectively of the `Set-SqlAvailabilityGroup` cmdlet. Below is a sample code to configure backup preference to prefer secondary.

```
Set-SqlAvailabilityGroup -Path SQLSERVER:\Sql\AlwaysOnN1\DEFAULT\AvailabilityGroups\AGCorp
-AutomatedBackupPreference Secondary
```

The following is a sample code to configure backup priority of 20 for AlwaysOnN1 replica, 30 for AlwaysOnN2 replica, and 10 for AlwaysOnN3 replica.

```
Set-SqlAvailabilityReplica -BackupPriority 20 -Path SQLSERVER:\Sql\AlwaysOnN1\DEFAULT\
AvailabilityGroups\AGCorp\AvailabilityReplicas\ALWAYSONN1
Set-SqlAvailabilityReplica -BackupPriority 30 -Path SQLSERVER:\Sql\AlwaysOnN1\DEFAULT\
AvailabilityGroups\AGCorp\AvailabilityReplicas\ALWAYSONN2
Set-SqlAvailabilityReplica -BackupPriority 10 -Path SQLSERVER:\Sql\AlwaysOnN1\DEFAULT\
AvailabilityGroups\AGCorp\AvailabilityReplicas\ALWAYSONN3
```

Automating Backups on Secondary Replicas

To automate the backups on secondary replicas and ensure that the backups run on the preferred replica and follow the replica priorities, you need to script the backup jobs for the availability group databases. To check if the current replica is the preferred backup replica, you can use the built-in system function `sys.fn_hadr_backup_is_preferred_replica`. We discussed this function in chapter 9. As a refresher, this function takes a database name as a parameter and returns a 1 if the availability replica that is hosted by the current instance is the preferred backup replica. If not, the function returns a 0.

The following is a sample code to use this function in backup jobs:

```
If sys.fn_hadr_backup_is_preferred_replica( @dbname ) <> 1
BEGIN
-- If this is not the preferred backup replica, exit
END
-- If this is the preferred replica, continue to do the backup.
```

If you use the default SQL Server Maintenance Plan for your backups, then you will not need to do anything extra as the maintenance plan uses this function by default to decide if the backups need to occur on a particular replica. If you do not use maintenance plans and have custom backup jobs, then you will need to modify the backup job using something similar to the sample code shown earlier.

To ensure that the backups will occur on the current preferred backup replica at the time of starting the backup job, you need to create the same jobs (using maintenance plan for backups or custom backup jobs) with the same schedule on all replicas. Say, for example, you configure the backup preference and priority as shown in Figure 11-3 and you want to take transaction log backups every 15 minutes as per these backup configuration settings. You can create the automated transaction log backup job very easily by creating a database maintenance plan wizard on each replica to take log backups every 15 minutes with the same schedule. The jobs will run on each replica at the same time but the actual backup will occur only on the replica that is the current preferred backup replica. The jobs on non-preferred replicas will do nothing and exit. The same logic applies for all supported backup types.

If you are creating a database maintenance plan to take full backups, you will see the warning message shown in Figure 11-4.

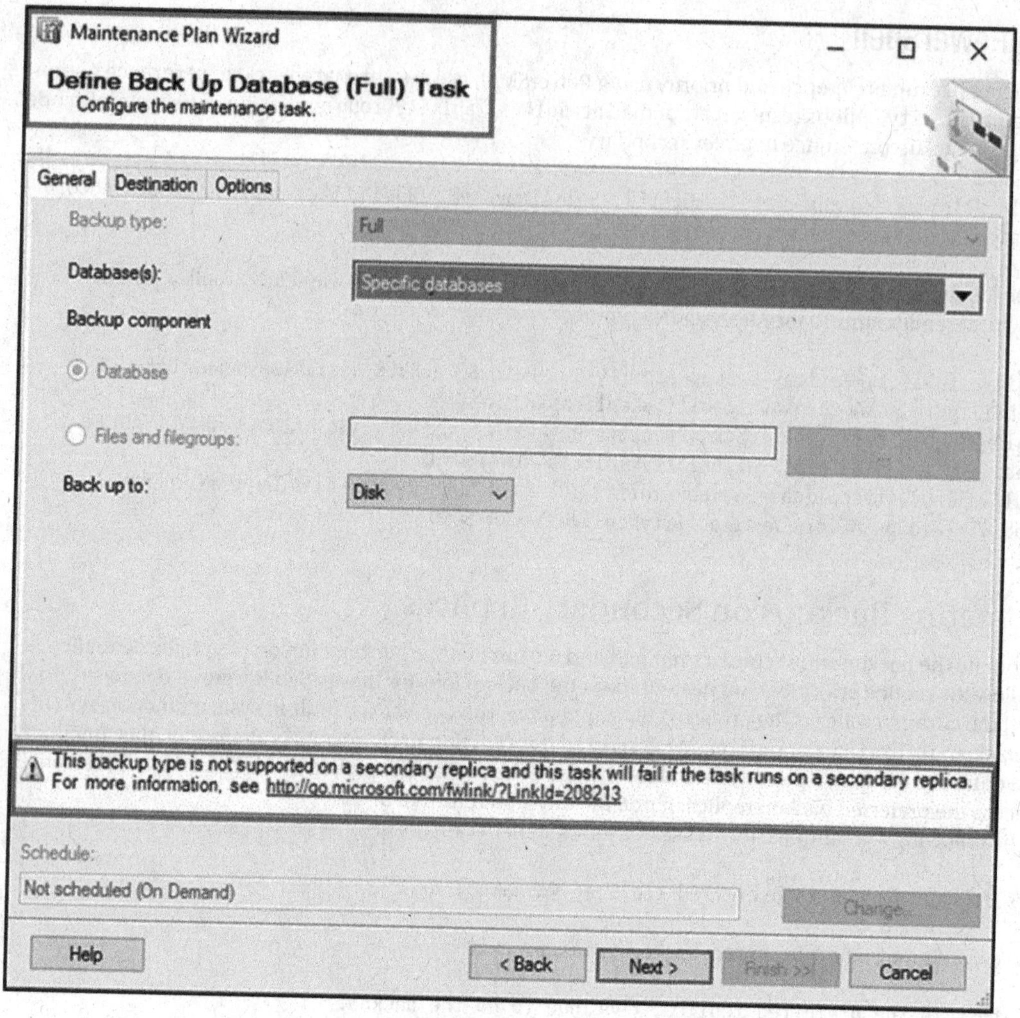

Figure 11-4. Warning message while creating database maintenance plan for full backup

This is expected as regular full backups are not supported on a secondary replica. To clear the warning, click the Options tab and select Copy-only backup check box as shown in Figure 11-5.

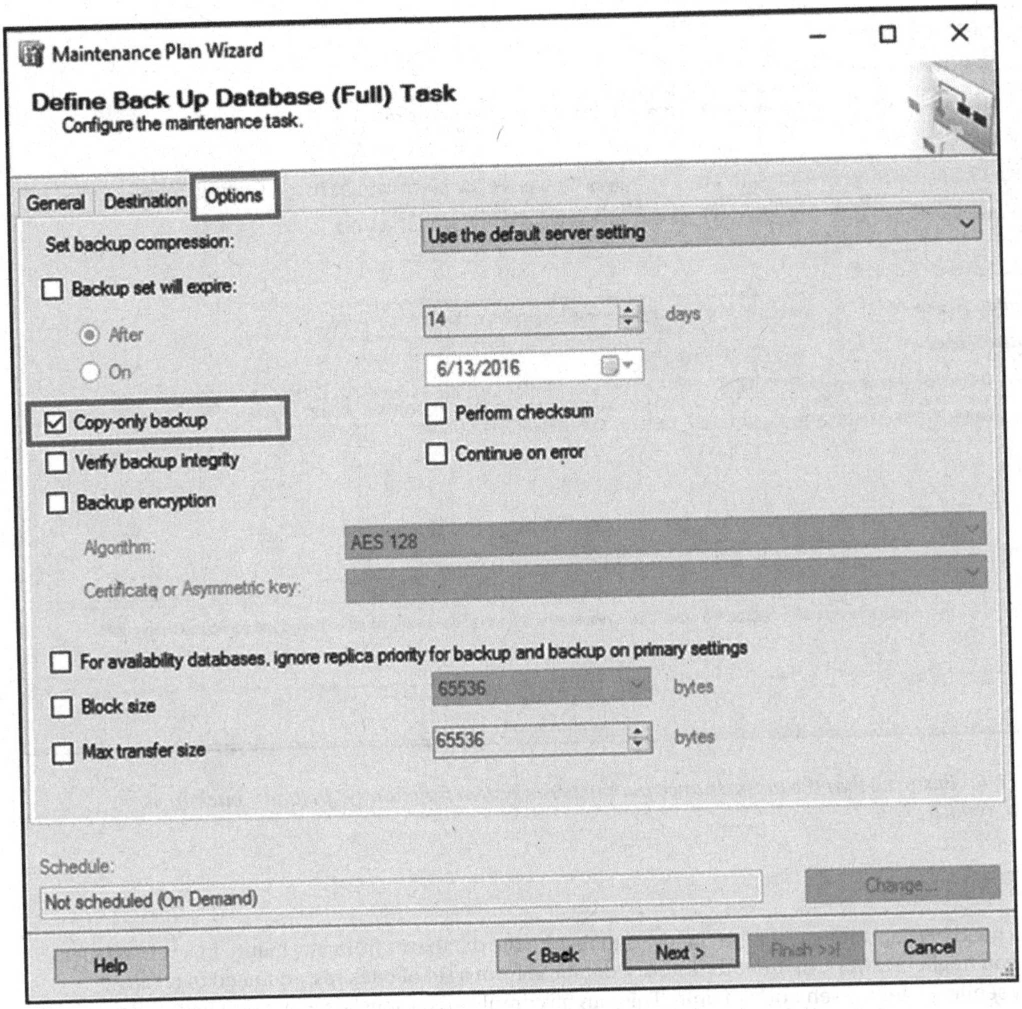

Figure 11-5. Selecting copy-only backup option for full backups

Also, notice the check box labelled For availability databases, ignore replica priority for backup and backup on primary settings. This option allows us to override the backup preference settings if we need to.

To see how the database maintenance plan uses the system function sys.fn_hadr_backup_is_the preferred_replica, right-click the maintenance plan, and select Modify. In the Design Maintenance Plan page, right-click Backup Database Task (Full), select Edit, and click the View T-SQL button in the Back Up Database Task page. Notice the function used in the backup script, as shown in Figure 11-6.

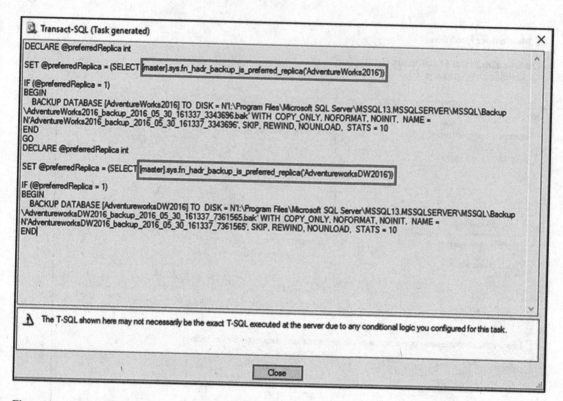

Figure 11-6. Ensuring that the maintenance plan uses the system function sys.fn_hadr_backup_is_preferred_replica

Best Practices

Having a good backup strategy in place helps us to restore the databases from any failure in a very efficient way. As you might be aware, in order to restore a database from a set of backups, you need to create a recovery sequence for a given point of time. This can be complicated especially since you have different types of backups. Also, since now you can take backups on any replica, you can have a bigger problem when you need to restore all the backups in the same order it was taken. If you miss a backup, then you will break the backup chain.

■ **Note** MSDB database is only aware of the backups taken on the local SQL Server instance. It does not know about the backups that are taken on the other replicas.

To ensure that you do not have to search all the replicas for all the backup files during recovery, it is highly recommended to maintain a central location for all backups, which is accessible from all replicas. This will ensure that during a failure, anyone can find all the backup files. Also, if the centralized location is separate from the replicas then you can ensure that you will not lose the backup files if any of the replicas fail.

Also, you can use the SSMS built-in tool *Recovery Advisor* to quickly create a correct and optimal restore sequence.

■ **Tip**   To open the *Recovery Advisor* tool in SSMS, right the Databases node and select Restore Database…. Click the ellipses next to the Device dialog box and add the path(s) to the backup locations. To perform point-in-time restore, click Timeline button on the Restore Database dialog box.

All you need to provide is the location of the backup sets and the Recovery Advisor tool automatically comes up with the correct restore sequence based on the header and LSN information available in the backup files. Again, if you have a centralized backup location, then you will only need to provide the path to the centralized backup location. But if for some reason, there are multiple backup locations, the Recovery Advisor tool allows us to add the paths to all the backup locations. Of course, if you forget about one or more backup paths then the tool will not be able to create the correct restore sequence and may throw an error. This tool can also be used to perform point-in-time restores easily too. You can select a point-in-time to restore by simply moving the slider on the time line or by entering the date and time values in the text boxes. The tool automatically chooses the right backup files required to restore the database to that point.

■ **Note**   To restore a database that is a part of an availability group, you will first need to remove it from the availability group.

We mentioned earlier that availability groups do not support taking differential backups on the secondary replicas. Also, copy-only full backups that are supported on the secondary replicas cannot be used as a base for differential backups. So, how do we handle this if our backup strategy requires differential backups? If you need to take differential backups, then you can set the backup preference to be Primary so that the full and differential backups will always be taken from the current primary replica. But this also will mean that the transaction log backups will take place on the current primary replica.

We know that transaction log backup jobs typically run every 15 to 30 minutes whereas the full and differential backups jobs run once a day after business hours. So, the transaction log backups that are running during business hours will have the maximum impact on the production load. What if you want to offload the transaction log backups to the secondary replica and only take the full and differential log backups on the primary replica? To achieve this, one method is to set the backup preference to Prefer Secondary as you saw in Figure 11-3 to ensure that the transaction log backups created using maintenance plans execute on secondary replicas. And for the full and differential backups, you can create custom jobs that will identify the primary replica before executing the backup. You can use the built-in system function sys.fn_hadr_is_primary_replica for this purpose. As per our discussion about this function in chapter 9, this function takes a database name as a parameter and returns a 1 when the database on the current instance is the primary replica. If not, the function returns 0. Below is some sample code that you can use to perform full and/or differential backups on the primary replica.

```
If sys.fn_hadr_is_primary_replica ( @dbname ) = 1
BEGIN
-- This is the primary replica. Perform the backup job.
END
-- This is not the primary replica, exit.
```

Running Integrity Checks

Running database integrity checks using DBCC CHEKDB is an important part of database maintenance. This allows us to identify any database consistency issues well in advance so that we can take appropriate actions to fix the issue before we incur data corruption and/or data loss. The rule of thumb is to run database integrity checks once a week. Most DBAs follow this rule but tend to delay the schedule to once every two weeks or once every month or sometimes even disable the job due to the time and resources this operation takes. As the databases becomes bigger, these checks take longer and soon the maintenance windows become too small to accommodate these jobs. You don't want to run these checks during business hours as these jobs are resource intensive and may affect performance of your mission critical production workload especially when there is a lot of activity on the server.

What if you can run the database integrity checks while minimizing the impact on the production workload? If that is possible, then most DBAs will happily run these checks regularly again. Availability groups allow us to do just that. It allows us to perform DBCC CHECKDB jobs on the secondary replica while minimizing the performance impact on the production load on the primary replica. Let's look if running DBCC CHECKDB on the secondary replicas is enough and what the considerations are to run it on the secondary replicas.

Running DBCC CHECKDB on Secondary Replicas

To be able to run DBCC CHECKDB on secondary replicas, you need to configure the secondary replicas as *readable* as discussed in chapter 10. If you try to run DBCC CHECKDB on a non-readable secondary replica, you will get the following error message:

```
Msg 976, Level 14, State 1, Line 1
The target database, 'AdventureWorks2016', is participating in an availability group
and is currently not accessible for queries. Either data movement is suspended or the
availability replica is not enabled for read access. To allow read-only access to this and
other databases in the availability group, enable read access to one or more secondary
availability replicas in the group.  For more information, see the ALTER AVAILABILITY GROUP
statement in SQL Server Books Online.
```

As you might be aware, DBCC CHECKDB creates an internal snapshot and performs copy-on-write activity in order to check a specific point-in-time while allowing redo to progress. While performing DBCC CHECKDB on the secondary replica, it is possible that the secondary replica is behind the primary replica. If you want to avoid creating an internal snapshot, you can execute DBCC CHECKDB WITH TABLOCK. This operation requires a database lock and to obtain the database lock you need to first suspend the HADR activity on the database, run DBCC CHECKDB WITH TABLOCK and then resume the HADR activity.

■ **Note**   Suspending the HADR activity on the database will cause a backlog of log blocks and cause the transaction log file(s) to grow on the primary and other remaining replicas that do not have data synchronization suspended.

Running integrity checks on the secondary minimizes the impact of the production load on the primary replica but it does not completely replace the act of running it on the primary replica. This is due to the fact that the primary cause of corruption issues that we see is due to I/O subsystem corruption. As we are aware, each replica has a separate copy of the databases that are stored on a different I/O subsystem (or different portion of the I/O subsystem) and hosted on different servers with different memory.

■ **Note**   SQL Server 2016 supports running DBCC CHECKDB on databases that contain memory-optimized tables. However, validation only occurs on the disk-based tables. Also, DBCC repair options are not available for memory-optimized tables. Therefore, you must continue to back up your databases regularly and test the backups. You will need to restore from the last good backup if there are any data integrity issues in the memory-optimized tables. Also, as part of database backup and recovery, a CHECKSUM validation is done for files in memory-optimized filegroups.

Running DBCC CHECKDB only on the secondary replica is not sufficient. It is possible that one availability replica may be corrupted while the other replica may not be corrupted, and the only way to detect any corruption to the database files from the I/O subsystem on a particular replica is via running DBCC CHECKDB on that replica.

Different Options to Run DBCC CHECKDB

To ensure that you are running DBCC CHECKDB on all the replicas while minimizing the performance impact on the production replica, consider the below options:

1. Run on secondary replica and failover periodically (recommended).

2. Run on all replicas but more frequently on the secondary replicas.

3. Run lightweight checks on primary replica.

In option 1 - Run on secondary replica and failover periodically is the preferred option if the secondary replicas are built exactly similar to the primary replica and you don't have any concerns running the integrity checks on the secondary replicas for a long time. In this option, you will schedule DBCC CHECKDB jobs on all the replicas and use the sys.fn_hadr_is_primary_replica function to run the DBCC CHECKDB only on the current secondary replica. Below is a sample code that performs DBCC CHECKDB for database AdventureWorks2016 only on the secondary replica.

```
IF sys.fn_hadr_is_primary_replica('AdventureWorks2016')<>1
BEGIN
        DBCC CHECKDB(AdventureWorks2014)
END
ELSE
        PRINT 'This is the primary replica, exit!'
```

You will perform availability group failover periodically (say once every other week) so that the next DBCC CHECKDB will run on the new secondary. This way, databases on both primary and secondary replicas are checked for corruption while minimizing the performance impact caused by DBCC CHECKDB. Also another benefit of this option is that you will know that all our replicas are functional and operating optimally and in case of a real disaster you can confidently failover to any replica and continue to operate normally. If you always use a particular server as your primary replica and use the secondary replica only for DR purposes, then you may not be 100% sure how it will perform when you do a failover.

If for some reason, you cannot use option 1, then you can consider using option 2 - Run on all replicas but more frequently on the secondary replicas. In this option, run DBCC CHECKDB on all replicas but run it more frequently (once a week, for example) on the secondary replicas as compared to the primary replica (monthly, for example). This option will not fully compensate for database integrity checks on the primary replica but it will reduce the impact on the primary replica.

If you cannot use either options 1 or 2, consider using option 3 - Runlight weight checks on primary replica. In this method, you run DBCC CHECKDB WITH PHYSICAL_ONLY to reduce the impact on the primary replica. This option has a small overhead and a shorter run time as compared to running the full DBCC CHECKDB and it checks the physical consistency of the database, detect torn pages, checksum failures, and common hardware failures that can corrupt user databases.

■ **Note**   It is still recommended to run the full DBCC CHECKDB periodically to check both the physical and logical integrity of the user databases.

Summary

In this chapter, you learned the benefits of active secondary replicas and how to leverage the hardware of the secondary replicas to run database backup and integrity check jobs. In the next chapter, we will discuss other common management tasks that DBAs need to perform on an availability groups HADR solution.

PART V

■ ■ ■

Managing Availability Groups

CHAPTER 12

■ ■ ■

Common Management Tasks

In this chapter we will take a look at all the common management tasks that an administrator would need to perform on an availability group. Creation of availability group is a one-time operation; however, you would need to manage the availability groups on an ongoing basis.

Suspend Secondary Database Synchronization

If the primary replica is experiencing performance degradation with queries and transactions taking longer, then suspending the synchronization on one or more secondary databases briefly might be useful to temporarily improve performance on the primary replica. By suspending the synchronization, the primary doesn't have to send the transaction log blocks to the secondary replica and can perform the commits more quickly.

To suspend the synchronization using SQL Server Management Studio, connect to the secondary replica, then under Availability Groups right-click the database and click Suspend Data Movement.

Figure 12-1 shows the Suspend Data Movement option in the SSMS GUI on Secondary Replica instance.

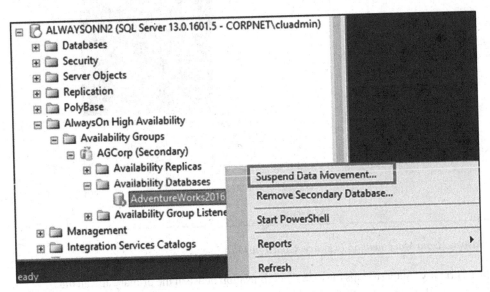

Figure 12-1. Suspend Data Movement on Secondary Replica Instance

© Uttam Parui and Vivek Sanil 2016
U. Parui and V. Sanil, *Pro SQL Server Always On Availability Groups*, DOI 10.1007/978-1-4842-2071-9_12

Suspending an Always On secondary database does not directly affect the availability of the primary database. However, it can impact redundancy and failover capabilities for the primary database.

After the secondary database synchronization is suspended, the transaction log of the corresponding primary database cannot be truncated. This causes log records to accumulate on the primary database. Therefore, try to resume or remove a suspended secondary database as quickly as possible. Also consider adding some temporary space for logs on the primary and other secondaries as it starts growing when the data synchronization is suspended.

Suspend Primary Database Synchronization

If multiple secondary replicas are causing performance issues on the primary replica for the same database(s) then it might be easier and faster to suspend the synchronization on the primary databases itself instead of going to each and every one of the secondary databases and suspending the synchronization.

■ **Note**   Starting SQL Server 2014, you can have up to eight secondary replicas for an availability group.

To suspend the synchronization using SQL Server Management Studio, connect to the primary replica, then under Availability Groups right-click the database and click Suspend Data Movement.

Figure 12-2 shows the Suspend Data Movement option in the SSMS GUI on Primary Replica instance.

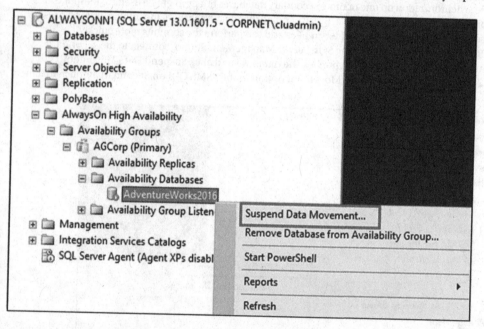

Figure 12-2. *Suspend Data Movement on Primary Replica Instance*

Suspending a primary database stops the data synchronization between the primary and all the secondary databases. In this case, the transaction log of the primary database cannot be truncated, and also changes made to the primary databases are not propagated to any of the secondary databases. Hence in case of a disaster on the primary replica instance there can be data loss. Therefore, try to resume the primary database synchronization as quickly as possible. Also consider adding some temporary space for logs on the primary and other secondaries, as it starts growing when the data synchronization is suspended.

Resume Database Synchronization

Resuming a suspended database puts the database into the SYNCHRONIZING state. Resuming the primary database also resumes any of its secondary databases that were suspended as the result of suspending the primary database.

To resume the synchronization using SQL Server Management Studio, connect to the replica database and then under Availability Groups, right-click the database and click Resume Data Movement.

Figure 12-3 shows the Resume Database Movement option in the SSMS GUI.

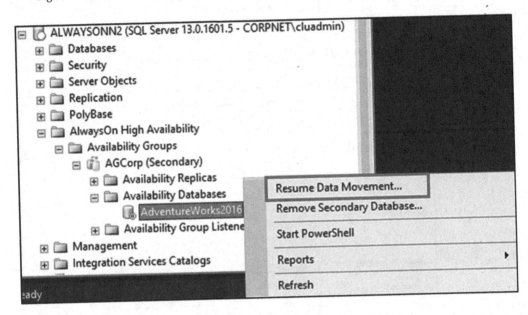

Figure 12-3. Resume Data Movement

If a secondary database was suspended locally, that is, from the SQL Server instance that hosts the secondary replica, then that secondary database must be resumed locally.

Once the primary database is in the SYNCHRONIZING state, we know that the synchronization has resumed on the secondary database.

Change the Availability Mode

The availability mode is a replica property that controls whether the replica commits asynchronously or synchronously. Availability mode can only be changed from the primary replica instance.

When synchronous-commit availability mode is used, the primary replica waits for the secondary replica to commit the transaction to the transaction log before confirming the commit back to the application. This can cause performance issues on the primary if the commits to synchronous secondary replica are delayed. In such scenarios, the Availability Mode of the secondary replica could be changed to asynchronous-commit, so that the primary replica doesn't have to wait for the confirmation from the secondary anymore. This will provide temporary relief to the SQL transaction performance on the primary. However, this temporary relief measure increases the chances of data loss as the Availability mode is now set to asynchronous-commit.

To change the Availability Mode of a replica using SQL Server Management Studio, connect to the primary replica and then under Availability Groups, right-click the availability group and click on Properties. Use the Availability Mode drop-down list to change the availability mode of the replica.

Once Availability Mode is changed, review the availability group configuration to ensure that the availability group will be able to meet the RTO and RPO requirements in the SLA.

Figure 12-4 shows the Availability Mode setting in the Availability Group Properties.

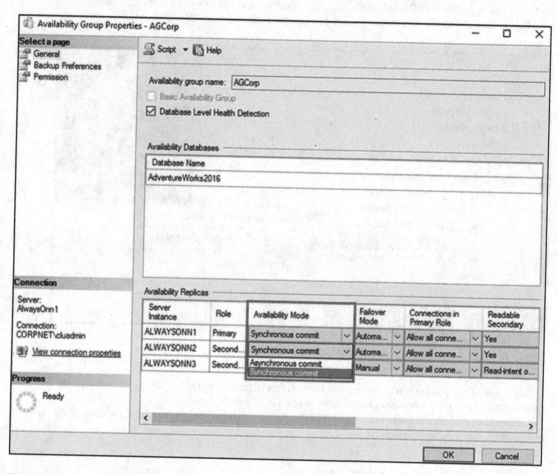

Figure 12-4. *Availability Mode*

Add a Database

A database can be added to an availability group by adding it first to the primary replica instance and then restoring and adding it to the secondary replica instances. A database can also be added to a secondary replica instance if it is already present on the primary replica instance. This is possible if the availability group was created with Skip Initial Synchronization option or if the secondary database was removed from the availability group due to performance bottleneck.

If the database is added to the primary replica instance, then add it to all the secondary replica instances at the earliest chance. If automatic seeding is enabled for an availability group, SQL Server automatically creates the secondary replicas when you add a database to the availability group. That means you no longer have to manually back up and restore secondary replicas. For automatic seeding to work, the data and log file path should be the same on every SQL Server instance participating in the availability group. Also the database should be in full recovery model and should have a current full and transaction log backup.

To add a database to an availability group using SQL Server Management Studio, connect to the primary replica instance and under Availability Groups right-click Availability Group and click Add Database to launch the Add Database to the Availability Group wizard.

Figure 12-5 shows the Add Database option in the SSMS GU.I

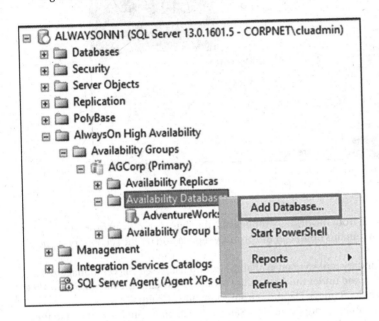

Figure 12-5. *Add Database*

To add a database to a secondary replica of an availability group using SQL Server Management Studio, first ensure that the database is prepared for availability group. Then connect to the secondary replica instance and under Availability Groups, right-click the Availability Group and click Join to Availability Group to launch the Join Database to Availability Group wizard.

Remove a Database

The transaction log can start growing when database synchronization is suspended. If the synchronization cannot be resumed, then the database should be removed from the secondary replica. The removed secondary database goes into the RESTORING state.

Figure 12-6 shows the Remove Database option in the SSMS GUI.

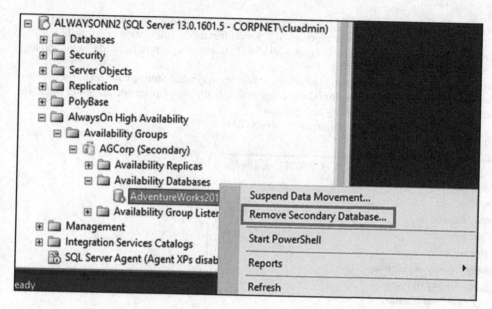

Figure 12-6. *Remove Database*

When a replica database is removed from the primary replica, the database is removed from the Availability Group on all the replicas. It remains online on the primary replica and on the secondary replicas it goes into the RESTORING state.

To remove a database from a secondary replica of an availability group using SQL Server Management Studio, connect to the secondary replica and under the Availability Groups, right-click the database and click Remove Secondary Database to launch the Remove Database from Availability Group wizard.

To remove a database from an availability group using SQL Server Management Studio, connect to the primary replica instance and then under Availability Groups, right-click the database to launch the Remove Database from Availability Group wizard.

If the database was removed due to performance considerations, then plan to add it back to the availability group at the earliest chance.

Add a Replica

A new replica can be added to an existing availability group.

Before you add an instance to an availability group as a secondary replica, first ensure that the instance satisfies all the prerequisites discussed in the prerequisites chapter.

To add a replica to an availability group using SQL Server Management Studio, connect to the primary replica and then under Availability Groups, right-click the Availability Group and click Add Replica to launch the Add Replica to the Availability Group wizard.

Once the replica is added, review the replica properties such as Availability Mode, Backup Preference, etc.

Figure 12-7 shows the Add Replica option in the SSMS GUI.

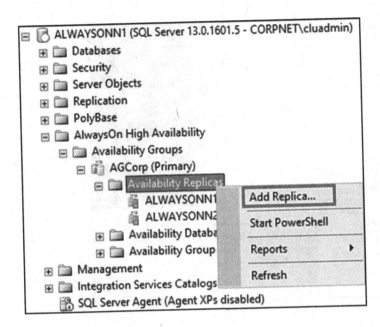

Figure 12-7. Add Replica

Remove a Replica

A replica can be removed from an existing availability group. If an availability group has multiple databases and if a secondary replica is causing performance issues to the primary replica, it might be better to remove the secondary replica than removing selected replica databases.The most common reason to remove the secondary replica is that it is either disconnected or down and you no longer want to be part of the availability group.

To remove a replica from an availability group using SQL Server Management Studio, connect to the primary replica instance and under the Availability Groups, right-click the replica that you want to remove and click Remove from Availability Group to launch the Remove Secondary Replica from the Availability Group wizard.

Figure 12-8 shows the Remove Replica option in the SSMS GUI.

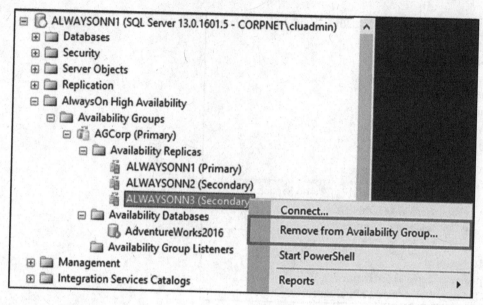

Figure 12-8. Remove Replica

Once the replica is removed, review the availability group properties such as Availability Mode, Backup preference, etc. to ensure that you will still be able to achieve RTO and RPO objectives with the change in the configuration.

Remove an Availability Group

An availability group can be deleted from the following locations:

1. **Primary replica instance**

   Post availability group deletion, the replica databases on the (former) primary replica instance will be online and available for operations. ˙

2. **Any of the secondary replica instances** (use this in emergency scenarios only)

   Post availability group deletion, the (former) secondary replica databases are left in the RESTORING state. They can be manually bought online.

3. **Windows Server Failover Cluster (WSFC)**

   Use this option only if none of the nodes hosting the replica instances of the availability group are online. It can be deleted from any node in the (WSFC) that possesses the correct security credentials for the Availability Group.

Ensure that the WSFC has quorum, before attempting to remove the Availability Group. Figure 12-9 shows the Delete Availability Group option in the SSMS GUI.

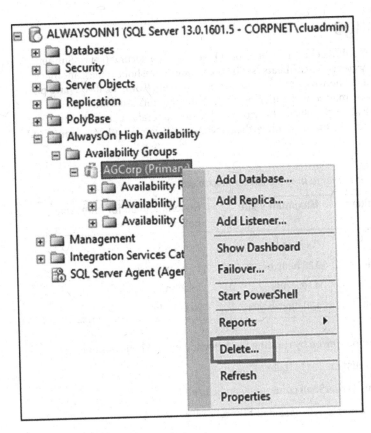

Figure 12-9. Delete Availability Group

Deleting an availability group also deletes the listener. However, the Virtual Computer Object (VCO) for the listener still remains in the Active Directory. Clean up the VCO from the AD OU post availability group deletion.

Add a File to a Replica Database

As part of the prerequisites, we had recommended using the same file path or the database on all the replicas in the prerequisites chapter. If the data path is the same, then adding the file on the primary database automatically adds it to the secondary database when the secondary replica performs the REDO activity. However, If the data path is different on a secondary database as compared to the primary database, the add-file operation will cause the secondary database synchronization to be suspended.

To resolve this problem, you will have to perform the following steps:

1. Remove the secondary database from the availability group.

2. Then restore a full backup that contains the added file and a transaction log backup to the secondary replica, using WITH NORECOVERY and WITH MOVE.

3. Restore any other outstanding log backups from the primary replica and then rejoin the secondary database to the availability group.

Tune Heartbeat Settings

By default, for single subnet and multi-subnet clusters, a heartbeat is sent every 1 second (set by Subnet Delay parameter). If a node misses a series of 5 heartbeats (set by the Subnet Threshold value), another node initiates failover. Normally, for most networks the default values work well. However, if you have poor/unreliable network connection then you may consider increasing the SameSubnetThreshold to 10 and CrossSubnetThreshold to 20. This will allow the cluster heartbeat to be more tolerable across the subnets. Table 12-1 lists the cluster properties to tune the cluster heartbeats along with their default, maximum and recommended values.

Table 12-1. Cluster properties and their values to tune the cluster heartbeats

Parameter	Default Value	Maximum Value	Recommended for unreliable networks
SameSubnetDelay	1 second	2 seconds	1 second
SameSubnetThreshold	5 heartbeats	120 heartbeats	10 heartbeats
CrossSubnetDelay	1 second	4 seconds	1 second
CrossSubnetThreshold	5 heartbeats	120 heartbeats	20 heartbeats

The existing heartbeat settings can be viewed by running the following PowerShell command:

```
PS C:\Windows\system32> get-cluster | fl *subnet*
```

To change the setting, the following PowerShell command can be used

```
PS C:\Windows\system32> (get-cluster).CrossSubnetThreshold = 20
```

Create Multiple Listeners for the Same Availability Group

There might be some scenarios where you may need to create additional listeners for your availability group. For example, you might have multiple legacy clients that use different instance names to connect to the databases that are now part of the availability group. In that case, if client connection strings cannot be changed, then you would need multiple listener names that the clients could connect to using the same connection string.

■ **Note** You cannot create multiple listener names using the SSMS GUI.

To create multiple listeners, follow the steps below:

1. Pre-stage the listener names as Virtual Computer Objects (VCO) in the Organizational Unit (OU) where the Cluster Name Object (CNO) resides. Give the CNO full permissions on the VCOs.

2. In the Windows Server Failover Cluster (WSFC) manager, create Client Access Points (CAP) for the new listener IP and Name.

3. After all the listener names are online, in the WSFC add them as OR dependencies to the availability group resource.

4. Assign the port(s) to the listeners using T-SQL.

5. Set RegisterAllProvidersIP=1 for all the listeners using PowerShell.

6. Connect to the listeners to confirm that the listener creation was successful.

Summary

In this chapter we covered some of the common management tasks that you might have to perform on availability groups. In the next chapter we will take a look on how to upgrade, update, and migrate availability groups.

CHAPTER 13

■ ■ ■

Upgrading and Migrating

Microsoft SQL Server team announced the general availability of the SQL Server 2016 on June 1, 2016. Your company's mission-critical production application currently uses SQL Server 2014 Always On Availability Groups. Your business unit wants you to start testing the upgrade to SQL Server 2016 so that the production availability group (AG) environment can be upgraded in six months. Everything needs to be tested and one of the critical requirements for the upgrade is that the downtime for the production client applications needs to be minimum as it is a 24/7 application. You have been asked to keep the actual downtime that the client applications will experience during the upgrade to only few minutes (say less than 5 mins.). You might be wondering that this is wishful thinking and if it is even possible to perform an upgrade from SQL Server 2014 to SQL Server 2016 with less than 5 minutes of downtime. From past experiences, you know that even for a regular stand-alone SQL Server instance upgrade, the typical downtime is around 1 to 4 hours. And this is an Always On Availability Group environment with multiple SQL Server instances running on a Windows Server Failover Cluster (WSFC). How are you going to achieve this task?

Upgrading and Updating SQL Server

We have found that most database administrators (DBAs) are aware of the various advantages and capabilities of Always On Availability Groups as discussed in chapters 10 and 11. Very few, though, are aware of the advantage that Always On environment allows us to perform *rolling upgrades* and *rolling updates*. *Rolling upgrade* process is a way to upgrade the SQL Server version with minimum downtime and maximum uptime with minimum risk. *Rolling update* process is a way to install an SQL Server/Windows Server update, security patch, or cumulative update and/or service pack. A rolling update process also helps minimize downtime and maximize availability with minimum risk. In the following sections, we will discuss how to reduce the downtime of the primary replica to only one or two manual failovers by performing a rolling upgrade of an SQL Server Always On Availability Group.

■ **Note** The rolling upgrade and update process are exactly the same. Even though the following sections discuss about rolling upgrade, you can simply replace the word upgrade with update and use the same process to apply an update to availability group replicas.

Prerequisites

Even though rolling upgrade lets us minimize the *actual downtime* for the client applications, it does not mean the actual process of upgrading takes only a few minutes. The actual upgrade itself takes much longer but business is happy as long as the client applications are not experiencing any outage and can

© Uttam Parui and Vivek Sanil 2016
U. Parui and V. Sanil, *Pro SQL Server Always On Availability Groups*, DOI 10.1007/978-1-4842-2071-9_13

perform their work normally. We cannot stress enough that it is very important to plan and test the upgrade thoroughly in a test environment to achieve minimal downtime and risk. Only after thorough testing is completed and all your time requirements are met, can you perform the upgrade on the production environment.

Here are some important prerequisites that should be completed before the upgrade to SQL Server 2016:

- Review the hardware and software requirements for installing SQL Server 2016.

- Review your current SQL Server and Windows Server versions and editions. Do they have a supported upgrade path to SQL Server 2016? If you are on SQL Server 2012 and want to upgrade to SQL Server 2016 then you will need a minimum of SP1 for SQL Server 2012 installed. You can upgrade SQL Server 2014 release to manufacturing (RTM) and up to SQL Server 2016. For more information, review the Microsoft MSDN article titled "Supported version and edition upgrades" at https://msdn.microsoft.com/en-us/library/ms143393.aspx

---

■ **Note** When you upgrade availability group replicas from a prior version of SQL Server Enterprise Edition to SQL Server 2016, you will need to choose between Enterprise Edition: Core-based licensing and Enterprise Edition. Enterprise Edition: Core-based licensing supports all the cores as reported by the operating system whereas the Enterprise Edition (not available for new agreement) is limited to a maximum of 20 cores per SQL Server instance.

- Review the SQL Server 2016 backward compatibility topic to review the changes in behavior between SQL Server 2016 and the SQL Server version you are upgrading from.

- Run the SQL Server 2016 Data Migration Assistant tool to see if there are any upgrade blockers, and if any modifications have to be made to scripts or applications due to breaking changes. You can download the SQL Server 2016 Data Migration Assistant tool from http://www.microsoft.com/en-us/download/details.aspx?id=53595. SQL Server Upgrade Advisor tool is deprecated and replaced with Data Migration Assistant tool.

- Run the SQL Server 2016 System Configuration Checker tool to see if the SQL Server setup programs detect any blocking issues before actually upgrading. To run the System Configuration Checker tool, run SQL Server 2016 setup.exe, click Tools on the left-hand side, and then click System Configuration Checker on the right-hand side.

- Plan and Thoroughly Test the Upgrade Plan and Document All the Steps with Detailed Information.

Rolling Upgrade Best Practices

Similar to the best practices list for upgrading a regular SQL Server instance, we have a list of best practices for performing rolling upgrade for availability group replicas. Following the best practices will avoid data loss, maximize the uptime, and minimize the downtime for client applications using the availability groups.

- Take a full database backup of all databases (if you already don't have one).

- Run DBCC CHECKDB on all databases and ensure that there are no errors.

- Manually failover on at least one of your synchronous-commit secondary replicas and ensure that it fails over as expected.

- Remove automatic failover from all synchronous-commit replicas. This is to avoid any unintended failovers during the upgrade process.

- Change the automated backup preference as discussed in chapter 11 to ensure that the backups will not run on the replica being upgraded.

- Always upgrade the remote secondary replicas first followed by the local secondary replicas, and the primary replica the last.

- Before upgrading the primary replica, fail over the availability group to an upgraded synchronous-commit secondary replica with a SYNCHRONIZED state. If you fail over to an asynchronous-commit secondary-replica, then you can have data loss and all availability databases will be suspended requiring us to manually resume them.

■ **Note**   Failure to fail over to an upgraded secondary replica before upgrading the primary replica will affect the applications and users and will extend the downtime during the primary replica upgrade.

- If the replicas are SQL Server failover clustering instances (FCIs), then upgrade the inactive node of the FCI before you upgrade the active node.

Rolling Upgrade Process

Rolling upgrade process involves multiple steps in a certain order. The actual steps depend on the availability group topology and the availability of replica-commit mode. Figure 13-1 shows the rolling upgrade process for the availability group environment that we created in chapter 8. In this environment we have three replicas: primary replica (AlwaysOnN1) and secondary replica (AlwaysOnN2) are in the primary datacenter. They are configured with synchronous-commit availability mode and automatic failover mode. The remote secondary replica (AlwaysOnN3) is in the disaster recovery datacenter configured with asynchronous-commit availability mode.

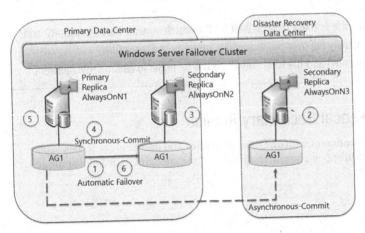

Figure 13-1. *Rolling Upgrade Process for an AG environment used for HA and DR*

The steps for rolling upgrade for our availability group environment are as follows:

1. Remove automatic failover from all synchronous-commit replicas (AlwaysOnN1 and AlwaysOnN2). This is to prevent any automatic failovers during the upgrade process.

2. Upgrade remote secondary replica (AlwaysOnN3).

3. Upgrade local secondary replica (AlwaysOnN2). At this point, we have upgraded all secondary replicas and the client applications connected to the primary replica (AlwaysOnN1) have not experienced any downtime.

■ **Note** During the upgrade process, the secondary replica is not available for failover or for read-only reporting workloads. But the production OLTP workload on the primary replica is not affected. After the upgrade of the secondary replicas, depending upon the activity on the primary replica, it may take some time for the secondary replica to catch up with the primary replica.

---

4. Ensure that the local secondary replica (AlwaysOnN2) has caught up with the primary replica and is in a SNYCHRONIZED state. Whenever you have some downtime, manually fail over the availability group to the SYNCHRONIZED secondary replica. After the availability group fails over to AlwaysOnN2, client applications can get connected again and work normally. The only downtime they will experience is the time it takes the availability group to fail over from AlwaysOnN1 to AlwaysOnN2, which is typically a few seconds. To find the exact downtime, it is important to test in your test environment.

5. Upgrade the former primary replica (AlwaysOnN1).

6. Configure the automatic failover mode for the replicas (AlwaysOnN1 and AlwaysOnN2).

■ **Note** If you need AlwaysOnN1 to be the primary replica, wait for it to catch up with the AlwaysOnN2 and achieve SYNCHRONIZED state. Then manually fail over the availability group from AlwaysOnN2 to AlwaysOnN1. This will cause some downtime (few seconds) and the total downtime will be equal to two manual failovers.

Availability Group with One Local Secondary Replica

Let's consider an availability group environment with one primary replica and one local secondary replica used for only high availability with synchronous-commit availability mode and automatic failover mode. Figure 13-2 shows such an environment.

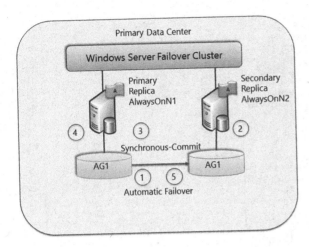

Figure 13-2. Rolling Upgrade Process for an AG environment used for only HA

The rolling upgrade process for such an environment is as follows:

1. Remove automatic failover from the synchronous-commit replicas (AlwaysOnN1 and AlwaysOnN2).

2. Upgrade local secondary replica (AlwaysOnN2).

3. Ensure that the local secondary replica (AlwaysOnN2) has caught up with the primary replica and is in a SNYCHRONIZED state. Whenever you can take some downtime, manually fail over the availability group to the SYNCHRONIZED secondary replica.

4. Upgrade the former primary replica (AlwaysOnN1).

5. Configure the automatic failover mode for the replicas (AlwaysOnN1 and AlwaysOnN2).

■ **Note** If you need AlwaysOnN1 to be the primary replica, wait for it to catch up with the AlwaysOnN2 and achieve SNYCHRONIZED state. Then manually fail over the availability group from AlwaysOnN2 to AlwaysOnN1. This will cause some downtime (few seconds) and the total downtime will be equal to two manual failovers.

Availability Group with One Remote Secondary Replica

Let's consider an availability group environment with one primary replica and one remote secondary replica used for only disaster recovery with asynchronous-commit availability mode and manual failover mode. Figure 13-3 shows such an environment.

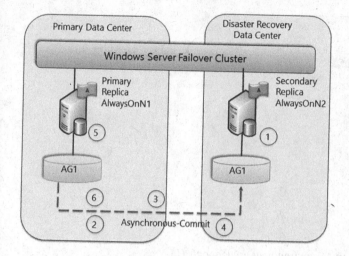

Figure 13-3. *Rolling Upgrade Process for an AG environment used for only DR*

The rolling upgrade process for such an environment is as follows:

1. Upgrade remote secondary replica (AlwaysOnN2).

2. To avoid data loss, change the availability mode to synchronous-commit.

3. Wait for the secondary replica to catch up and the synchronization state is SYNCHRONIZED. The following is a sample TSQL code to check if the database is ready for failover on the remote secondary replica AlwaysOnN2. If the is_failover_ready column in the DMV sys.dm_hadr_database_replica_cluster_states equals to 1 on a database, you can fail over without any data loss. If the value is 0 and you force the failover to your secondary replica, data loss is possible.

```
SELECT is_failover_ready, *
FROM sys.dm_hadr_database_replica_cluster_states
WHERE replica_id = (SELECT replica_id FROM sys.availability_replicas
WHERE replica_server_name = 'AlwaysOnN2');
```

4. Whenever you can take some downtime, manually fail over the availability group to the SYNCHRONIZED secondary replica (AlwaysOnN2) on the disaster recovery data center.

5. Upgrade the former primary replica (AlwaysOnN1).

6. Manually fail over the availability group from AlwaysOnN2 to AlwaysOnN1 and change the commit mode to asynchronous-commit.

Distributed Availability Groups

We learned about distributed availability groups (DAGs) in chapter 3. As a refresher, a distributed availability group can be thought of as an "availability group of availability groups." Figure 13-4 shows such an environment.

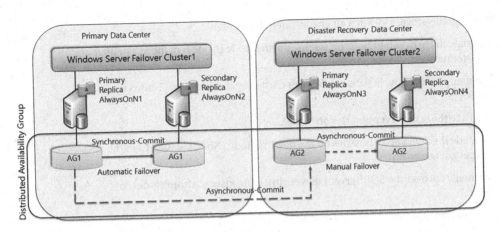

Figure 13-4. *Rolling Upgrade Process for Distributed AG*

The rolling upgrade process for distributed availability groups is as follows:

1. Perform rolling upgrade for AG2 in the disaster recovery datacenter. Follow the steps as explained in the section titled "Availability Group with One Remote Secondary Replica" in this chapter.

2. Perform rolling upgrade for AG1 in the primary recovery data center. Follow the steps as explained in the section titled "Availability Group with One Local Secondary Replica" in this chapter.

Availability Group with Failover Cluster Nodes

Let's consider an availability group environment where in both the primary replica and remote secondary replicas are SQL Server failover clustering instances (FCIs) for HA and DR. Figure 13-5 shows such an environment.

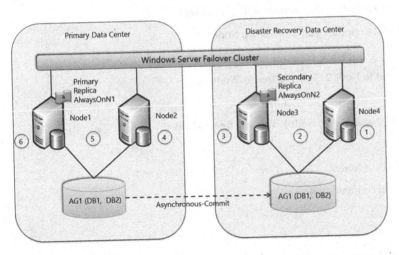

Figure 13-5. *Rolling Upgrade Process for an AG environment with SQL Server FCIs*

The rolling upgrade process for such an environment is as follows:

1. Upgrade the SQL Server binaries on the inactive node (Node4) of the FCI in the disaster recovery datacenter.

2. Manually fail over the SQL Server failover clustering instance from Node3 to Node4.

3. Upgrade the SQL Server binaries on Node3.

4. Upgrade the SQL Server binaries on the inactive node (Node2 of the FCI in the primary data center).

5. Manually fail over the SQL Server failover clustering instance from Node1 to Node2.

6. Upgrade the SQL Server binaries on Node1.

Multiple Availability Groups

So far we have considered availability group environments with only one AG. If you are running multiple AGs with primary replicas on separate nodes, the rolling upgrade path will involve more failover steps to preserve high availability. Suppose you have a three-node Windows Server Failover Cluster (WSFC) with the availability groups as shown in Table 13-1.

Table 13-1. *Availability groups on a 3-node WSFC*

Availability Group	Node1	Node2	Node3
AG1	Primary		
AG2		Primary	
AG3			Primary

The rolling upgrade process in such an environment will be as follows:

1. Manually fail over AG2 to Node3. This will free up Node2.

2. Upgrade Node2.

3. Manually fail over AG1 to Node 2. This will free up Node1.

4. Upgrade Node1.

5. Manually fail over AG2 and AG3 to Node1. This will free up Node3.

6. Upgrade Node3.

7. Manually fail over AG3 to Node3.

Table 13-2 shows the resulting configuration.

Table 13-2. *Resulting availability groups configuration after rolling upgrade*

Availability Group	Node1	Node2	Node3
AG1		Primary	
AG2	Primary		
AG3			Primary

■ **Note** In this environment, the rolling upgrade process causes an average downtime of less than two failovers per availability group.

Upgrading the Operating System

So far we have discussed the steps to upgrade SQL Server and/or apply an update or service pack to SQL Server or Windows Server in an availability group environment. There are situations you may need to upgrade the operating system. As you know, availability groups run on top of a WSFC and upgrading the Windows operating system hosting the WSFC is not supported before Windows Server 2012 R2. In this section we will discuss the steps that will need to be taken to upgrade Windows Server 2012 R2 (and below).

Cluster OS Rolling Upgrade

Windows Server 2016 introduced a new feature called *Cluster OS Rolling Upgrade*. Cluster OS Rolling Upgrade feature introduced a new concept called *Mixed-OS mode*, which allows us to start with a Windows Server 2012 R2 failover cluster and upgrade the operating system of the cluster nodes from Windows Server 2012 R2 to Windows Server 2016 with minimum downtime. Figure 13-6 shows high-level sequential steps that need to be performed for each Windows Server 2012 R2 cluster node during a Cluster OS Rolling Upgrade.

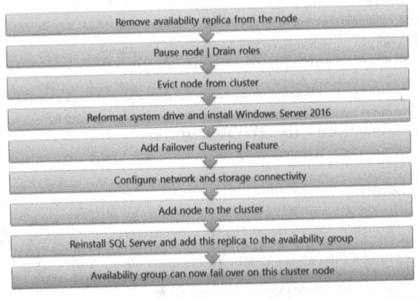

Figure 13-6. *Cluster OS Rolling Upgrade Workflow for each Windows Server 2012 R2 cluster node*

■ **Note** During a Cluster OS Rolling Upgrade, it is recommended to use a clean Windows Server 2016 install, which means you will need to reinstall SQL Server and add the replica to the availability group. In-place Windows upgrade is not encouraged although it may work in some cases where default drivers are used. The actual downtime for availability group primary replica during a Cluster OS Rolling Upgrade is the time taken for one manual failover. Once Windows Server 2016 is released, we recommend you review the Technet article at `https://technet.` `microsoft.com/windows-server-docs/compute/failover-clustering/cluster-operating-` `system-rolling-upgrade` to see if they are any updates to the Cluster OS Rolling Upgrade process.

Cluster OS Rolling Upgrade starts with a Windows Server 2012 R2 cluster and includes the following high-level steps:

1. Select half of the cluster nodes that have the secondary replicas. Remove the secondary replicas from the existing availability group.

2. Pause, drain, evict, reformat, and install Windows Server 2016 on these cluster nodes.

3. On the Windows Server 2016 nodes, add Failover Clustering feature, configure networking and storage connectivity, and add the node to the existing Windows Server 2012 R2 cluster.

4. Reinstall SQL Server and add the replica to the availability group. At this time, availability group can fail over to this cluster node if required. The time required to perform the manual fail over is the only downtime that the clients connecting to the primary replica will experience.

5. Perform steps 2, 3, and 4 to the remaining half nodes.

6. At this time, all the cluster nodes are upgraded to Windows Server 2016. At this point, the process can be fully reversed, and Windows Server 2012 R2 nodes can be added to the cluster.

7. The cluster is still running at the Windows Server 2012 R2 functional level.

8. When you are certain that you want to run at Windows Server 2016 functional level, run the Update-ClusterFunctionalLevel PowerShell cmdlet.

■ **Note** After you update the cluster functional level, you cannot go back to Windows Server 2012 R2 functional level and Windows Server 2012 R2 nodes cannot be added to the cluster.

Cross-Cluster Migration

Let's say the operating system on your availability group cluster nodes is Windows Server 2008 R2 and you have been asked to plan and upgrade to Windows Server 2012 R2. You know that upgrading the operating system hosting the WSFC nodes is not supported before Windows Server 2012 R2. So how are you going to upgrade the operating system? To address this, Microsoft introduced *cross-cluster migration* starting in SQL Server 2012 SP1. The *cross-cluster migration* lets us move one or more availability groups from one WSFC (source cluster) to a new version WSFC (destination cluster) with little downtime.

■ **Note**   Cross-cluster migration of Always On Availability Groups is intended primarily for an operating system upgrade to a Windows Server 2012 (or R2) cluster.

To support cross-cluster migration, an equal or higher version of SQL Server (a minimum of SQL Server 2012 SP1) must be installed on two or more nodes of the destination cluster, and these SQL Server instances must be enabled for Always On. Figure 13-7 shows two WSFCs. The first one (source cluster) is a two-node Windows Server 2008 R2 cluster, each hosting a stand-alone SQL Server instance (SQL Server 2012 SP1 or higher). Both the instances are part of an availability group AG1 with instance 1 being the primary replica and instance 2 being the synchronous secondary replica. The second cluster (destination cluster) is a two-node Windows Server 2012 R2 cluster. The goal is to migrate AG1 from source cluster to destination cluster with minimum downtime.

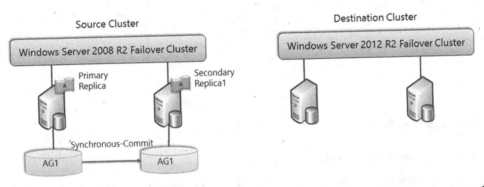

Figure 13-7. *Upgrading operating system from Windows Server 2008 R2 to 2012 R2 using cross-cluster migration*

Cross-cluster migration involves the following high-level phases:

1. Preparation of the destination cluster. This step has no downtime.

2. Data migration. This step has no downtime.

3. Availability group resource migration. This step has planned minimal downtime.

Preparation

This phase prepares the destination cluster and involves the following steps:

1. Create a new Windows Server 2012 R2 cluster.

2. Install SQL Server 2012 SP1 or higher on each cluster node.

3. Configure each SQL Server instance to support availability group.

4. On each source cluster node, grant cluster registry permissions to the service account of each SQL Server instance on the destination cluster node.

5. For each availability group listener that needs to be migrated, grant the destination cluster full permission on the virtual network name (VNN) computer object in the Active Directory Server.

Data Migration

This phase involves creating and configuring two new secondary replicas on the destination cluster for each availability group. Figure 13-8 depicts the data migration phase.

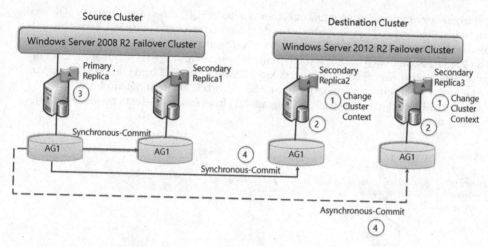

Figure 13-8. Data migration phase

The data migration phase involves the following steps:

1. On each destination SQL Server instance, switch the HADR cluster context to the source cluster name. This step enables the destination server instances to host availability replicas for availability groups on the source cluster. Below is a sample TSQL command to switch the HADR cluster context.

   ```
   ALTER SERVER CONFIGURATION SET HADR CLUSTER CONTEXT = 'cluster_name'
   ```

   ■ **Note**   Switching HADR cluster context is supported starting from SQL Server 2012 SP1.

   ---

2. For each availability group to be migrated in a given batch, choose two destination instances. Seed new secondary databases on these instances.

3. Connect to the primary replica on the source cluster, and create secondary replicas on the destination SQL Server instances.

4. Connect to the destination instances and join the secondary replicas and databases to AG1. Configure a synchronous-commit secondary replica on one destination instance and an asynchronous-commit secondary replica on the second destination instance.

■ **Note**   The Add Replica Wizard can automate steps 2, 3, and 4.

Resource Migration

This phase moves the availability group resources from the source cluster to the destination cluster. Figure 13-9 depicts the resource migration (planned downtime) phase.

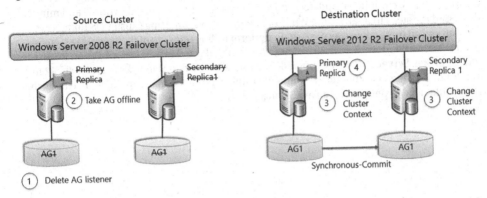

Figure 13-9. *Resource migration phase*

Resource migration phase involves the following steps:

1. Delete the availability group listener on the primary replica.

2. Take the availability group offline from Failover Cluster Manager.

■ **Note** SQL Server 2012 SP1 introduced a new ALTER AVAILABILITY GROUP option for taking an availability group offline.

---

3. On each destination SQL Server instance, switch the HADR cluster context to LOCAL cluster.

4. For each availability group in the batch, create new availability group on the destination instance.

5. Create new availability group listener.

After migrating your availability groups, remember to perform the post-installation tasks as discussed in chapter 9. For example, create the SQL Agent jobs on the destination SQL Server instances for the databases that were migrated.

■ **Note** Starting with SQL Server 2016, distributed availability groups (DAGs) as discussed in chapters 3 and 8 are another option to perform rolling upgrades of the operating system. After upgrading the operating system on the second WSFC, wait until the second availability group catches up. Then perform a manual failover to the second availability group and drop the distributed availability group using the DROP AVAILABILITY GROUP T-SQL command. As distributed availability groups associate two availability groups that have their own listeners, you could use the old database mirroring connection string syntax for transparent client redirection after failover. For example:
"Server=AGCorp1_listen; Failover_Partner=AGCorp2_listen; Database=AdventureWorks2016"

Summary

In this chapter, we discussed Always On Availability Group rolling upgrade and rolling update features. These features enable us to upgrade the SQL Server version and apply SQL Server and Windows Server updates like security patches, cumulative updates, and service packs with minimal downtime and minimal risk. We also discussed the steps to upgrade the Windows operating system using Cluster OS Rolling Upgrade feature introduced in Windows Server 2016 to perform rolling upgrade of the operating system Windows Server 2012 R2 to Windows Server 2016. Last, we discussed the cross-cluster migration feature that was introduced in SQL Server 2012 SP1 to upgrade the operating system Windows Server 2008 R2 to Windows Server 2012 R2. In the next chapter, we will review the common database maintenance tasks that an administrator would need to perform on an availability group.

CHAPTER 14

■ ■ ■

Performing Database Maintenance Tasks

In this chapter we will take a look at some of the considerations for the database maintenance tasks that an administrator would need to perform on an availability group.

Since the secondary replica databases are read-only, index maintenance and statistics updates need to be performed on the primary replica SQL Server instance.

Index Maintenance

As Index maintenance is performed on the primary, it not only impacts the primary replica, but it can also impact the data synchronization between replicas. Index maintenance operations can involve massive amounts of data, and this data change would also need to be synchronized with the secondary replicas. This impacts the performance of data synchronization causing data transfer delays in case of asynchronous-commit and performance impact on the primary in case of synchronous-commit.

Assess the Impact in a Test Environment First

Index maintenance tasks can stress the system depending on the workload, system configuration, and fragmentation on the indexes. Hence it would be better to test the index maintenance tasks in a test environment first and assess the impact before performing them on a production SQL Server instance.

Run during Off-Peak Hours

One way to reduce the impact of index maintenance is to run it during off-peak hours for the reorganize operation and preferably during no activity for rebuilds.

Selective/Smart Index Rebuilds/Reorganize

A smart rebuilding strategy of only rebuilding or reorganizing selective indexes based on the index fragmentation percentage and number of pages in the index could also help relieve the stress on the system. Rebuilding an index will drop and re-create the index. Reorganizing an index will use minimal system resources to defragment the leaf level of clustered and nonclustered indexes. However, reorganization swaps one page at a time to reduce fragmentation. Hence it may cause the transaction log to grow and cause

© Uttam Parui and Vivek Sanil 2016
U. Parui and V. Sanil, *Pro SQL Server Always On Availability Groups*, DOI 10.1007/978-1-4842-2071-9_14

additional synchronization overhead for databases in an availability group. Take this into consideration while deciding on rebuild vs reorganize. Also it is recommended to rebuild if the fragmentation is more than 30% and reorganize if less than 30% and more than 10%. Defragmenting small tables may not provide any performance benefit, hence it is better to check for fragmentation in tables with page count greater than 1000 pages.

Switch Availability Mode

Significant amounts of data get written to the transaction log on the primary replica instance while rebuilding, which it then sends to the secondary replica instances. Hardening of transaction logs on a secondary replica instance can be slowed down due to this additional workload. In case of a synchronous-commit replica, this can result in a higher than normal *HADR_SYNC_COMMIT* wait on the primary. To avoid this situation, consider switching the availability Mode of all the secondary replicas to asynchronous-commit during the maintenance period and then switch it back to the original mode after the maintenance is completed.

Statistics Updates

Although temporary statistics are created and maintained on the Read-only replica, there are some maintenance tasks still that need to be performed on the primary replica. The permanent statistics on the primary replica are replicated to the secondary replicas.

■ **Note** Missing statistics are automatically created both on primary and secondary replica.

Update Statistics on the Primary Replica

If the primary replica instance holds statistics that the secondary replica instance is using for its read workload, then updating those statistics often on the primary replica can help speed up the read workload on the secondary replica. If you run heavy reporting on the secondary replica, then consider reviewing the temporary stats to convert some of them to permanent stats on the primary replica. Temporary stats are stored in tempdb. Once created on the primary replica, update them frequently for the read-only replica workload to benefit from them. If for some reason you need to create the reporting workload index and statistics on the secondary replica itself, then consider using transactional replication to maintain a secondary copy instead of using Always On Availability Groups. The subscriber data in transactional replication can be updated and indexes and statistics can also be created on the subscriber.

Use the following query to gather temporary stats information:

```
USE tempdb
GO

SELECT OBJECT_NAME(s.object_id) AS object_name,
    COL_NAME(sc.object_id, sc.column_id) AS column_name,
    s.name AS statistics_name
FROM sys.stats AS s JOIN sys.stats_columns AS sc
    ON s.stats_id = sc.stats_id AND s.object_id = sc.object_id
WHERE s.is_temporary <> 0
ORDER BY s.name;
```

> ■ **Note**   Transactional replication can be configured on Always On Availability Group databases.

Memory-Optimized Tables

Memory-optimized tables are supported in availability groups. However, automatic statistics update for memory-optimized tables on the primary or secondary replica is not supported prior to SQL Server 2016. Hence monitor the query performance and execution plans on the secondary replica and manually update the statistics on the primary replica when needed.

> ■ **Note**   Automatic update of statistics is now supported starting SQL Server 2016 when using database compatibility level of 130, for memory-optimized tables.

Summary

In this chapter we covered some of the database maintenance tasks that you might have to perform on availability groups. In the next chapter we will take a look how to monitor availability groups.

PART VI

Monitoring and Troubleshooting Availability Groups

CHAPTER 15

■ ■ ■

Monitoring Availability Groups

Now that you have successfully deployed Always On Availability Groups and configured them per Microsoft best practices, it's time to discuss monitoring the health of the availability groups. Monitoring availability groups is an important activity that allows us to review the availability groups quickly to ensure that everything is working as expected. Also, the data generated by the monitoring tools are invaluable while troubleshooting a problem and finding the root cause of the problem. In this chapter, we will explore different ways to monitor the current health and synchronization status of availability groups.

Using Dashboard

We discussed about the Always On Availability Groups dashboard in chapter 9. As a refresher, the dashboard is a graphical user interface (GUI) that, similar to your automobile's dashboard, organizes and presents the information about availability groups in a way that is easy to interpret. The dashboard displays the health and details of the availability groups, availability replicas, and availability databases that allow database administrators (DBAs) to make quick operational decisions. It shows the synchronization states and provides performance indicators that allow us to monitor the availability groups without writing a single line of code. Figure 15-1 shows a sample Always On dashboard when launched from the primary replica.

© Uttam Parui and Vivek Sanil 2016
U. Parui and V. Sanil, *Pro SQL Server Always On Availability Groups*, DOI 10.1007/978-1-4842-2071-9_15

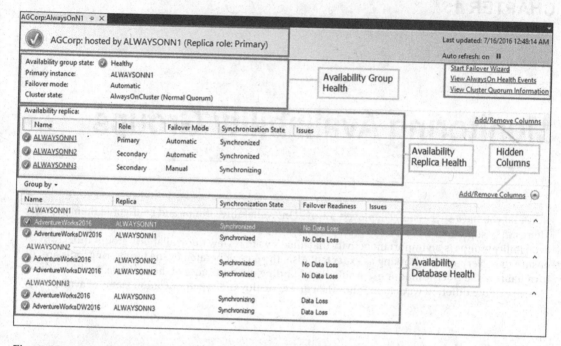

Figure 15-1. *Sample availability group dashboard launched from the primary replica*

The dashboard displays a lot of information and is also highly configurable. There are many hidden columns that can be added for additional information. Below we will discuss some of the useful columns:

- *Failover Mode* lets us know the failover mode for which the replica is configured. The possible values are Automatic or Manual.

- *Availability Mode* lets us know the availability mode for which the replica is configured. The possible values are synchronous or asynchronous.

- *Synchronization State* column is in both the availability replica health section and the availability database health section. In the availability replica health section, it tells us whether the secondary replica is currently synchronized with the primary replica. The typical values are synchronized, synchronizing, or not synchronized. If the local SQL Server instance cannot communicate with WSFC then the value is *NULL*. In the availability database health section, it tells us whether the availability database is currently synchronized with the primary replica. The possible values here are synchronized, synchronizing, not synchronizing, reverting, or initializing.

■ **Note** Do not force failover to the secondary replica when a database is in the reverting or initializing state as that may leave the database in a state in which it cannot be started.

- *Issues* tells us if there is any issue. The possible values are Warnings or Critical. To review the issue details, click the hyperlink for the Warning or Critical.

- *Connection State* indicates whether the secondary replica is currently connected to the primary replica. The possible values are connected and disconnected.

- *Last Connection Error No., Description and Timestamp* columns provide us with the timestamp of the last connection error along with the number and brief description.

- *Failover Readiness* tells us to which replica can the availability group be failed over with or without potential data loss.

- *Estimated Data Loss (seconds)* is a very useful column to monitor recovery point objective (RPO). It tells us the time in seconds that the data is not synchronized to the secondary database. If the primary replica fails, all data within this time window will be lost.

- *Estimated Recovery Time (seconds)* is a very useful column to monitor the recovery time objective (RTO). It tells us the time in seconds it will take for the secondary replica to catch up with the primary replica.

- *Log Send Queue Size (KB)* indicates the amount of log records in KB needed to be sent from the primary database to the secondary database to complete synchronization.

- *Log Send Rate (KB/sec)* indicates the rate in KB per second at which the log records are being sent from the primary replica to the secondary replica.

- *Redo Queue Size (KB)* indicates the amount of log records in KB needed to be redone in the secondary database to complete synchronization.

- *Redo Rate (KB/sec)* indicates the rate in KB in second at which the log records are being redone in the secondary database to complete synchronization.

Figure 15-2 shows the dashboard with some of the useful hidden columns displayed.

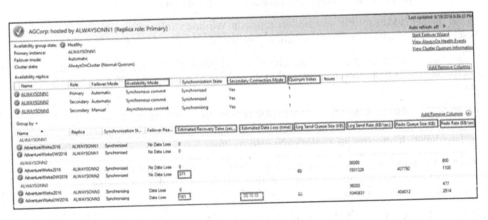

Figure 15-2. Customized dashboard displaying useful hidden columns

Using Transact-SQL

SQL Server 2016 availability groups has a rich set of catalog views, dynamic management views (DMVs), and functions (DMFs) that allow us to monitor the availability groups and availability replicas and availability databases.

Following are some commonly used catalog views:

- `sys.availability_groups` reports the configuration information for each availability group, such as failure condition level, health check timeout, and automated backup preference.

- `sys.availability_replicas` reports the configuration information for all availability replicas, such as availability mode, failover mode, and primary/secondary connectivity.

- `sys.availability_read_only_routing_lists` reports information about the read-only routing list of each availability replica.

- `sys.availability_listeners` reports configuration information for each availability group listener, such as port, IP address, and IP subnet mask.

- `sys.databases` reports additional information if the database is enabled for Always On. The replica_id and group_database_id columns are added, which identifies the database in the replica and the availability group respectively.

Here are some commonly used dynamic management views and functions:

- `sys.dm_hadr_availability_replica_states` return information about the state of the availability replicas. It returns a row for each replica when run from the primary replica.

- `sys.dm_hadr_database_replica_states` return information about the state of each database in a given availability group. It returns a row for each replica database per replica when run from the primary replica. When this is run from the secondary replica, it returns a row of each replica database for the local replica.

- `sys.dm_hadr_cluster` return information about the Windows Server Failover Cluster, such as cluster name and quorum information.

- `sys.dm_hadr_auto_page_repair` returns a row for the latest automatic page-repair attempts on any availability database on that server with a maximum of 100 rows per database.

- `sys.dm_hadr_automatic_seeding` (new in SQL Server 2016) provides information on successful or failed database seeding and error messages explaining why the seeding may have failed. It returns one row for each seeding process.

- `sys.dm_hadr_physical_seeding_stats` (new in SQL Server 2016) provide statistical information on completed and ongoing availability databases seeding. It returns rows when seeding is running.

The following T-SQL script can be used to monitor the health of the availability group:

```
SELECT ag.name AS 'AG Name', ar.replica_server_name AS 'Replica Instance',
dr_state.database_id AS 'Database ID',
Location = CASE
WHEN ar_state.is_local = 1 THEN N'LOCAL'
ELSE 'REMOTE' END,
Role = CASE
WHEN ar_state.role_desc IS NULL THEN N'DISCONNECTED'
```

```
ELSE ar_state.role_desc   END,
ar_state.connected_state_desc AS 'Connection State', ar.availability_mode_desc AS 'Mode',
dr_state.synchronization_state_desc AS 'State'
FROM ((sys.availability_groups AS ag JOIN sys.availability_replicas AS ar  ON ag.group_id =
ar.group_id )
JOIN sys.dm_hadr_availability_replica_states AS ar_state ON ar.replica_id = ar_state.
replica_id)
JOIN sys.dm_hadr_database_replica_states dr_state ON
ag.group_id = dr_state.group_id and dr_state.replica_id = ar_state.replica_id;
```

Results for the preceding script are shown in Figure 15-3.

	AG Name	Replica Instance	Database ID	Location	Role	Connection State	Mode	State
1	AGCorp	ALWAYSONN1	5	LOCAL	PRIMARY	CONNECTED	SYNCHRONOUS_COMMIT	SYNCHRONIZED
2	AGCorp	ALWAYSONN1	6	LOCAL	PRIMARY	CONNECTED	SYNCHRONOUS_COMMIT	SYNCHRONIZED
3	AGCorp	ALWAYSONN2	5	REMOTE	SECONDARY	CONNECTED	SYNCHRONOUS_COMMIT	SYNCHRONIZED
4	AGCorp	ALWAYSONN2	6	REMOTE	SECONDARY	CONNECTED	SYNCHRONOUS_COMMIT	SYNCHRONIZED
5	AGCorp	ALWAYSONN3	5	REMOTE	SECONDARY	CONNECTED	ASYNCHRONOUS_COMMIT	SYNCHRONIZING
6	AGCorp	ALWAYSONN3	6	REMOTE	SECONDARY	CONNECTED	ASYNCHRONOUS_COMMIT	SYNCHRONIZING

Figure 15-3. Monitoring the health of the availability groups using T-SQL

The next T-SQL script can be used to monitor the current workload and synchronization status of the availability group:

```
SELECT ag.name AS 'AG Name', ar.replica_server_name AS 'Replica Instance',
dr_state.database_id as 'Database ID',
Location = CASE
WHEN ar_state.is_local = 1 THEN N'LOCAL'
ELSE 'REMOTE' END ,
Role = CASE
WHEN ar_state.role_desc IS NULL THEN N'DISCONNECTED'
ELSE ar_state.role_desc END,
dr_state.log_send_queue_size AS 'Log Send Queue Size', dr_state.redo_qeue_
size AS 'Redo Queue Size',
dr_state.log_send_rate AS 'Log Send Rate',dr_state.redo_rate AS 'Redo Rate'
FROM (( sys.availability_groups AS ag JOIN sys.availability_replicas AS ar
ON ag.group_id = ar.group_id )
JOIN sys.dm_hadr_availability_replica_states AS ar_state  ON ar.replica_id =
ar_state.replica_id)
JOIN sys.dm_hadr_database_replica_states dr_state on
ag.group_id = dr_state.group_id and dr_state.replica_id = ar_state.replica_id;
```

Results for that script are shown in Figure 15-4.

215

	AG Name	Replica Instance	Database ID	Location	Role	Log Send Queue Size	Redo Queue Size	Log Send Rate	Redo Rate
1	AGCorp	ALWAYSONN1	5	LOCAL	PRIMARY	NULL	NULL	NULL	NULL
2	AGCorp	ALWAYSONN1	6	LOCAL	PRIMARY	NULL	NULL	NULL	NULL
3	AGCorp	ALWAYSONN2	5	REMOTE	SECONDARY	0	0	36000	800
4	AGCorp	ALWAYSONN2	6	REMOTE	SECONDARY	0	3704876	13519372	1100
5	AGCorp	ALWAYSONN3	5	REMOTE	SECONDARY	0	0	36000	477
6	AGCorp	ALWAYSONN3	6	REMOTE	SECONDARY	0	3704428	48106337	2514

Figure 15-4. Monitoring current workload and synchronization status using T-SQL

The next T-SQL script can be used to monitor the automatic seeding progress and performance using the two new DMVs introduced in SQL Server 2016:

```
SELECT start_time,
       completion_time,
       is_source,
       current_state,
       failure_state,
       failure_state_desc
FROM sys.dm_hadr_automatic_seeding;

SELECT * FROM sys.dm_hadr_physical_seeding_stats;
```

Using Wait Statistics

Most DBAs are familiar and are using wait types and wait statistics to monitor SQL Server instances. They can continue to do the same for monitoring SQL Server configured with Always On Availability Groups. This methodology is great as waits indicates where SQL Server is spending lots of time working. The biggest waits point out the most important and relevant Performance Monitor counters for the workload, which in turn provides us with the next troubleshooting steps.

SQL Server 2016 tracks 872 different wait types. There are around 75 wait types related to Always On. Always On wait type names begin with HADR. Execute the following T-SQL query to review all wait statistics with the Always On wait types:

```
SELECT * FROM sys.dm_os_wait_stats
WHERE wait_type LIKE '%hadr%'
ORDER BY wait_time_ms DESC;
```

■ **Note** A lot of the Always On wait types are expected waits when everything is running normally. Just because a wait type appears on the top of the list, it does not mean that there is some issue. For a description of all the wait types, refer to the MSDN article https://msdn.microsoft.com/en-us/library/ms179984.aspx. It is recommended to have a baseline of the wait types when everything is working normally so that the values can be compared with the wait types when there is a performance issue.

Let's review some of the Always On wait types that are commonly seen when you are monitoring the wait types:

- HADR_SYNC_COMMIT is expected for synchronized availability groups. This wait type tracks the time it takes the primary to send the transaction log blocks to the secondary, for the secondary to receive them, harden them, and sent the commit acknowledgement back to the primary. A consistently high value for this wait type could mean that the synchronous secondary has a performance bottleneck that is affecting the commits on the primary replica instance. This wait type is also reflected by the *Transaction Delay* performance monitor counter.

- HADR_CLUSAPI_CALL is very frequently seen when reviewing the wait statistics in an availability group environment. There is nothing to be worried about it even if you see this at the top of your wait statistics list. All this wait type tells us is that the SQL Server thread is waiting to switch from non-preemptive mode (scheduled by SQL Server) to preemptive mode (scheduled by Windows Server) to invoke the WSFC APIs. As you know, availability groups work very closely with the WSFC, there are many cluster APIs and activities that are being executed and it is very natural to see this one at the top of the list.

- HADR_LOGCAPTURE_WAIT indicates the time SQL Server is waiting for the log records to be become available. If the hardening is completely caught up and there are no log blocks that are waiting to be hardened to the transaction log on the disk, SQL Server will wait to get the next log block. So if the log scan is completely caught up, you will actually see a high value for this wait type. This is expected and does not mean that something is necessarily wrong.

- HADR_SYNCHRONIZING_THROTTLE indicates the time it takes a synchronizing secondary database to catch up with the primary database in order to transition from synchronizing state to synchronized state. This is an expected wait when a secondary database is trying to catch up with the primary database. If you are having latency issues and you see this wait type on the top, you may consider switching the secondary replica to asynchronous commit and later during off-peak hours when the estimated data loss on that secondary nears zero, you can switch back to synchronous-commit mode and it will quickly change its status to synchronized.

- WRITELOG is not an Always On wait type but you see this quite often in an availability group environment. This wait type indicates the time it takes for SQL Server to harden the log blocks to the transaction log. If you see a high value for this wait type, it typically means that you may have a disk subsystem bottleneck. It means that SQL Server is sending writes to the transaction log but the writes are not happening quickly enough. This is when you want to review the disk subsystem, review disk performance monitor counters, and work with storage administrators as a high value of this wait type can have a direct impact on the availability group synchronization, which in turn will affect your service level agreements (SLAs).

Using Performance Monitor

Performance Monitor is still very useful and popular in monitoring SQL Servers. SQL Server Always On performance monitor counters are a part of the *Availability Replica* and *Database Replica* objects. Also some counters in the *Databases* object are useful for monitoring Always On availability group synchronization.

For every availability replica that you have, there are some performance counters that are specific to the replica. These counters are a part of the *SQL Server: Availability Replica* object.

■ **Note**   All the availability replica performance counters can be traced on both the primary and the secondary replicas. Some counters may show a zero value depending on the current role of the local replica.

- *Bytes Received from Replica/sec* indicates the number of bytes received from the availability replica per second.

- *Bytes Sent to Replica/sec* indicates the number of bytes sent per second to the remote replica. On a primary replica, this counter indicates the number of bytes sent per second to the secondary replica. On a secondary replica, this counter indicates the number of bytes sent per second to the primary replica.

■ **Note**   *Bytes Sent to Replica/sec* on the primary replica reflects the same values as *Bytes Received from Replica/sec* on the secondary replica.

- *Bytes Sent to Transport/sec* indicates the actual number of bytes sent per second to the remote replica over the network. This counter closely follows the same pattern as *Bytes Sent to Replica/sec* but it averages higher as the transport bytes also contain control block overhead.

- *Resent Messages/sec* indicates the number of Always On messages resent in the last second. Basically it means that SQL Server has sent the message but something happened (may be corruption) and SQL Server has to send the message again. A non-zero value for this performance counter should be further investigated to see why messages are being sent over and over again. Trace this counter at the primary and secondary replicas.

The preceding counters are specific to the availability replica. The next set of counters are specific to every availability database. These counters are part of the *SQL Server: Database Replica* object.

- *Log Send Queue* indicates how much log (in KB) has not been sent from the primary database to the secondary database. This counter tells us the amount of log the secondary database does not have at the time of failover and the amount of data loss customers will experience. A high value of log send queue counter may directly mean that you may not be able to achieve our RPO. You may be looking at data loss if you have a high log send queue value and the only available replicas are asynchronous replicas. The log send queue is also reported in the log_send_queue_size column of the sys. dm_hadr_database_replica_states DMV. Trace this counter at the primary replica.

■ **Note**   As *Log Send Queue* counter rises, the *Log Bytes Received/sec* counter trends down.

- *Transaction Delay* indicates the time (in milliseconds) it takes the primary to send the transaction log blocks to the secondary, for the secondary to receive them, harden them, and sent the acknowledgement commit back to the primary. This is similar to the HADR_SYNC_COMMIT wait type. Since asynchronous commit mode does not need acknowledgement to commit a transaction, this counter reports 0 for database in asynchronous commit mode. For multiple secondaries, this counter measures the total time all transactions wait for the secondary acknowledgement. Trace this counter at the primary replica.

- *Mirrored Write Transactions/sec* indicates the number of transactions per second that were written to the primary database and waited for the log to be sent to the secondary database in order to commit. This counter is a measure of transactions that are waiting to be hardened to the primary because synchronous availability mode requires that they harden at the secondary too. This counter reports 0 for asynchronous availability mode or an unhealthy synchronous mode. Trace this counter at the primary replica.

- *Recovery Queue* indicates the number of log records in the log file of the secondary database that has not yet been redone. Trace this counter at the secondary replica.

- *Redone Bytes/sec* indicates the number of log records that were redone on the secondary database in the last second. Trace this counter at the secondary replica.

■ **Note**   *To measure recovery time, divide Recovery Queue by Redone Bytes/sec.*

- *Redo Bytes Remaining* indicates the amount of log records that is remaining to be redone to finish the reverting phase. Trace this counter at the secondary replica.

■ **Note**   If *Log Bytes Received/sec* trends higher than *Redone Bytes/sec* for a sustained period of time, then it indicates that *REDO* latency is building up between the primary and the secondary replicas. If *Redo Bytes Remaining* and *Recovery Queue* are growing, then it also indicates that *REDO* is the bottleneck.

- *Redo Blocked/sec* indicates the number of times the redo thread is blocked per second on locks held by database readers.

While monitoring the Always On performance counters, you may also want to monitor the *Log Bytes Flushed/sec* counter in the *SQL Server: Databases* object. This is not an Always On performance counter but is very useful. This counter indicates the total number of log bytes flushed per second. It tells us at what rate you are writing to the transaction log. If the *Log Bytes Flushed/sec* is very low, then it may indicate some disk subsystem bottleneck. Review other disk performance counters to review the disk subsystem and collaborate with your storage administrators as required.

■ **Note**   You may have noticed that we haven't provided any threshold values for the performance counters because none exist. There are no magic values for these counters. Hence, it is very important to have a baseline by monitoring these performance counters when everything is working fine. That way when things are not working fine, you can collect the performance counters and compare the values with the baseline.

Mapping DMVs, Wait Statistics, and Performance Monitor

Now that we have discussed the DMVs, wait statistics, and the performance monitor counters, we will map them together and provide an overview of the data that can be collected during the replication of the transaction log blocks from the primary replica to a secondary replica in a synchronous mode. To understand this section, it is important to review the data synchronization in synchronous-commit mode that we discussed in chapter 4.

As a refresher, data synchronization in synchronous-commit mode is shown in Figure 15-5 and the useful metrics that can be collected during the data synchronization are discussed next:

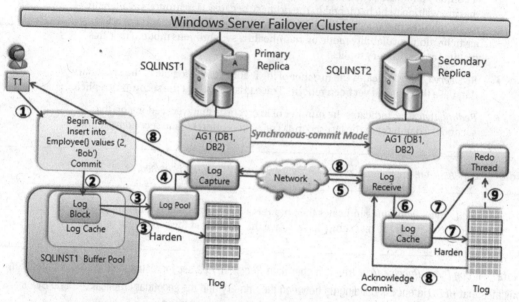

Figure 15-5. *Data synchronization in synchronous-commit mode*

1. A client issues a transaction against the database participating in the availability group on the primary replica.

2. Primary replica generates transaction log blocks. In the background, the secondary replica initiates a request to the primary, asking for the log blocks to be shipped.

3. When the log block becomes full or the primary replica issues a commit operation, the log blocks from the *Log Cache* are flushed to the log file to make it persistent. At this point you can track the performance monitor counter *Log Bytes Flushed/sec* in the *SQL Server: Databases* object and track the rate at which the log hardening is occurring on the primary. In an Always On Availability Group configuration, when the log block is being flushed to the log file on the primary replica, they also get copied to the *Log Pool*.

4. The log blocks in the *Log Pool* are read by the *Log Capture* thread. The rate at which the *Log Capture* is reading the log blocks can be tracked by capturing the performance monitor counter *Bytes Sent to Replica/sec*, which in the *SQL Server: Availability Replica* object. Also, you can look at the log_send_queue_size (KB) and log_send_rate (KB/sec) in the dmv sys.dm_hadr_database_replica_ states to track the amount of log records of the primary database that has not been sent to the secondary database and the rate at which log records are being sent to the secondary database respectively.

■ **Note**   If the primary replica were to fail at this time and there is only asynchronous secondary replica available then you may lose data. You can divide log_send_queue_size (KB) by log_send_rate (KB/sec) to calculate the data loss and see if you are meeting your RPO.

In case of multiple secondary replicas, there is one *Log Capture* thread for each replica, which ensures that the log blocks are sent across multiple replicas in parallel. The log content gets compressed and encrypted before being sent over to the secondary replicas. The actual number of bytes that are sent can be tracked by the performance monitor counter *Bytes Sent to Transport/sec* in the *SQL Server: Availability Replica* counter.

5.   On the secondary replica, *Log Receive* thread receives the log blocks from the network. The number of bytes received from the replica per second can be tracked by capturing the performance monitor counter *Bytes Received from Replica/sec* in the *SQL Server: Availability Replica* object.

6.   It writes to the log cache on the secondary replica.

7.   When the log block on the secondary replica becomes full, or it receives a commit log record, it hardens the content of log cache onto the log disk on the secondary replica. This can be tracked by capturing the performance monitor counter *Log Bytes Flushed/sec* in the *SQL Server: Databases* object to track the rate at which the log hardening is occurring on the secondary.

8.   If the secondary replica is configured to run in synchronous mode, it will send an acknowledgement on the commit to the primary node indicating that it has hardened the transaction, and so it is safe to tell the user that the transaction is committed. At this point you can monitor the wait type HADR_SYNC_COMMIT. What if the primary replica is having some disk bottlenecks or the primary is so slow with the amount of workload running on the primary that it still hasn't hardened the transaction log blocks on the primary replica? The additional wait that is being introduced due to this issue will be tracked using the WRITELOG wait type. So if you see high values of WRITELOG wait type on the primary replica, it means that as far as transaction log hardening is concerned, the primary replica is slower than the synchronous-commit secondary replica. At this point, if you see the commits are delayed or queries are timing out, focus on the primary replica instead of worrying about the secondary replicas.

9.   The redo thread runs independently of how log blocks are being generated on the secondary or being copied and persisted. If the redo thread is a running few minutes behind, those log blocks may not be available in the *Log Cache*. In that case, the redo thread will pick up those log blocks from the log disk, and that is what is shown in the dotted line on the right side of the figure above. You can track the redo thread activity by monitoring the performance monitor counters *Redone Bytes/sec* and *Recovery Queue* in the *SQL Server: Database Replica* object and the redo_queue_size (KB) and redo_rate (KB/sec) in the dmv sys. dm_hadr_database_replica_states. To track the RTO, divide redo_queue_size (KB) by redo_rate (KB/sec).

Using Policy-Based Management

Have you ever wondered how the health information, errors, and warnings are generated in the Always On Availability Group dashboard that we discussed earlier in this chapter? For example, if you suspend the data synchronization for a secondary database, the dashboard gives us a warning at the secondary database level saying that the data synchronization state of this availability database is unhealthy. So where does all these errors and warnings come from on the dashboard? When you create an availability group, it creates certain Always On system policies on the availability replicas that evaluate whether the availability group is healthy or not and displays the results on the dashboard. Always On health model is built on top of the Policy-Based Management (PBM) feature of SQL Server. To review the system policies, open SQL Server Management Studio (SSMS) Object Explorer, connect to any of the availability replicas, expand Management, expand Policy Management, expand Policies, and then expand System Policies as shown in Figure 15-6. The Always On policy names start with Always On.

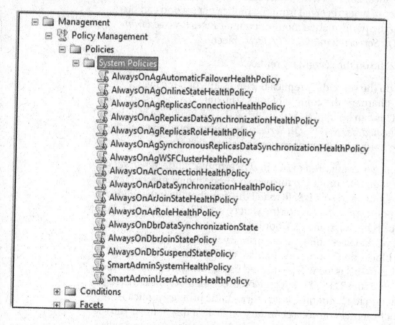

Figure 15-6. *System policies created after deploying availability groups*

If a system policy evaluates to false, you will see an error/warning in the dashboard. If you click the hyperlink for the error/warning, you will see the underlying policies that evaluated to false and their corresponding messages.

■ **Note**　Policy-Based Management (PBM) is a feature that was originally introduced in SQL Server 2008 to manage SQL Server instances. PBM allows us to define and enforce policies for the SQL Server instances. If you are not familiar with PBM, refer to Microsoft's MSDN article "Administer Servers by Using Policy-Based Management" at https://msdn.microsoft.com/en-us/library/bb510667.aspx for more information.

Monitoring Your Availability Groups for RTO and RPO Metrics

You are not restricted to using only the system policies. In fact, Microsoft encourages us to create our own PBM policies and alter a few settings so that our policies will be automatically evaluated by the Always On dashboard. The two key metrics that you want to monitor in an Always On Availability Groups environment are the recovery time objective (RTO) and recovery point objective (RPO) metrics.

Recovery Time Objective (RTO) is the maximum allowable downtime when a failure occurs. RTO depends on the failover time of your Always On Availability Group implementation at any given time and can be expressed as

Tfailover = Tdetection + Tredo + Toverhead

Tdetection is the time it takes for the availability group to detect the failure. This time depends on Windows cluster level settings. It can be as fast as the `sp_server_diagnostics` error report is sent to the cluster (the default interval is 1/3 of the health check timeout) or as long as the timeout interval (higher of health check timeout and lease timeout).

Tredo is the time taken for the redo thread to catch up to the end of the log. It is calculated as `redo_queue_size(kb)` divided by `redo_rate(kb/sec)`.

Toverhead is the time taken to fail over the cluster and to bring the databases online. This time is usually short and constant.

Recovery Point Objective (RPO) is the maximum acceptable level of data loss after a failure occurs. RPO depends on the possible data loss of your Always On Availability Group implementation at any given time and can be expressed as

Tdata_loss = log_send_queue_size / (Log Bytes Flushed/sec)

■ **Note** If an availability group contains more than one availability database, then the availability database with the highest *Tfailover* and *Tdata_loss* becomes the limiting value for RTO and RPO compliance respectively.

Next we'll walk through the process of creating a policy to monitor the RTO and RPO metrics, and integrating this policy into the Always On health model. We will create two policies that will have the following characteristics:

- An RTO policy that is evaluated every 5 minutes and will fail when the estimated failover time exceeds 10 minutes.

- An RPO policy that is evaluated every 30 minutes and will fail when the estimated data loss exceeds 1 hour.

- The policy is evaluated only if the local availability group replica is the primary replica.

- Policy failures are displayed on the primary replica's dashboard.

If you have used PBM before, you may already know that the process for creating and managing polices includes four steps:

1. Select a facet and configure its properties.

2. Set the condition that specifies the state of the facet.

3. Create a policy with the condition/s that you have created, the targets that are to be evaluated with the condition, and its evaluation mode.

4. Execute the policy to verify if the SQL Server instance is in compliance with the policy.

Follow the step-by-step instructions below on all the SQL Server instances that are participating in your Always On Availability Group environment.

Step 1: Select a Facet and Configure its Properties

Open the Facets folder under Policy Management, and scroll through them as shown in Figure 15-7.

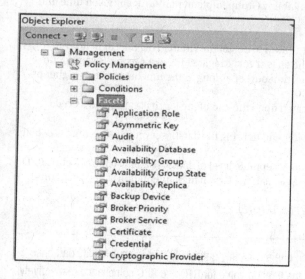

***Figure 15-7.** Reviewing the available facets*

Once you find a facet that seems to describe what you are looking for, right-click it and select Properties. For our example, we will be using the *Availability Group* and *Database Replica State* facets.

■ **Note**   For more information on all the properties of *Availability Group* facet, visit https://msdn.
microsoft.com/en-us/library/microsoft.sqlserver.management.smo.availabilitygroupstate
(v=sql.130).aspx.

For more information on all the properties of Database Replica State facet, visit https://msdn.microsoft.com/
en-us/library/microsoft.sqlserver.management.smo.databasereplicastate(v=sql.130).aspx.

The *Availability Group* facet has eight different properties as shown in Figure 15-8. One of the property is *LocalReplicaRole* that is used to get the role (primary, secondary, resolving or unknown) of the local availability replica.

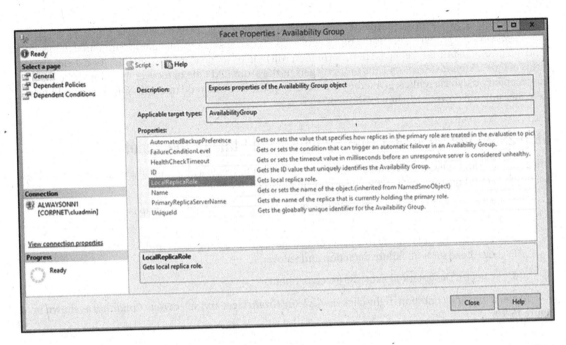

Figure 15-8. *Properties of availability group facet*

The *Database Replica State* facet has 36 different properties as shown in Figure 15-9.

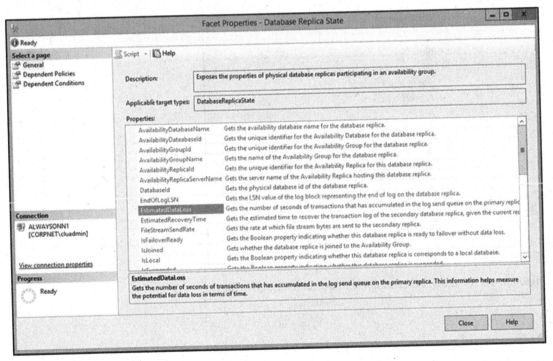

Figure 15-9. *Properties of Database Replica State facet*

We are going to use the properties, *EstimatedDataLoss* and *EstimatedRecoveryTime*. The *EstimatedDataLoss* property gets us the number of seconds of transactions that has accumulated in the log send queue on the primary replica. This information will help us to measure the potential for data loss in terms of time. *EstimatedRecoveryTime* property gets us the estimated time to recover the transaction log of the secondary database replica, given the current redo queue size and redo rate. This information will help us to measure the downtime when a failure occurs.

Step 2: Set the Condition That Specifies the State of the Facet

Once you have identified the facet and the property you want to create a policy on, the next step is to create the property condition. You will create the following three conditions:

1. Check whether the local availability replica for a given availability group is the primary replica.

2. Check if the potential failover exceeds 10 minutes, including 60 seconds overhead for both failure detection and failover.

3. Check if the potential data loss exceeds 1 hour.

To create the first condition, right-click *Availability Group* facet and select *New Condition* as shown in Figure 15-10.

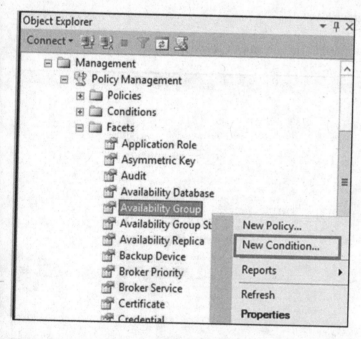

Figure 15-10. *Creating new condition for the availability group facet*

Enter the following specifications to create the condition and click OK:

- Name: IsPrimaryReplica
- Field: *@LocalReplicaRole*
- Operator: =
- Value: *Primary*

Figure 15-11 shows the condition that will check whether the local availability replica for a given availability group is the primary replica.

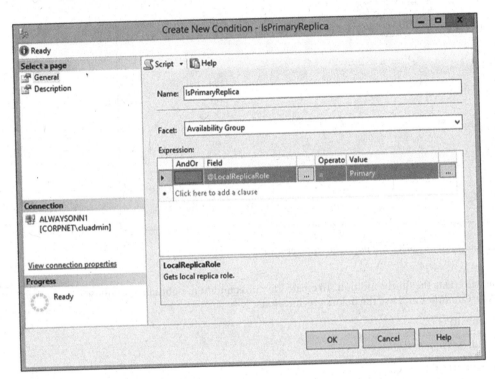

Figure 15-11. *Condition to check if the role for the local replica is primary*

Next, you will create the second condition. To create the second condition, right-click *Database Replica State* facet, select *New Condition* and use the below specifications:

- Name: RTO
- Field: *Add(@EstimatedRecoveryTime, 60)*
- Operator: <=
- Value: 600

This condition as shown in Figure 15-12 will fail when the potential failover time exceeds 600 seconds (i.e., 10 minutes), including a 60-second overhead for both failure detection and failover.

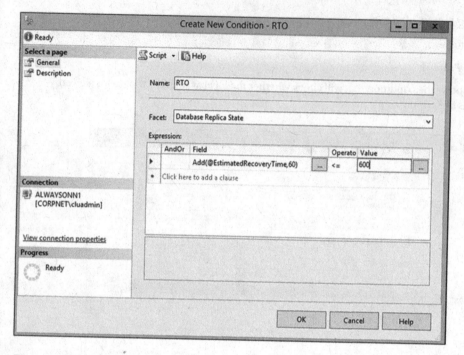

Figure 15-12. *Condition to check the potential failover time*

Next, you will create the third condition. To create the third condition, right-click *Database Replica State* facet, select *New Condition,* and use the below specifications:

- Name: RPO

- Field: *@EstimatedDataLoss*

- Operator: <=

- Value: 3600

This condition as shown in Figure 15-13 will fail when the potential data loss exceeds 3600 seconds (i.e., 1 hour).

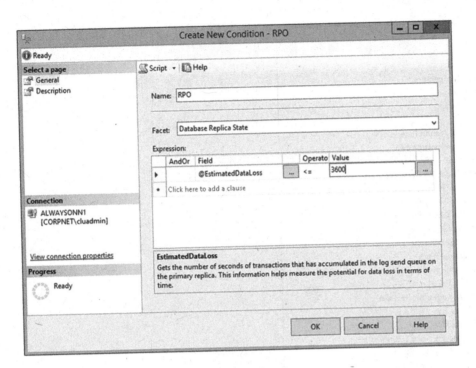

Figure 15-13. *Condition to check the potential data loss*

Step 3: Create the Policy

After creating the conditions for the facets, our next step is to create the policy. You will create two policies:

- *RTOPolicy* – This policy will fail when the estimated failover time exceeds 10 minutes and is evaluated every 5 minutes.

- *RPOPolicy* – This policy will fail when the estimated data loss exceeds 1 hour and is evaluated every 30 minutes.

To create the first policy, right-click *Database Replica State* facet and select *New Policy* as shown in Figure 15-14.

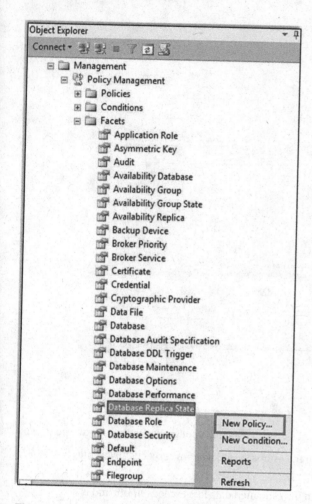

Figure 15-14. *Creating new policy for the Database Replica State facet*

Use the below specifications to create the RTOPolicy:
General Page:

- Name: RTOPolicy

- Check condition: RTO

- Against targets: *Every DatabaseReplicaState* in *IsPrimaryReplica AvailabilityGroup*

- Evaluation mode: On schedule

- Schedule: CollectorSchedule_Every_5_min

- Enabled: checked

The general page for the RTOPolicy is shown in Figure 15-15.

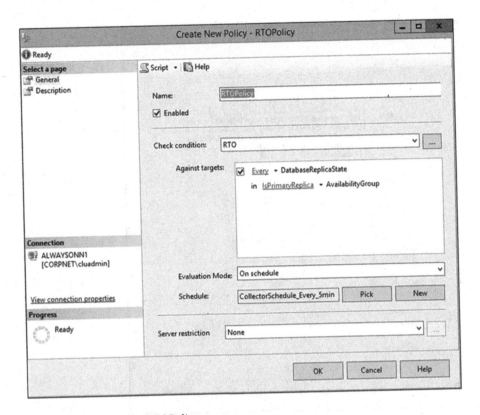

Figure 15-15. *Creating RTOPolicy*

Description Page:

- Category: Availability database warnings. This setting will display the policy evaluation results on the Always On dashboard.

- Description: The current availability replica has a Recovery Time Objective (RTO) that exceeded 10 minutes, assuming an overhead of one minute for failure detection and failover. Troubleshoot performance issues on the respective SQL Server instance immediately.

- Text to display: Recovery Time Objective (RTO) exceeded!

The description page for the RTOPolicy is shown in Figure 15-16.

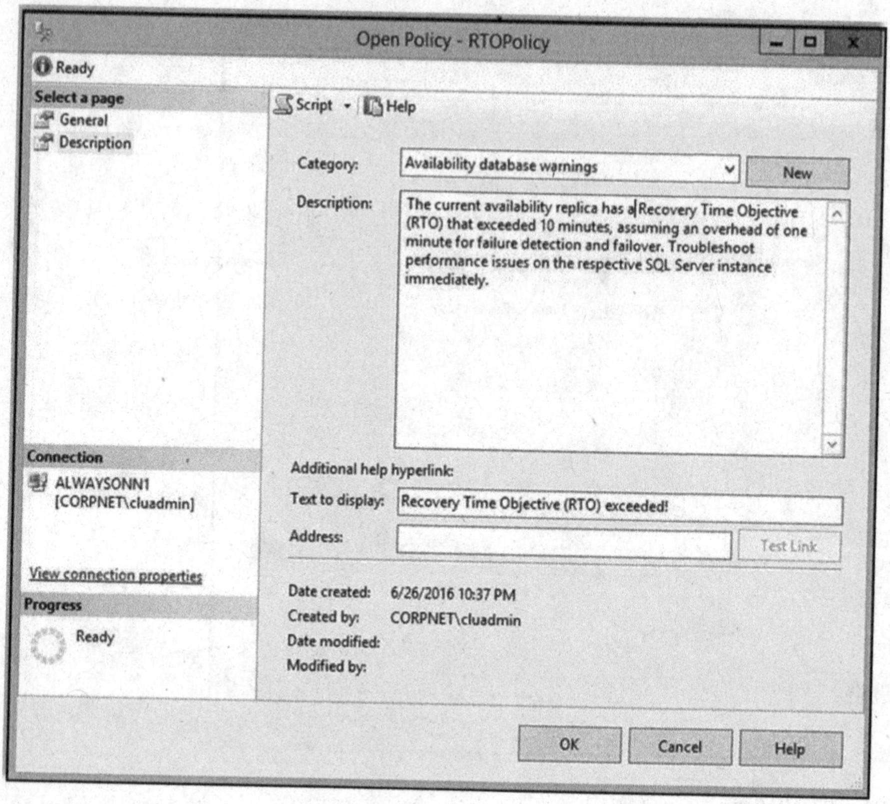

Figure 15-16. *Description page for the RTOPolicy*

To create the second policy, right-click Database Replica State facet, select New Policy, and use the below specifications to create the RTOPolicy:

General Page:

- Name: RPOPolicy

- Check condition: RPO

- Against targets: *Every DatabaseReplicaState* in *IsPrimaryReplica AvailabilityGroup*

- Evaluation mode: On schedule

- Schedule: CollectorSchedule_Every_30_min

- Enabled: checked

The general page for the RPOPolicy is shown in Figure 15-17.

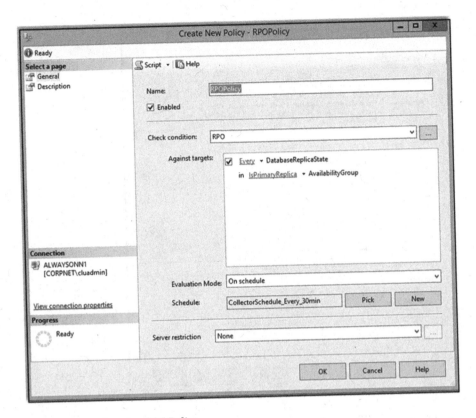

Figure 15-17. Creating RPOPolicy

Description Page:

- Category: Availability database warnings.

- Description: The availability database has exceeded your Recovery Point Objective (RPO) of 1 hour. Troubleshoot performance issues on the availability replicas immediately.

- Text to display: Recovery Point Objective (RPO) exceeded!

The description page for the RPOPolicy is shown in Figure 15-18.

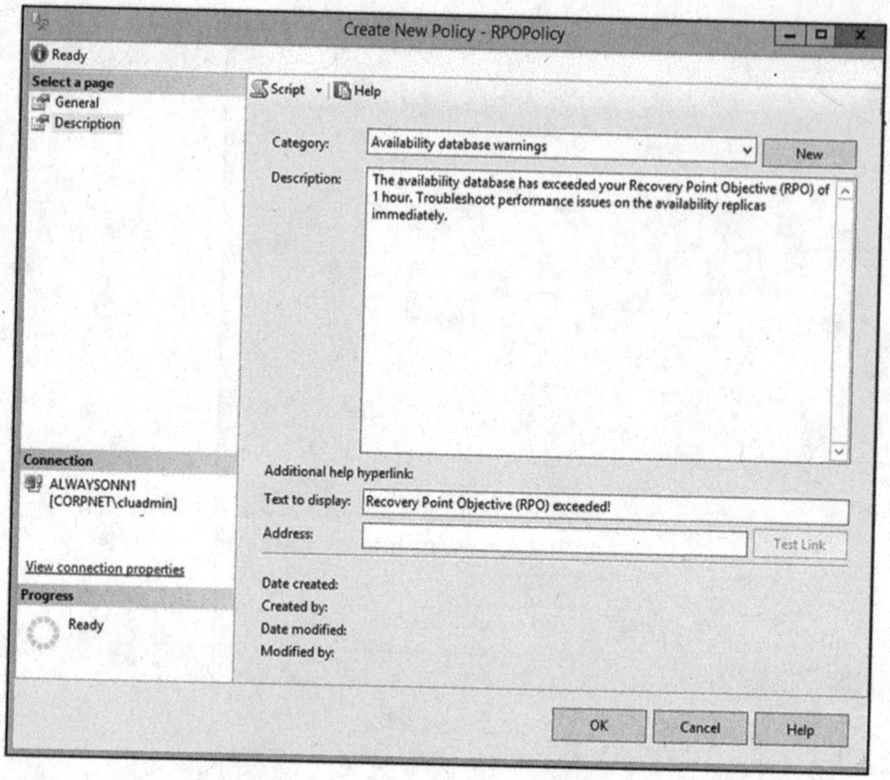

Figure 15-18. *Description page for the RPOPolicy*

After completing the above three steps, you will have three new conditions; two new policies; and two new SQL Server Agent jobs, one for each policy evaluation schedule as shown in Figure 15-19. These jobs have names that start with *syspolicy_check_schedule*.

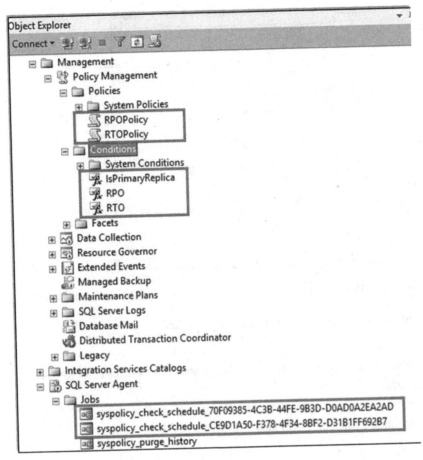

Figure 15-19. *Reviewing the conditions, policies, and jobs created for monitoring RTO and RPO metrics*

Step 4: Execute the Policy and Inspect the Evaluation Results

After creating the policy, the only thing left to do is to execute the policy and inspect the evaluation results. You created the above two policies to run on a schedule. You can also run the policy on demand by right-clicking the policy and selecting *Evaluate*. To inspect the evaluation results, view the job history. Evaluation failures will also be recorded in the Windows application log with the event ID *34052*. You can also create an alert on error number *34052* to get automatic notification of the policies evaluating to *False*.

To display the messages on Always On dashboard, click Tools menu, select Options, expand SQL Server Always On, expand Dashboard, and check Enable user-defined Always On Policy check box as shown in Figure 15-20.

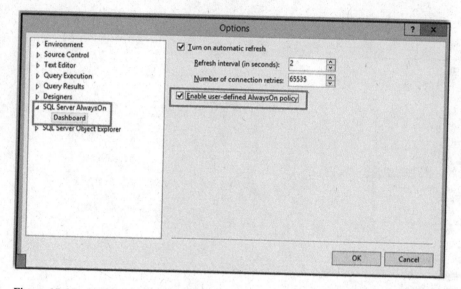

Figure 15-20. *Enabling user-defined Always On Policy checkbox to display the messages on the dashboard*

Now the Always On dashboard will pick up our RTOPolicy and RPOPolicy.

■ **Tip** If the Always On dashboard is already open, then refresh the dashboard or close the dashboard and reopen it to display the new policies.

Figure 15-21 shows the dashboard when the policy fails.

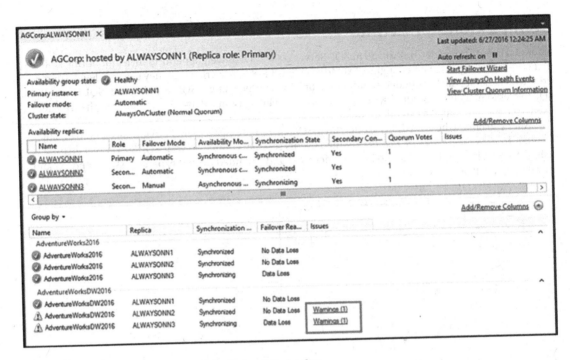

Figure 15-21. Always On dashboard displaying failed policy

Click on the Warnings (1) hyperlink to display the issue details as shown in Figure 15-22.

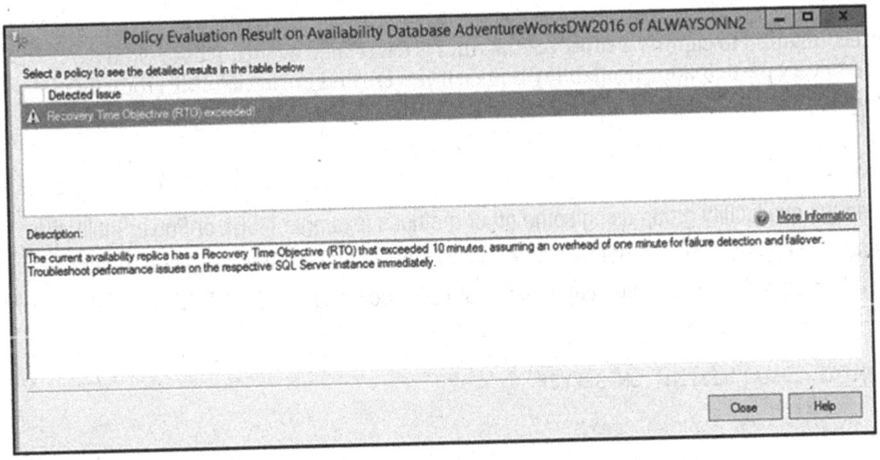

Figure 15-22. Reviewing the detailed results for a failed policy in Always On dashboard

Using Extended Events

Extended Events originally introduced in SQL Server 2008 is a lightweight performance monitoring system that is built into the SQL Server engine. Extended events have less overhead as they use very few resources. Prior to SQL Server 2012, extended events could only be created using T-SQL. Starting with SQL Server 2012, SQL Server Management Studio (SSMS) provides an excellent graphical user interface (GUI) that can be used to create and manage extended events.

After you create the availability group, *AlwaysOn_health* extended events session gets automatically created. To view the *AlwaysOn_health* extended events session, connect to your SQL Server instance using SSMS Object Explorer, expand Management, expand Extended Events, expand Sessions and expand AlwaysOn_health as shown in Figure 15-23.

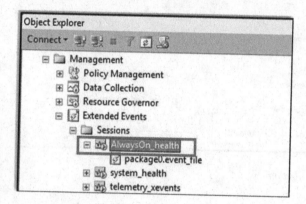

Figure 15-23. *Viewing AlwaysOn_health extended events session in SSMS*

This session is preconfigured to capture a subset of the Always On related events. This session is automatically started on every participating availability replica if you created the availability group using the *New Availability Group* wizard. The green arrow next to the AlwaysOn_health session indicates that it is currently running.

■ **Note**   If you created the availability group using some other methods (example T-SQL or PowerShell), the *AlwaysOn_health* extended event session may not be automatically started. To start the *AlwaysOn_health* session and configure it to start automatically, you can use the GUI or execute the below T-SQL script.

```
ALTER EVENT SESSION [AlwaysOn_health] ON SERVER
WITH (STARTUP_STATE = ON)
GO
ALTER EVENT SESSION [AlwaysOn_health] ON SERVER
STATE = START
```

Preconfigured AlwaysOn_health Extended Events

To review the events that the *AlwaysOn_health* session captures to monitor the availability groups, right-click the session and select Properties. Under Select a page, click Events to display the events as shown in Figure 15-24.

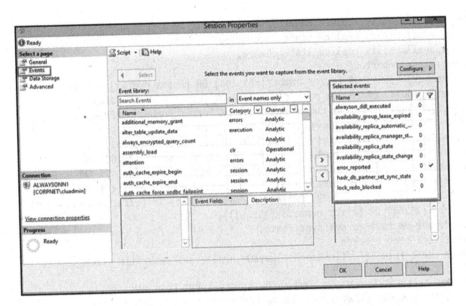

Figure 15-24. *Viewing the preconfigured events in AlwaysOn_health session*

Below is a brief description of the preconfigured events:

- *alwayson_ddl_executed* – occurs when Always On data definition language (DDL) statement is executed, including CREATE, ALTER, or DROP.

- *availability_group_lease_expired* – occurs when the cluster and availability group has a connectivity issue and the lease is expired.

- *availability_replica_automatic_failover_validation* – occurs when the automatic failover validates the readiness of an availability replica as a primary replica.

- *availability_replica_manager_state_change* – occurs when the state of the availability replica manager has changed.

- *availability_replica_state* – occurs when the availability replica is starting or shutting down.

- *availability_replica_state_change* – occurs when the state of the availability replica has changed.

- *error_reported* – occurs when an error is reported.

- *hadr_db_partner_set_sync_state* – occurs when the hadr partner sync state has changed.

- *lock_redo_blocked* – occurs when the redo thread blocks when trying to acquire a lock.

To view the definition of the *AlwaysOn_health* session, right-click the session, click Script Session as, click CREATE To, and then click New Query Editor Window. This will create the following T-SQL script:

```
CREATE EVENT SESSION [AlwaysOn_health] ON SERVER
ADD EVENT sqlserver.alwayson_ddl_executed,
ADD EVENT sqlserver.availability_group_lease_expired,
ADD EVENT sqlserver.availability_replica_automatic_failover_validation,
```

```
ADD EVENT sqlserver.availability_replica_manager_state_change,
ADD EVENT sqlserver.availability_replica_state,
ADD EVENT sqlserver.availability_replica_state_change,
ADD EVENT sqlserver.error_reported(
    WHERE ([error_number]=(9691) OR [error_number]=(35204) OR [error_number]=(9693)
    OR [error_number]=(26024) OR [error_number]=(28047) OR [error_number]=(26023)
    OR [error_number]=(9692) OR [error_number]=(28034) OR [error_number]=(28036) OR
    [error_number]=(28048) OR [error_number]=(28080) OR [error_number]=(28091) OR
    [error_number]=(26022) OR [error_number]=(9642) OR [error_number]=(35201) OR
    [error_number]=(35202) OR [error_number]=(35206) OR [error_number]=(35207) OR
    [error_number]=(26069) OR [error_number]=(26070) OR [error_number]>(41047) AND
    [error_number]<(41056) OR [error_number]=(41142) OR [error_number]=(41144) OR [error_
    number]=(1480) OR [error_number]=(823) OR [error_number]=(824) OR [error_number]=(829)
    OR [error_number]=(35264) OR [error_number]=(35265))),
ADD EVENT sqlserver.hadr_db_partner_set_sync_state,
ADD EVENT sqlserver.lock_redo_blocked
ADD TARGET package0.event_file(SET filename=N'AlwaysOn_health.xel',max_file_size=(5),max_
rollover_files=(4))
WITH (MAX_MEMORY=4096 KB,EVENT_RETENTION_MODE=ALLOW_SINGLE_EVENT_LOSS,MAX_
DISPATCH_LATENCY=30 SECONDS,MAX_EVENT_SIZE=0 KB,MEMORY_PARTITION_MODE=NONE,TRACK_
CAUSALITY=OFF,STARTUP_STATE=ON)
GO
```

Debug Events for Always On Availability Groups

In addition to the above events, SQL Server defines an extensive set of debug events for Always On Availability Groups. To review the debug events, open *AlwaysOn_health* session properties. Under Select a page, click Events. In the event library, select always on in the Category column and Debug in the Channel column and clear all other selections. This will display all the Always On debug events as shown in Figure 15-25.

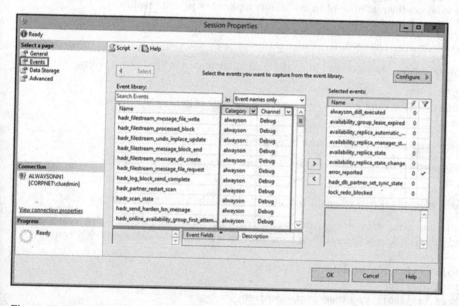

Figure 15-25. Viewing the Always On Debug events

To view all the Always On extended events along with a brief description, execute the below T-SQL statement:

```
SELECT name, description FROM sys.dm_xe_objects WHERE name LIKE '%hadr%' order by name;
```

Configuring AlwaysOn_health Session Target File

To configure the AlwaysOn_health session, follow these steps:

1. Open the AlwaysOn_health session properties.

2. Under Select a page, select Data Storage.

3. Select the event_file target from Targets and click on the Remove button.

4. This will pop up a window saying that the target data will be deleted. If you need the old event files, then make a backup of the files and then click Yes.

5. Click Add button to add a target with your own properties. For example, Figure 15-26 will configure the event file with a maximum of 4 files and a maximum of 1GB file size.

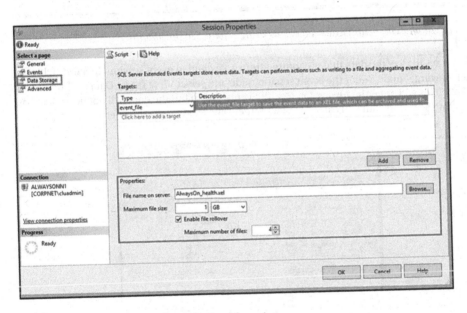

Figure 15-26. Configuring AlwaysOn_health session

Viewing Always On Health Events Data

To view the Always On health events, simply open the dashboard and click the link View Always On Health Events on the right-hand top corner of the dashboard. This will open the Always On Health Events screen as shown in Figure 15-27 below. You can add columns by right-clicking the column headers and then select what you need. Also, when you click a specific row, you can see the details of the rows below.

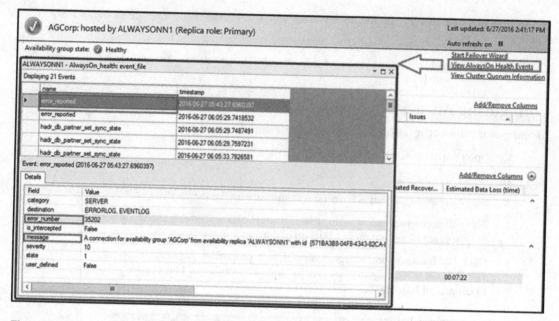

Figure 15-27. *Viewing AlwaysOn_health extended events using Always On dashboard*

There are other ways to view the data that is captured from an extended event session. In SSMS, Object Explorer, right-click the target node under the event session node and select View Target Data as shown below in Figure 15-28. This will open the Always On Health Events screen but the data will not be updated as new data is reported by the events. But you can click View Target Data again to get the latest data.

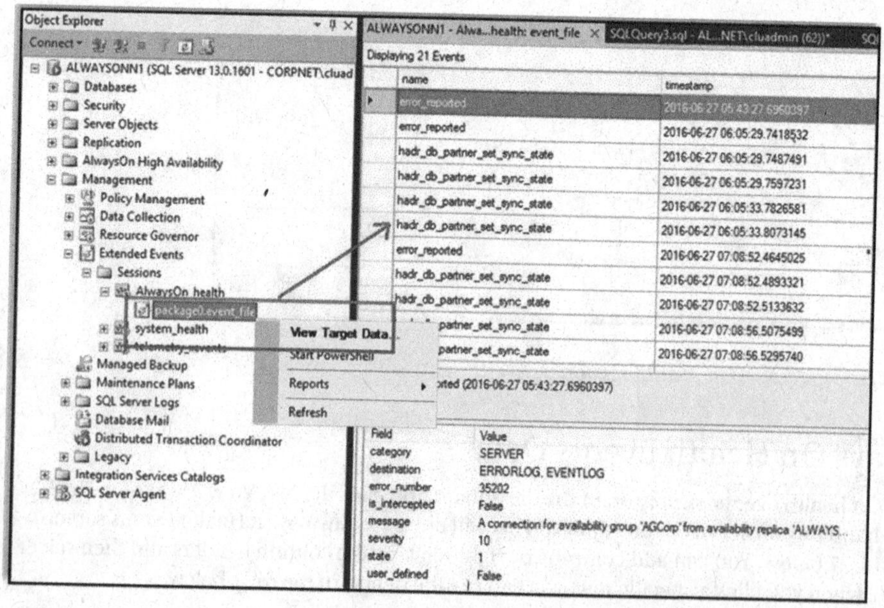

Figure 15-28. *Viewing AlwaysOn_health extended event_file using SSMS Object Explorer*

If you want to watch the data as it continues to arrive in real time, you can right-click the event session node and select Watch Live Data as shown below in Figure 15-29.

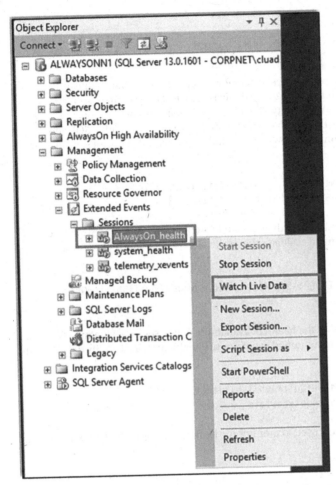

Figure 15-29. *Viewing live AlwaysOn_health extended events data using SSMS Object Explorer*

If you want to view the AlwaysOn_health extended events using T-SQL, then you can use the T-SQL function sys.fn_xe_file_target_read_file as shown below. You can click a cell in the event_data_XML column and/or copy the long XML string from the event_data column and paste into your text editor (example Notepad), save the file with extension .xml and then open the .xml file with a browser.

```
SELECT
        object_name,
        file_name,
        file_offset,
        event_data,
        CAST(event_data AS XML) AS [event_data_XML]
FROM
```

```
sys.fn_xe_file_target_read_file(
    'ENTER FULL PATH OF YOUR AlwaysOn_health event file name',
    null, null, null
);
```

Using PowerShell

SQL Server 2016 Always On Availability Groups provides a set of PowerShell cmdlets that enable us to deploy, manage, and monitor availability groups, availability replicas, and availability databases. The following PowerShell cmdlets are available to monitor the health of availability groups:

Test-SqlAvailabilityGroup – assesses the health of an availability group by evaluating SQL Server PBM policies. As an example, the below command shows all availability groups with a health state of *Error* on the server instance AlwaysOnN1\Default

```
Get-ChildItem SQLSERVER:\Sql\AlwaysOnN1\Default\AvailabilityGroups | Test-
SqlAvailabilityGroup | Where-Object { $_.HealthState -eq "Error" }
```

Test-SqlAvailabilityReplica – assesses the health of availability replicas by evaluating SQL Server PBM policies. As an example, the below command evaluates the health of the availability replica AlwaysOnN1 in the availability group AGCorp

```
Test-SqlAvailabilityReplica -Path SQLSERVER:\SQL\AlwaysOnN1\Default\AvailabilityGroups\
AGCorp\AvailabilityReplicas\AlwaysonN1
```

Test-SqlDatabaseReplicaState – assesses the health of availability databases by evaluating SQL Server PBM policies. As an example, the below command evaluates the health of all availability databases in the availability group AGCorp

```
Get-ChildItem SQLSERVER:\Sql\AlwaysOnN1\Default\AvailabilityGroups\AGCorp\
DatabaseReplicaStates  | Test-SqlDatabaseReplicaState
```

Figure 15-30 shows the PowerShell cmdlets used to monitor the health of the availability group AGCorp and the corresponding results.

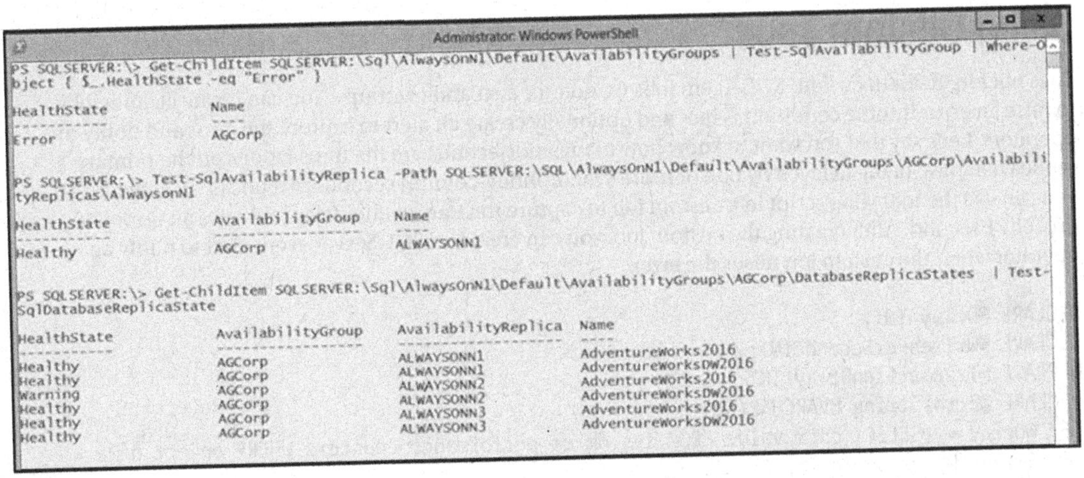

Figure 15-30. Monitoring availability groups using PowerShell

Using Alerts

You can use the in-built alerts feature in SQL Server Agent to monitor availability groups. As you might be aware, events are generated by SQL Server and entered into Windows application log. SQL Server Agent reads the application log and compares the events in the log with the alerts that you create. When a match is found it fires an alert, which basically is an automated response to an event. SQL Server Agent also monitors performance conditions and Windows Management Instrumentation (WMI) events.

You can create the following alerts to monitor the health of the availability groups.

- *Alerts over Always On errors* – To get a complete list of Always On system error messages, run the below T-SQL command. This will return 17 rows in SQL Server 2016.

  ```
  SELECT * FROM sys.messages WHERE text LIKE ('%availability%') AND
  language_id = 1033 AND  is_event_logged = 1;
  ```

- *Alerts over other relevant errors* – You can create alerts on non-Always On errors too if they are relevant and need to be monitored to ensure the health of the availability group. To get a complete list of errors that can be monitored for an availability group, go to the properties of AlwaysOn_health extended events session, click on Events, click Configure and select the event error_reported.

- *Alerts over Always On Perfmon counters* – We discussed some of the important Performance monitor counters earlier in this chapter. You can create alerts to monitor these counters.

- *Alerts over custom conditions* – You can create alerts for specific conditions that need to be evaluated. For example, to get an alert if our recovery time objective (RTO) will be exceeded, you can create a SQL Server Agent job that divides *Redo Queue Size* by *Redo Rate* and throw an error if the result exceeds the RTO value. You can then configure an alert to capture these errors and notify the operators accordingly.

Using Custom Jobs

Let's not forget about custom SQL Agent jobs to monitor availability groups. You can create custom jobs to raise an error if some condition is met and optionally create an alert to capture the error and notify the operators. Let's say that you want to know how many milliseconds are the transactions on the primary replica database being delayed by one or more synchronous-commit secondary replicas. To achieve this, you can use the following script in a custom job to capture the transaction delay and raise an error if it exceeds 1 second. After creating the custom job, you can create an SQL Server event alert to notify an operator when the custom job raises the error.

```
DECLARE @Delay INT;
DECLARE @WritesPerSecond INT;
DECLARE @TransactionDelay INT;
DECLARE @ErrorString NVARCHAR(50);
SET @Delay = (SELECT cntr_value FROM sys.dm_os_performance_counters WHERE object_name =
'SQLServer:Database Replica'
AND counter_name = 'Transaction Delay' AND instance_name = '_Total');
SET @WritesPerSecond = (select cntr_value FROM sys.dm_os_performance_counters WHERE object_
name = 'SQLServer:Database Replica'
AND counter_name = 'Mirrored Write Transactions/sec' AND instance_name = '_Total');
SET @TransactionDelay = (@Delay/@WritesPerSecond);
SET @ErrorString = CONCAT('Transactions are being delayed by ', @TransactionDelay, '
milliseconds');
IF (@TransactionDelay > 1000)
BEGIN
RAISERROR (@ErrorString,16,1) WITH LOG;
END
```

■ **Note**   The preceding script captures two Performance Monitor counters from the *SQLServer:Database Replica* object. The first one is *Transaction Delay* that shows the wait time for an unterminated commit acknowledgement (in milliseconds). The second one is *Mirrored Write Transactions/sec* that shows the number of transactions that are waiting to be hardened to the primary because synchronous availability mode requires that they harden at the secondary also. Dividing these two counters tells us by how many milliseconds are the transactions on the primary replica database being delayed by one or more synchronous-commit secondary replicas.

Using System Center Operations Manager (SCOM)

In the preceding sections, we have discussed multiple ways to monitor availability groups using in-built SQL Server and operating system tools. Last but not least, we will discuss System Center Operations Manager (SCOM). Many of our customers are already using SCOM to monitor their private and public datacenters. SCOM provides predictable performance and availability of applications and offers a comprehensive, flexible and cost-effective infrastructure monitoring system. You can download the management pack for SQL Server (SQLMP) to monitor your SQL Servers and Always On Availability Group deployments. SQLMP provides performance, availability, and configuration monitoring, along with performance data collection and default thresholds. Additionally, SQLMP includes dashboard views, diagram views and extensive knowledge with embedded inline tasks, and views that enable near real-time diagnosis and resolution of detected issues. Here are some of the monitoring features that are relevant to availability groups:

- Easily track your Always On Availability Groups inventory by automatically discovering availability groups, availability replicas and availability databases from hundreds of computers.

- Enable faster resolution to problems by utilizing SCOM's alerting and ticketing feature.

- Create custom tasks to manage availability groups from the SCOM console.

- Easily roll up health from availability databases to availability replicas.

Summary

In this chapter, we reviewed multiple ways to monitor the health and synchronization status of Always On Availability Groups. It's good to know about all the in-built SQL Server monitoring tools that you have at your disposal. Sometimes, you may only need to use one tool while other times you may have to use multiple tools to gather as much data as possible to troubleshoot a problem. In the next chapter, we will discuss troubleshooting techniques and review some common troubleshooting scenarios that we see at our customer sites in the field.

CHAPTER 16

■ ■ ■

Troubleshooting Availability Groups

This chapter discusses how to use different logs to troubleshoot errors encountered during availability group setup and usage. You will also learn how to troubleshoot some of the common availability group failures and performance issues.

An unplanned failover of an availability group can happen for various reasons. The cause is usually outside of SQL Server. SQL Server is just an application that is using external resources to perform its duties and availability group is one of its components. Hence, unless the error message clearly indicates that the issue is due to SQL Server, start troubleshooting in the following order:

1. Hardware

2. Operating system

3. Network

4. Security

5. Windows Server failover cluster

6. SQL Server

When an outage occurs, the first step is to define what actually went wrong. Ask the following questions:

- What resource(s) failed?

    - Was it the disk? Or was it the network?

    - Was it the SQL Server? Or was it the SQL Server Agent?

    - Was it the file share?

- Were the users not able to connect even when the SQL Server instance was online?

- Did the problem occur on one node or all nodes?

To determine the root cause of the failure, determine exactly what failed, on which nodes, and what actions the cluster performed to try to resolve the problem.

Useful Reports and Logs

Let's take a look at some useful reports and logs that can help in troubleshooting issues with availability groups.

© Uttam Parui and Vivek Sanil 2016
U. Parui and V. Sanil, *Pro SQL Server Always On Availability Groups*, DOI 10.1007/978-1-4842-2071-9_16

Always On Dashboard

For a quick overview of the availability group, look at the Always On dashboard. It provides information on the availability group states and other performance indicators allowing you to easily make high availability operational decisions using the following types of information:

- Replica state

- Synchronization mode and state

- Estimate Data Loss

- Estimated Recovery Time (redo catch up)

- Database Replica details

- Time to restore log

- And more...

This is a centralized report and the replica status can be viewed from the primary replica itself. You do not need to go to each replica to view the state of that replica.

Figure 16-1 shows the Always On dashboard in the SSMS GUI on Primary Replica instance. As you can see there is a lot of useful information on the dashboard. Important information and report links have been highlighted.

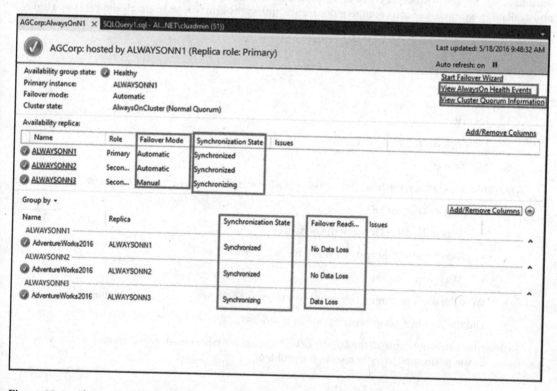

Figure 16-1. *Always On Dashboard*

Figure 16-2 shows the Always On dashboard in the SSMS GUI on Primary Replica instance. More columns can be added to the dashboard result by clicking on the Add/Remove columns option above the column header and then selecting the columns to add. The below figure shows the options available for the first result set on the dashboard. The columns highlighted in red are some important columns that you may want to consider adding to the dashboard.

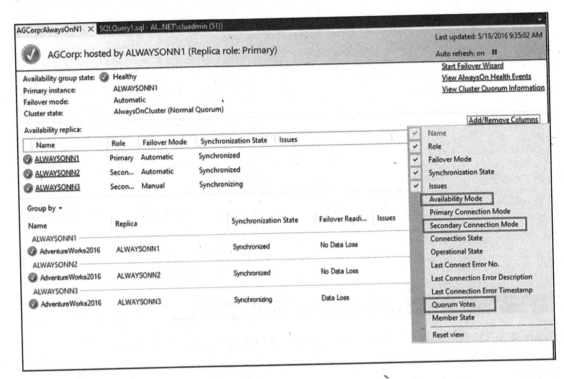

Figure 16-2. *Columns available to add to the first result set in the Always On Dashboard*

Figure 16-3 shows the options available for the second result set on the dashboard. The columns highlighted in red are some important columns that you may want to consider adding to the dashboard.

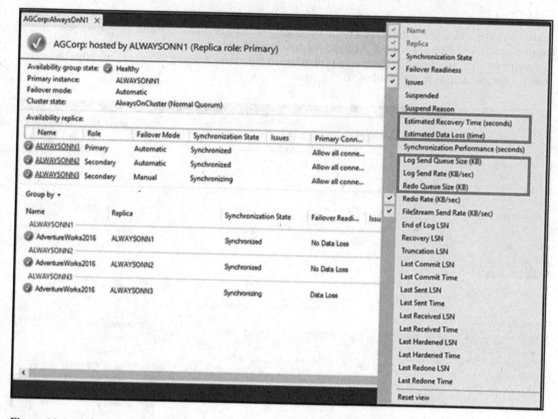

Figure 16-3. *Columns available to add to the second result set in the Always On Dashboard*

DMVs

There are various DMVs and catalog views (that start with sys.dm_hadr_ and sys.availability), which expose lot of useful information related to availability group troubleshooting. Here are some common ones:

- **sys.dm_hadr_availability_group_states** - Displays the states that define the health of a given availability group

- **sys.dm_hadr_availability_replica_states** – Displays information about the state of a given availability replica

- **sys.dm_hadr_database_replica_states** - Returns a row for each database that is participating in an availability group

- **sys.dm_hadr_cluster** – Displays information about the cluster and the quorum

- **sys.dm_hadr_cluster_members** - Returns a row for each of the members that constitute the quorum and the state of each of them

- **sys.availability_groups_cluster** – Displays information on the availability group metadata from the WSFC cluster

- **sys.availability_replicas** - Returns a row for each of the availability replicas that belong to any availability group in the WSFC failover cluster

- **sys.dm_tcp_listener_states** – Displays information on the TCP listener
- **sys.dm_hadr_physical_seeding_stats** – Displays physical stats of each seeding process currently running on the primary replica
- **sys.dm_hadr_automatic_seeding** – Displays the status of the automatic seeding process on the primary replica

Extended Event Logs

The Always On Health Extended Event logs cover the availability group related diagnostics such as state changes for the group or replica or databases, errors reported, lease expiration, and any availability group related DDL that is executed. It is created automatically when the availability group is created and captures availability groups related events The format of the logs is: *AlwaysOn_health*.xel* and is located by default under the SQL Server log folder. It is a preconfigured session and is useful for troubleshooting an availability group.

Figure 16-4 shows the Always On Extended Events session in the SSMS GUI on Primary Replica instance.

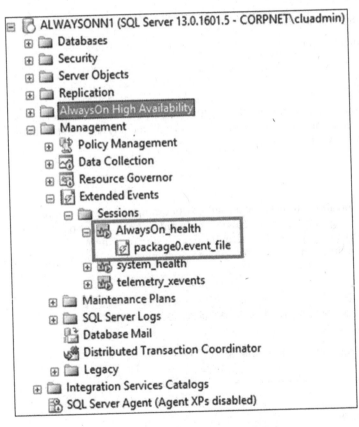

Figure 16-4. *Always On Health Extended Events Session*

■ **Note** If you created the availability group using the wizard, then this session is automatically started on every participating availability replica. If the availability group wasn't created using the wizard, then this session should be manually started.

SQL Server Error Logs

Check the SQL Server Error Log for events affecting availability groups, such as the following:

- Communication with the Windows Server Failover Clustering (WSFC) cluster
- State transitions of availability replicas
- State transitions of availability databases
- Connectivity state of availability databases between primary and secondary replicas
- Statuses of the availability group endpoints
- Statuses of the availability group listeners
- Lease status between the SQL Server resource DLL
- Error events in the availability group

Event Logs

The Cluster Service adds messages about the resource status to the cluster log and the system-event log. The system-event log is generally easier to read than the cluster logs. You can usually identify failed resources by searching for event ID 1069 in the system-event log.

Cluster Log

If the system-event log has no information about the cause of the failure (for example, the system stops writing events to the log), use the cluster log. The Cluster.log files can be found in the <systemroot>\cluster\reports directory (usually c:\windows\cluster\Reports) on each node. Get-ClusterLog is the Windows PowerShell cmdlet that will generate the cluster.log on each server that is a member of the cluster and is currently running.

■ **Note** The cluster log is verbose and complex. It should be the last place you go, not the first.

Figure 16-5 shows the Get-ClusterLog PowerShell command.

```
PS C:\> Get-ClusterLog

Mode                  LastWriteTime         Length Name
----                  -------------         ------ ----
-a----      5/18/2016  10:17 AM           77274272 Cluster.log
-a----      5/18/2016  10:17 AM           53487966 Cluster.log
```

Figure 16-5. PowerShell Command to generate cluster log

■ **Note**   Cluster log timestamps are in GMT, while event log timestamps are in local time.

Use NET HELPMSG to decipher error codes or ERR.EXE. Start at the bottom and work your way upwards searching for the following:

- [ERR]
- -->failed – resource failure
- -->failed – group failure

Figure 16-6 shows the net helmsg command to help decipher error codes logged in the cluster log.

```
C:\>net helpmsg 5018

The cluster resource could not be brought online by the resource monitor.
```

Figure 16-6. *net helpmsg command*

Calculating Estimated Data Loss

If the primary replica is unhealthy and you do not have a secondary replica with a SYNCHRONIZED state, you may have to perform a forced failover of the availability group to bring it online. Doing so can cause data loss. It is not possible to estimate this data loss if the primary replica is not healthy. So it is imperative that you have monitoring set up to alert you if the estimated data loss grows beyond your RPO for the availability group.

You may want to be able to quickly check how much data loss may occur if a forced failover is to be performed at a particular moment.

Following are two of the ways to get this information:

- Dashboard - Monitor the "Estimated Data Loss" column values for your secondary replica databases. In the default dashboard view, this column is hidden. You can add it by clicking on the "Add/remove columns" link above the replica database table.

  Figure 16-7 shows the Always On dashboard with the estimated data loss column added to the view.

Availability replica:							
Name	▲ Role	Failover Mode	Synchronization State	Availability Mode	Issues	Secondary Co...	
✅ ALWAYSONN1	Primary	Automatic	Synchronized	Synchronous commit		No	
✅ ALWAYSONN2	Secondary	Automatic	Synchronized	Synchronous commit		Yes	
⚠️ ALWAYSONN3	Secondary	Manual	Synchronizing	Synchronous commit	Warnings...	Yes	

Group by ▾

Name	Replica	Synchronization St...	Failover Readiness	Issues	Estimated Recovery Time...	Estimated Data Loss
ALWAYSONN1						
✅ AdventureWorks2014	ALWAYSONN1	Synchronized	No Data Loss		0	
✅ AdventureWorksDW2...	ALWAYSONN1	Synchronized	No Data Loss		0	
ALWAYSONN2						
✅ AdventureWorks2014	ALWAYSONN2	Synchronized	No Data Loss		0	
✅ AdventureWorksDW2...	ALWAYSONN2	Synchronized	No Data Loss		103	
ALWAYSONN3						
✅ AdventureWorks2014	ALWAYSONN3	Synchronized	No Data Loss		0	
⚠️ AdventureWorksDW2...	ALWAYSONN3	Synchronizing	Data Loss	War...	99	00:02:26

Figure 16-7. *Estimated data loss column in the Always On Dashboard*

- System Views – The "last_commit_time" column from the sys.dm_hadr_database_
  replica_states DMV gives you an approximate time for the last commit record.
  If the value for this column for a secondary replica database is subtracted from its
  primary replica counterpart, then you get an estimate of data loss that can occur if a
  forced failover is performed to that secondary replica.

Following is the script to find out how many seconds a SYNCHRONIZING replica is behind the primary replica.

```
WITH PR(database_id, last_commit_time) AS
(
SELECT dr_state.database_id as database_id,
dr_state.last_commit_time FROM
((sys.availability_groups AS ag JOIN sys.availability_replicas AS ar ON ag.group_id=ar.
group_id)
JOIN sys.dm_hadr_availability_replica_states AS ar_state ON ar.replica_id = ar_state.
replica_id)
JOIN sys.dm_hadr_database_replica_states dr_state on ag.group_id=dr_state.group_id and dr_
state.replica_id=ar_state.replica_id
WHERE ar_state.role=1
)
SELECT ar.replica_server_name AS 'Replica Instance', dr_state.database_id as 'Database ID',
DATEDIFF(s,dr_state.last_commit_time,PR.last_commit_time) AS 'Seconds Behind Primary'
  FROM ((sys.availability_groups AS ag JOIN sys.availability_replicas AS ar ON ag.group_id =
  ar.group_id)
JOIN sys.dm_hadr_availability_replica_states AS ar_state ON ar.replica_id = ar_state.
replica_id)
```

```
JOIN sys.dm_hadr_database_replica_states dr_state
ON ag.group_id = dr_state.group_id and dr_state.replica_id = ar_state.replica_id
JOIN PR ON PR.database_id=dr_state.database_id
WHERE ar_state.role!=1 and dr_state.synchronization_state=1
```

Figure 16-8 shows the results from the preceding SQL query.

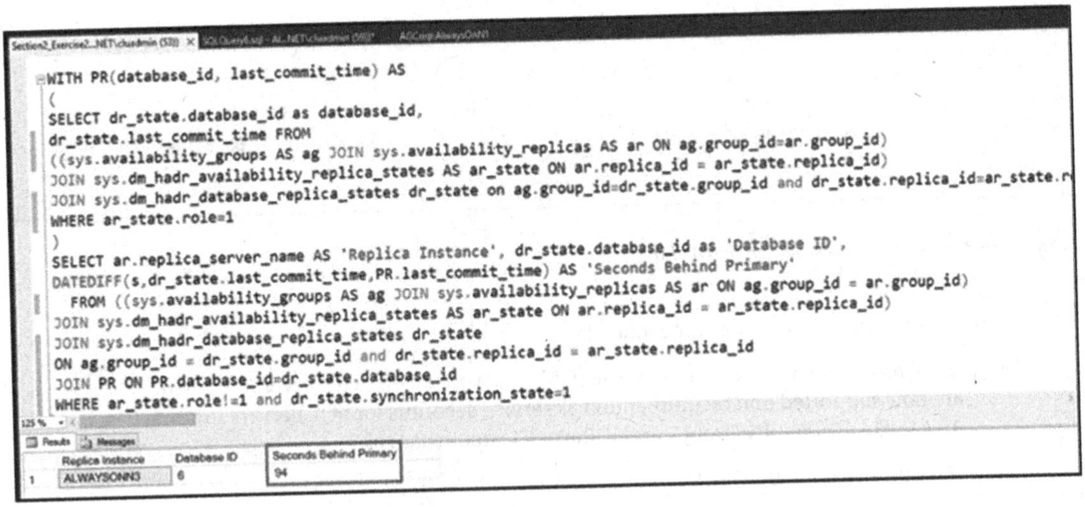

Figure 16-8. *Estimated data loss query result*

Common Failure Scenarios

Now let's take a look at some common failure scenarios and how to troubleshoot them.

Endpoint Connectivity Failure

For two replicas to connect to each other's database mirroring endpoint, the login account of each SQL instance requires access to the other instance. Also, each login account requires connect permission to the Database Mirroring endpoint of the other instance. If the permissions to the endpoint are insufficient, replicas cannot communicate with each other, resulting in connection handshake failure. When this happens, the Always On dashboard shows the replica state as "Disconnected." The SQL error log also shows the error message as shown in the figure below.

Figure 16-9 shows the error messages logged in the SQL error log due to insufficient service account permissions.

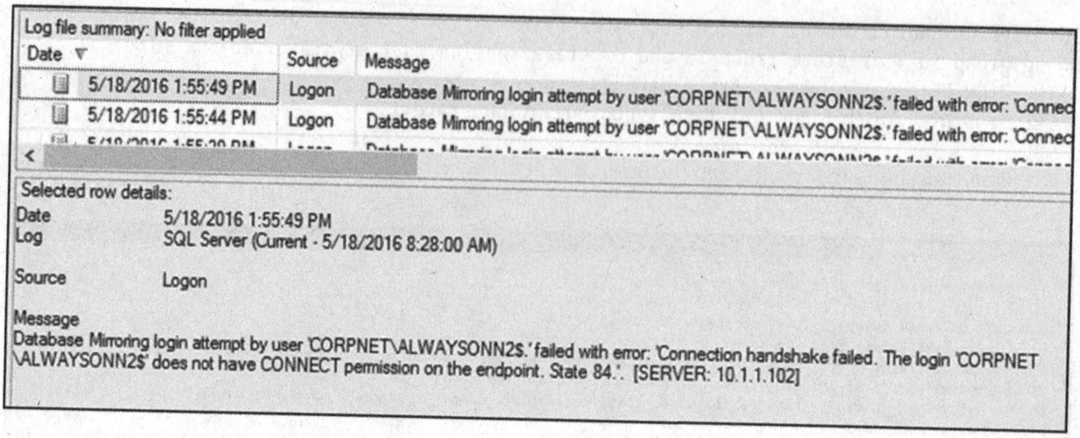

Figure 16-9. *Error message in SQL Error Log*

You can resolve this error in one of the following ways:

- Use Group Managed Service Accounts(GMSA) if you are on SQL Server 2016. They are now supported and recommended as service accounts for SQL Servers running Always On Availability Groups and Failover Cluster instances.

    GMSAs have the following benefits:

    - Domain-scoped and automatically managed service accounts
    - Automatic password rotation
    - Much more secure than regular domain accounts
    - Enables cross system security context

- In SQL 2012 and SQL 2014, as GMSAs are not supported, configure the replica SQL instances to run under the same domain user account. This user account will be automatically added to the master database in each SQL instance and granted CONNECT permissions. This will simplify the security configuration.

- If you need to run both SQL instances under different domain accounts for any reason, you then have to add each domain account as a login under the other SQL instance. You also need to manually grant this login CONNECT permissions to the database mirroring endpoin of the oher SQL Server instancet.

- If you are using non-domain accounts (local accounts or SIDs) as SQL service startup accounts, you must use certificates for the ENDPOINT authentication.

- If you are using Domain Independent availability groups in SQL Server 2016 then, synchronize the service accounts on all proposed cluster nodes. That means that there must be an account with the same name and the same password, on each node in the cluster. Certificates need to be used for ENDPOINT authentication.

Availability Group Creation Failure

A common error that can occur while attempting to create an availability group is "The connection to the primary replica is not active (35250)." The error can be seen on the last screen, when creating the availability group using the availability group wizard. The same error will also be logged in the SQL error log.

Figure 16-10 shows the error message generated while attempting to create an availability group.

> ↳ An exception occurred while executing a Transact-SQL statement or batch. (Microsoft.SqlServer.ConnectionInfo)
>
> ↳ The connection to the primary replica is not active. The command cannot be processed. (Microsoft SQL Server, Error: 35250)

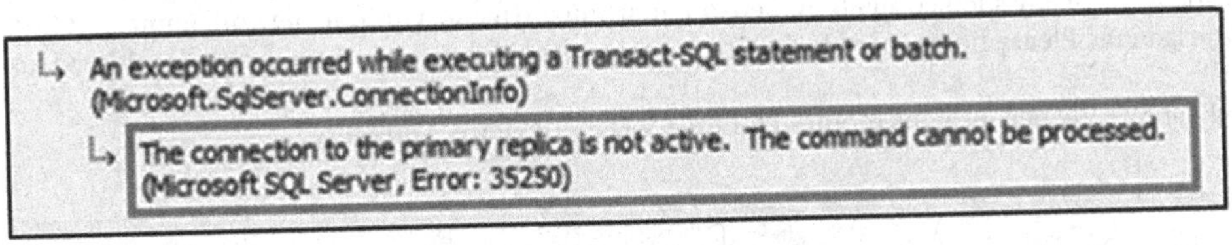

Figure 16-10. Error message while creating availability group

The following steps can be taken to resolve this error:

- **Create an inbound rule on each replica to open this port:**

  Inbound traffic to TCP port 5022 may be blocked by either windows firewall and/ or any external firewall between replicas. Traffic must be allowed on this port in order for the primary and secondary replica to communicate with each other during and after availability group creation.

- **Create and start database mirroring endpoint, if not done already:**

  Also, ensure that sufficient permissions are granted to the SQL service accounts on the endpoint. In addition, check SQL Server log to ensure that SQL Server is listening on port 5022 (or any other port being used for database mirroring endpoint).

Figure 16-11 shows the message logged in the SQL error log due to firewall restrictions on the database mirroring port.

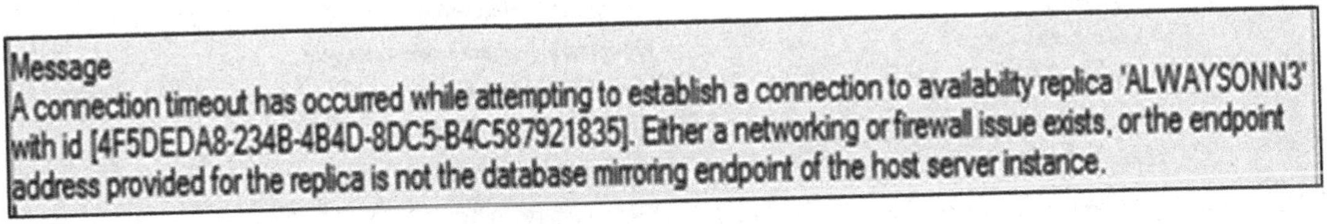

> Message
> A connection timeout has occurred while attempting to establish a connection to availability replica 'ALWAYSONN3' with id [4F5DEDA8-234B-4B4D-8DC5-B4C587921835]. Either a networking or firewall issue exists, or the endpoint address provided for the replica is not the database mirroring endpoint of the host server instance.

Figure 16-11. Error message in SQL Error Log

Listener Creation Failure

When you create an availability group listener thru SQL Server, it is creating a *client access point* (CAP) in the windows failover cluster. A CAP includes network name and associated IP address. Listener creation may fail due to issues at the windows failover cluster level.

Each network name being created in windows failover cluster is associated with a *Virtual Computer Object* (VCO) in Active Directory. If VCO with the same name already exists in an active directory, it will be used at the time of creation of the listener. If it does not exist, then *Computer Name Object* (CNO) will attempt to create it in the default computers OU (this is true even if CNO is in a different OU). If the CNO does not have appropriate permissions to the computer OU, the listener creation will fail.

To resolve this issue, either pre-stage the VCO in the computers OU or grant the following permissions to the CNO in the computers OU:

- Read all properties

- Create Computer objects

The listener creation may also fail if the same name and/or IP addresses are being used elsewhere in the same network. Resolve any such conflicts and ensure that you are using a unique network name and IP addresses for the listener. Please note that only the first 15 characters of the network name are considered for uniqueness.

Figure 16-12 shows the permissions required for the CNO in the Active Directory.

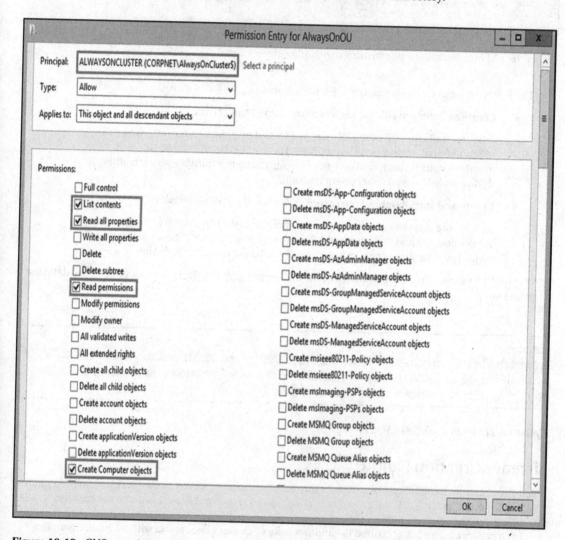

Figure 16-12. *CNO permissions*

Failover Troubleshooting

Availability groups can be configured for automatic or manual failover. Automatic failovers are triggered if a health issue is detected on the primary replica. Not all failovers might work as expected. Let's take a look at some common failover scenarios.

Automatic Failover Didn't Work

When an automatic failover is triggered on the primary replica, it may not be successful for multiple reasons. When the secondary replica fails to successfully transition to the primary role, the replica goes into the RESOLVING state and the databases report that they are in the *NOT SYNCHRONIZING* state. Hence applications will not be able to access these databases.

Following are some of the common reasons for an unsuccessful failover:

- Database synchronization state

  For an availability group to automatically fail over, all databases participating in the availability group must be in a SYNCHRONIZED state between the primary replica and the secondary replica. This synchronization condition must be met in order to make sure that there is no data loss. Hence, automatic failover will not successfully transition the secondary replica into the primary role if any one of the databases participating in the availability group is in the SYNCHRONIZING or NOT SYNCHORNIZING state.

■ **Note** Failover readiness of an availability group can be determined by querying the "is_failover_ready" column of the sys.dm_hadr_database_replica_cluster_states DMV.

Here is the SQL script to check for failover readiness of replicas:

```
Select rs.replica_server_name, r.role_desc,s.database_name, s.is_failover_ready
From sys.dm_hadr_database_replica_cluster_states s
inner join sys.dm_hadr_avalability_replica_states r on s.replica_id = r.replica_id
inner join sys.dm_hadr_availability_replica_cluster_states rs on rs.replica_id = s.replica_id
```

Figure 16-13 shows the failover readiness state of various replicas. In the below example, AlwaysOnN2 is ready for failover. However, AlwaysOnN3 replica is not.

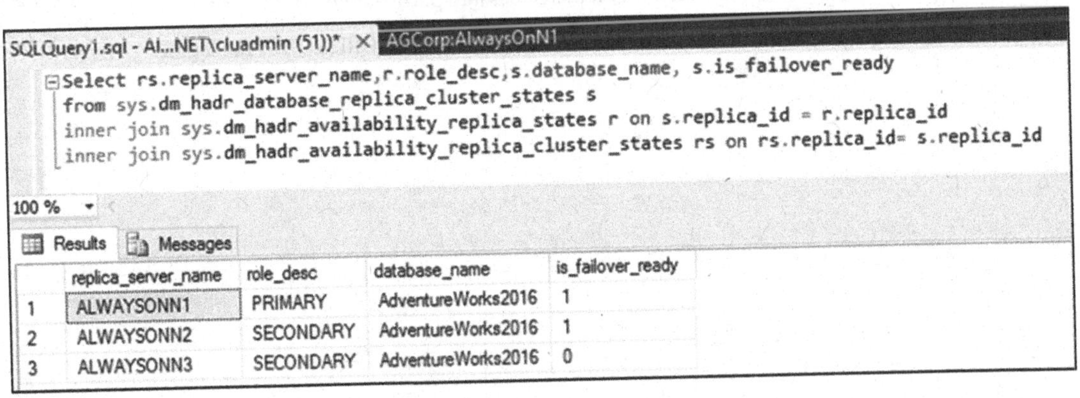

Figure 16-13. Query to check failover readiness of replicas

- No secondary replicas configured for automatic failover

  If none of the synchronous secondary replicas are configured for automatic failover then the availability group will not attempt a failover when a helth issue is detected on the primary. This could cause the database in the availability group to be unavailable to the users for read/write transactions. Hence ensure that automatic failover is enabled on the synchronous secondary repilicas.

■ **Note**   Prior to SQL 2016, only one out of the two synchronous replicas could be configured for automatic failover. Starting with SQL Server 2016, both synchronous secondary replicas can be configured as automatic failover partners with the primary replica. Even if one failover partner is lost, high availability can still be maintained in this case.

- SYSTEM account permissions

  To monitor health, the SQL Server resource DLL makes a connection to the primary replica by using ODBC and it uses the local SQL Server NT AUTHORITY\SYSTEM account logon credentials for the connection. This login account, by default, has the following permissions:

  - Alter Any availability group

  - Connect SQL

  - Create Availability Group

  - View Any Database

  - View server state

  If this account does not have any of these permissions on the automatic failover partner, that is, the secondary replica, then SQL Server cannot start health detection when an automatic failover occurs. Therefore, the secondary replica cannot transition to the primary role. To troubleshoot this issue, review the Windows cluster log. Errors like "failed to execute availability group command stored procedure" or "cannot alter the availability group... you do not have permission" will be logged. Review the permissions for the NT AUTHORITY\SYSTEM account to make sure that it has necessary permissions.

  Figure 16-14 shows the effective permissions of the NT AUTHORITY\SYSTEM login.

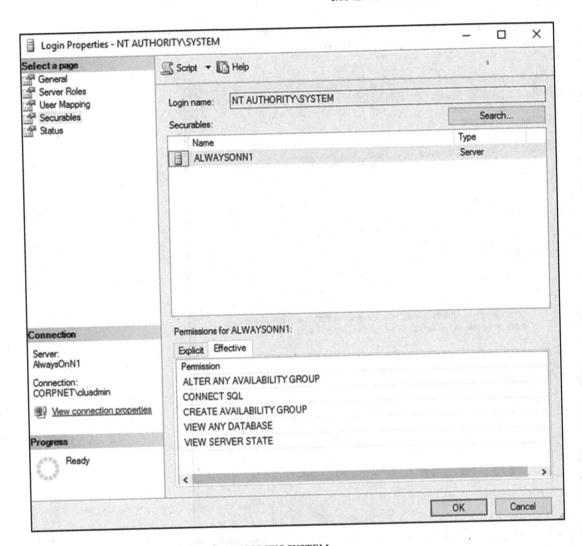

Figure 16-14. Login properties of NT AUTHORITY\SYSTEM

- Failover property value for "Maximum Failures in the Specified Period"

  This property is used to avoid the indefinite movement of a clustered resource when multiple node failures occur. By default, this is set to N-1, where N is the number of nodes in the cluster. If there are more failures than what is specified by this value, in a specific amount of time (6 hours by default), the resource will stay failed. This value can be manually adjusted. To check for this condition, review the cluster log and search for "failovercount" string.

■ **Note** Before you tweak this value, try to fix the underlying cause for the failover. Increasing this value may only cause the availability group to fail more times before transitioning to a failed state.

Figure 16-15 shows the availability group cluster resource property. In a three-node cluster the maximum failures in the specified period would be two.

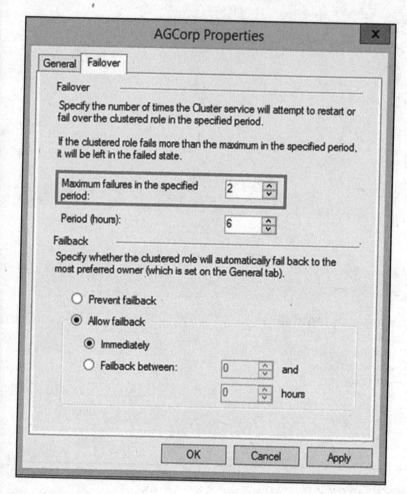

Figure 16-15. *Maximum failure in the specified period*

When to Force a Failover?

There might be situations where you have to force a failover. Let's look at some of the common scenarios that might need you to force a failover:

- Lost Cluster Quorum

  Quorum is required to keep the cluster up and running. If a catastrophic event like a datacenter failure occurs and it simultaneously brings down the majority of clustered nodes, then the entire cluster will go down due to loss of quorum. The availability groups will go into the RESOLVING state. The cluster log on the surviving node will have an error event logged for "lost quorum (status = 5925)."

The quorum needs to be reestablished or the quorum might need to be forced on the surviving nodes to bring the availability group back into the healthy state.

To force quorum, run the following PowerShell command:

```
Start Cluster-Node -FQ
```

Once the cluster quorum is forced, you will need to force the failover of availability group accepting data loss.

Figure 16-16 shows the command to force quorum in the case where the cluster quorum is lost.

```
Administrator: Windows PowerShell
PS C:\Windows\system32>
PS C:\Windows\system32> Start-ClusterNode -FQ

Name                    ID    State
----                    --    -----
ALWAYSONN3              2     Joining

PS C:\Windows\system32> _
```

Figure 16-16. *Force cluster quorum*

- Primary Replica unavailable

  If the primary replica goes down abruptly, and if there are no failover-ready secondary replicas, then the availability group on the secondary replicas goes into the RESOLVING state. If the primary replica cannot be brought up in a timely manner, the only option available is to force the failover to one of the surviving secondary replicas.

- No Synchronized Secondary

  If there is no synchronized secondary available, either because the availability mode of all secondary replicas is set to asynchronous-commit, or if the synchronization state of a synchronous secondary is SYNCHRONIZING at the time of a failover, then the only available option is to force a failover allowing data loss.

  Figure 16-17 shows the Always On dashboard with the secondary replicas in synchronizing state.

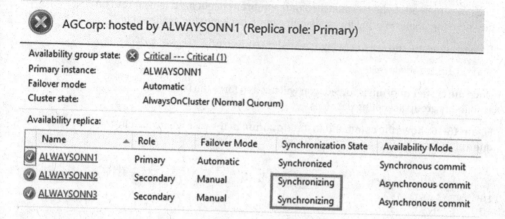

Figure 16-17. *Secondary replicas in Synchronizing state*

What Caused an Unexpected Failover?

- Network Connectivity issues

  Network connectivity issues between replicas is one of the common reason for unexpected failovers. WSFC depends on the heartbeat signals over the network to identify the availability of a node. If a network issue causes the heartbeats to miss more than a predefined threshold, this will trigger a failover of all resources owned by a node.

  To avoid these types of failovers, ensure that the network is stable, NIC drivers are up-to-date, and tune Receive Side Scaling (RSS)/TCP Chimney offload settings as per recommendations.

■ **Note** Information on the TCP Chimney Offload, Receive Side Scaling can be found in this KB article - http://support.microsoft.com/kb/951037.

Also consider tuning the cluster heartbeat settings. There are two settings that affect cluster heartbeat and health detection between nodes (i.e., delay and threshold).

Delay defines the frequency at which cluster heartbeats are sent between nodes.

Threshold defines the number of heartbeats that are missed before the cluster takes recovery action.

Table 16-1 shows the default and maxium values for the delay and threshold parameters in the same subnet, cross subnet and cross site for Windows Server 2012 R2 and Windows Server 2016.

Table 16-1. *Cluster Heartbeat default values and the maximums*

Parameter	Win2012 R2	Win2016	Maximum
SameSubnetDelay	1 second	1 second	2 seconds
SameSubnetThreshold	5 heartbeats	10 heartbeats	120 heartbeats
CrossSubnetDelay	1 second	1 seconds	4 seconds
CrossSubnetThreshold	5 heartbeats	20 heartbeats	120 heartbeats
CrossSiteDelay	NA	1 second	4 seconds
CrossSiteThreshold	NA	20 heartbeats	120 heartbeats

Figure 16-18 shows the command to view current heartbeat configuration values.

```
PS C:\> get-cluster | fl *subnet*

CrossSubnetDelay          : 1000
CrossSubnetThreshold      : 20
PlumbAllCrossSubnetRoutes : 0
SameSubnetDelay           : 1000
SameSubnetThreshold       : 10
```

Figure 16-18. *View current heartbeat configuration values*

■ **Note**   To be more tolerant of transient failures it is recommended on Win2008 / Win2008 R2 / Win2012 / Win2012 R2 to increase the SameSubnetThreshold and CrossSubnetThreshold values to the higher Win2016 values.

Figure 16-19 shows the command to change the heartbeat configuration values.

```
PS C:\> (get-cluster).SameSubnetThreshold = 20
PS C:\> get-cluster | fl *subnet*

CrossSubnetDelay          : 1000
CrossSubnetThreshold      : 20
PlumbAllCrossSubnetRoutes : 0
SameSubnetDelay           : 1000
SameSubnetThreshold       : 20
```

Figure 16-19. *Change heartbeat configuration values*

- System unhealthy event

  Availability group resource DLL monitors sp_server_diagnostics output to identify any unhealthy events. By default, the failure condition level of availability group resource is set to 3, which means that it will initiate a failover if there are any critical system events detected by the sp_server_diagnostics.

- Lease Timeout Expired

  The lease is a standard signaling mechanism between the SQL Server resource DLL and the availability group and is used to prevent split-brain from occurring for the availability group. The Least Timeout value defines this signaling interval. If the Least Timeout is exceeded without the signal exchange, then the lease is declared as Expired and the SQL Server resource DLL reports that the availability group no longer looks alive to the WSFC manager. The cluster manager then undertakes the configured corrective actions, which may include failover.

  Figure 16-20 shows the availability group resource properties. LeaseTimeout is set to 20 seconds by default.

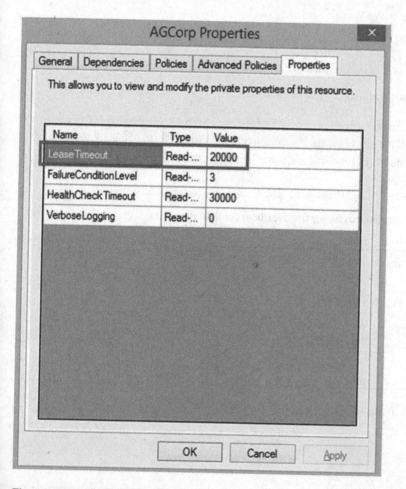

Figure 16-20. *LeaseTimeout setting*

Connectivity Failure

Following are some connectivity scenarios that you may encounter.

Listener Connection Fails

When you try to connect to the availability group using the Listener, your connection may fail. The following are some possible causes and their resolutions:

- **Cause:** The login for the listener does not exist on the primary replica instance.

  Resolution: Ensure that the login is created on the primary replica instance. If the availability group had failed over earlier, ensure that the login was transferred to the new primary replica instance. Alternately use contained database authentication if the replica database that you are trying to connect to is a Contained Database.

- **Cause:** The listener port was not specified during login

  Resolution: The availability group listener cannot use the SQL Browser service to resolve the listener name. If the listener was created with a non-default port, specify the port after the listener name when you try to connect to it.

- **Cause:** The listener connection timed out

  Resolution: If the availability group is spread over multiple subnets and if it was failed over from the primary replica to a secondary replica in another subnet, then the listener name may resolve to an IP address from a different subnet and connection to the IP address may time out. If supported by the client, set the MultiSubnetFailover parameter to true in the connection string. If you are connecting to the listener over a legacy client, set the RegisterAllProviderIPs value to 0 for the listener network name resource.

■ **Note** Always On availability groups set the Listener cluster resource RegisterAllProvidersIP property to 1 by default. .NET Framework 4.6.1 provides faster availability group connection by including "MultiSubnetFailover=True" in connection strings by default.

Read-Only Routing Fails

When you try to connect to a secondary replica instance using read-only routing, it may fail. If it does, ensure that the following prerequisites and recommendations are applied:

- Ensure that the routing list is configured and has an entry for the current primary replica instance.

- Ensure that the routing URLs are configured with the correct server name / IP address and port number.

- Ensure that the routing list for the current primary replica has at least one secondary replica that is in a healthy state and has its "Readable Secondary" value set to Yes or ReadIntentOnly.

- Connect to the listener, if the listener is configured with a non-default port, then specify the port number in the connection string.

- Add the ApplicationIntent=ReadOnly connection parameter in the connection string.

- Add the "Initial Catalog" or "Database" connection parameter and set its value to any replica database for that availability group.

- Ensure that the login that you are using in the connection string exists on the secondary replica instance that the listener will route you to.

- If the availability group is spread over multiple subnets, ensure that the "MultiSubnetFailover=True" parameter is specified in the connection string.

Transaction Log Growing Scenario

In a production environment with a high workload, it is possible for the transaction log to grow and fill up the disk. If the transaction log belongs to a replica database, the following actions can be taken to troubleshoot the transaction log growth and get the database back to a healthy state:

- Check the Log_Reuse_wait_Desc column from the sys.databases catalog view. If the value is not "AVAILABILITY REPLICA" then it means that something else is holding the transaction log from reusing the inactive portion of the log. Take appropriate action based on the value. For example, if the value is LOG_BACKUP, take a transaction log backup of the replica database and rerun the catalog view.

- If the value is "AVAILABILITY REPLICA," then check if all the secondary replicas are online. If there are one or more offline replicas, try to bring them online. If they fail to come online, consider removing them from the availability group.

- If all the replicas are online, check to see if they are connected to the primary replica. If they are not, investigate the disconnected replica(s).

- If all the replicas are connected, check their health state. For a synchronous-commit replica, the state should be SYNCHRONIZED and for an asynchronous-commit replica, the state should be SYNCHRONIZING. If there is an unhealthy replica, investigate it further. If the synchronization is suspended on that replica, try to resume the synchronization. If it cannot be resumed, consider removing the database from that replica.

- If all the replicas are healthy, check to see if one of the replicas is showing a high value for "Estimated Data Loss." If a replica is showing a high value for "Estimated Data Loss" compared to the baseline, then it means that the replica is falling behind in hardening the log blocks and sending the confirmations back to the primary replica. This could be caused by latency issue (disk, network, etc.) or a high read workload. Consider reducing the workload on the secondary replica or adding additional resources after further troubleshooting.

- If the "Estimated Data Loss" value is close to the baseline (or lower), this could mean that the primary replica may have latency issues or a high workload. Consider reducing the workload on the primary replica or adding additional resources after further troubleshooting.

Figure 16-21 shows the workflow to troubleshoot transaction log growing scenario.

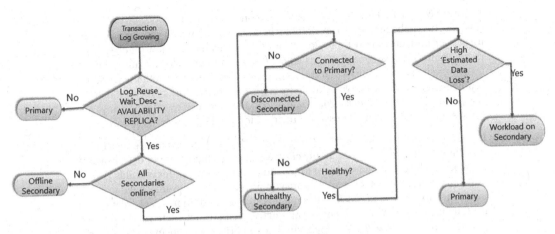

Figure 16-21. *Transaction Log growing scenario troubleshooting workflow*

Secondary Replica Falling Behind Primary Scenario

It is possible for a secondary replica to fall significantly behind the primary replica in terms of the transaction log blocks hardened. This can be observed by checking for a high value for the "Estimated Data Loss" column on the dashboard.

This has a direct impact on the RPO for the availability group in the event of a disaster.

The following actions can be taken to troubleshoot a secondary replica falling behind the primary replica:

- Check if the secondary replica is online and connected to the primary replica. If it is not, troubleshoot the secondary to see why it is offline or disconnected from the primary replica.

- If the secondary replica is online and connected to the primary, check if it is falling behind due to network latency between the primary and secondary replica. You can check for this by comparing the Bytes Sent to Replica/sec and Bytes Received from Replica/sec PerfMon counters (from the SQLServer:Availability Replica object) on the primary and secondary replicas. If they differ by a significant amount, troubleshoot for network latency. If the secondary replica is synchronous-commit, you may want to consider changing it to asynchronous-commit mode while you troubleshoot the network for latency.

- If there are no signs of network latency between the primary and secondary replicas, check if the primary replica is holding back the transactions log blocks by performing flow control. A primary replica performs flow control if a secondary replica fails to send acknowledgements for a certain number of messages received for the whole replica and also per database. In such case, primary replica only sends the next log blocks if the number of acknowledged messages drops below the threshold.

- There are two useful PerfMon counters, Flow control/sec and Flow Control Time (ms/sec) (from the SQLServer:Availability Replica object), which show you, within the last second, how many times flow control was activated and how much time was spent waiting on flow control. If the value for these counters is significantly above the baseline values, it may mean that the secondary is overwhelmed with the workload it is processing. In such case, you should troubleshoot the secondary to see if there are any performance bottlenecks. You could also reduce the read workload (if any) on the secondary replica and if possible provide additional resources to the secondary.

- If you do not see the flow control getting activated, check the primary replica for unusually high activity. Examples of activities causing a high number of transaction log blocks to be generated and sent to secondary replicas are index rebuilds, bulk operations, etc. If such activities are going on primary, they may need to be postponed to off-peak hours. If that is not possible then additional resources may need to be provided so that the environment can sustain such high workload. Before doing so, ensure that the high workload on primary is causing other secondary replicas to also fall behind the primary replica. If that is not the case, then troubleshoot the secondary replica in question further.

- If the primary replica doesn't show any unusually high activity, troubleshoot the secondary replica in question further with regards to performance bottleneck.

Figure 16-22 shows the workflow to troubleshoot secondary falling behind primary scenario.

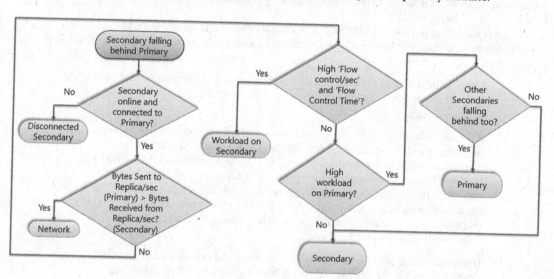

Figure 16-22. *Secondary falling behind primary scenario troubleshooting workflow*

Replica in Resolving State Scenario

A secondary replica may show up to be in Resolving state. Following are the scenarios during when this may happen:

- After an unsuccessful automatic failover – If the primary replica becomes unhealthy and the availability group does not failover automatically to a secondary replica, the secondary replicas show their state as Resolving. The secondary replicas revert back to their original state when either the primary replica becomes healthy again or the availability group is failed over to a secondary replica. The reasons for unsuccessful automatic failovers have been discussed earlier in this chapter.

- In the middle of an automatic failover – While an automatic failover of an availability group is in progress, all the secondary replicas (except the failover target) transition to a resolving state. As soon as the failover completes, they connect with the new primary replica and revert to their original state.

Summary

In this chapter we covered some of the common availability group failures and performance issues and how to go about troubleshooting them. In the next chapter we will take a look at Microsoft Azure.

PART VII

Availability Groups in Microsoft Azure

CHAPTER 17

■ ■ ■

Introduction to Microsoft Azure

So far in this book, we have discussed deploying SQL Server Always On Availability Groups that run on-premises in your organization. There are situations wherein you are unable to satisfy all the high availability (HA) and disaster recovery (DR) requirements and meet the service-level agreement (SLA) that the business unit requires for the SQL Server applications. In this chapter, we introduce you to Microsoft Azure, which assists you in meeting all the HADR requirements and stay within budget by deploying Always On Availability Groups as a hybrid solution or an Azure-only solution. In a hybrid environment, part of the availability group solution runs on-premises and the rest runs in Azure. In an Azure-only solution, the entire availability group runs in Microsoft Azure.

What Is Microsoft Azure?

Microsoft Azure is a public cloud computing platform and infrastructure created by Microsoft for building, deploying, and managing applications and services through a global network of Microsoft-managed datacenters.

■ **Note**   Azure was released as Windows Azure in February 2010 and was renamed Microsoft Azure in March 2014.

Microsoft Azure offers a collection of services that any organization can use or leverage for their IT solutions like file servers, database servers, virtual machines, web apps, etc., in their public cloud offering. Public cloud is cloud services that are available to anyone via the public Internet. The services are located all over the globe through Microsoft-managed global datacenters. You might be wondering why you need a public cloud when a private cloud can be created relatively easily.

Why Use Microsoft Azure?

Microsoft Azure has a lot of advantages, as depicted in Figure 17-1.

© Uttam Parui and Vivek Sanil 2016
U. Parui and V. Sanil, *Pro SQL Server Always On Availability Groups*, DOI 10.1007/978-1-4842-2071-9_17

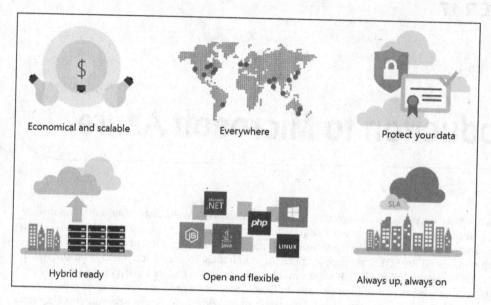

Figure 17-1. Advantages of Microsoft Azure

One of the biggest advantages is that Microsoft Azure allows you to perform virtually any compute or data storage operation by provisioning and scaling the necessary resources *on demand* and *on a pay-as-you-go basis*. Microsoft Azure not only allows you to scale your services dynamically to handle the increased demand that you may run into unexpectedly, it also involves descaling your services when demands shrink or traffic patterns slow down. It allows for immediate provisioning and de-provisioning and you have to pay only for what you use.

Microsoft Azure offers a world-wide solution. At the time of writing this chapter, Microsoft Azure has datacenters that operate in 24 regions around the world which is more than the other hyperscale cloud service providers (CSPs) Amazon Web Services (AWS), and Google Cloud combined. This allows us to deliver our services in a fast, low-latency fashion no matter where our customers are. It exposes the services to anyone anywhere they need to work from or anywhere they need to access the services from.

■ **Note**   Microsoft Azure is the first multinational cloud provider in mainland China.

You may be thinking, "All this is good, but is my data safe in the cloud?" In fact, this is one of the most frequently asked questions by our customers who are thinking of leveraging the cloud features. Microsoft Azure leads the industry in protecting the privacy of your data. It was the first CSP to adopt ISO 27018 that is the new international standard for cloud privacy. Also, it was the first CSP to be recognized by European Union's data protection authorities for its commitment to comply with rigorous EU privacy laws.

Another common question that we often get is, "We have made a big investment on our on-premises datacenters. Can we still use our resources in our on-premises datacenters and leverage the cloud?" Microsoft Azure is hybrid ready. It can seamlessly connect to your existing IT environment so that you can leverage the resources in your datacenters and within Microsoft Azure itself. You can use a wide set of hybrid connections, for example virtual private networks (VPNs), ExpressRoute connections, content delivery networks (CDNs), to ensure performance and ease of use.

Microsoft Azure is an open and flexible CSP. It supports the broadest selection of devices, operating systems, databases, programming languages, frameworks, and tools. It supports the same technologies most businesses trust and use today, including Windows, Linux, virtual machines and containers, and Active directory. This means you can use what you already know and there's no steep learning curve with Microsoft Azure.

Microsoft Azure offers enterprise grade SLAs on services, 24/7 tech support, and round-the-clock health monitoring. This is the reason more than 66% of Fortune 500 companies rely on Microsoft Azure. The web site https://azure.microsoft.com/en-us/support/legal/sla/ describes Microsoft's commitments for uptime and connectivity and lists the SLA for individual services.

■ **Note** Microsoft Azure is recognized by Gartner, a leading independent research firm, as a leader across six of their Magic Quadrants for enterprise cloud workloads for the second consecutive year. Visit https://azure.microsoft.com/en-us/campaigns/magic-quadrant/ to view Gartner's Magic Quadrant reports.

IaaS, PaaS, and SaaS

Microsoft Azure's compute offerings fall into three main categories

- *Infrastructure as a Service (IaaS),*

- *Platform as a Service (PaaS), and*

- *Software as a Service (SaaS).*

Figure 17-2 gives us a side-by-side view of each of these offerings compared to the on-premises model that you are already familiar with.

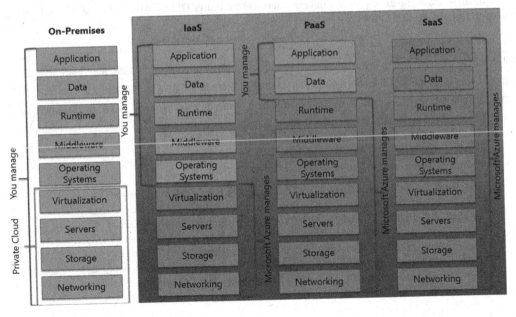

Figure 17-2. *What is IaaS, PaaS, and SaaS?*

In a traditional on-premises environment, you manage, own, and are responsible for everything from networking up through the applications. Private cloud is the first evolution wherein you automate and own the resources from virtualization down to the networking. This allows you to take the most advantage of the resources you have, control them in ways you can, and reallocate them in the best possible way.

The next evolution is the *Infrastructure as a Service (IaaS)*. IaaS looks into the pieces that can be automated and moves them over to Microsoft Azure. Microsoft Azure takes responsibility of the networking, storage, servers, and virtualization components. In short, IaaS gives you a server in the cloud (virtual machine). This frees up your time and allows you to work on the more important tasks like making sure that the applications are functioning correctly. You have complete control and are responsible for managing everything from the operating system on up to the application you are running. Some typical scenarios that organizations use IaaS for include testing and development, web site hosting, storage, backup and recovery, web apps, high-performance computing, and big data analysis.

The next evolution is the *Platform as a Service (PaaS)*. Here you focus only on application and data, that is, the things that really generate revenue for the business and let Microsoft Azure manage the other components starting from networking up through the runtime. PaaS is a complete development and deployment environment in the cloud that allows us to deliver everything from a simple cloud-based application to a sophisticated, cloud-based enterprise application. Like IaaS, PaaS includes infrastructure (storage, servers) and networking and also operating system, middleware, development tools, database management systems, business intelligence (BI) services, and more. This allows you to avoid the expense and complexity of buying and managing the infrastructure, software licenses, middleware, development tools, and more. It allows you to manage the applications and services and Microsoft Azure manages everything else. Some typical scenarios that organizations use PaaS for include development framework and analytics or business intelligence.

The next evolution is the *Software as a Service (SaaS)* where you let Microsoft Azure manage everything right from the networking layer up to the application layer. SaaS allows users to connect to and use cloud-based applications over the Internet. SaaS provides a complete software solution that you can purchase on as pay-as-you-go basis from a CSP. You rent the application for your organization, and your users connect to it over the Internet. This allows your organization to get quickly up and running with an application at minimal upfront costs. Some examples of SaaS are Microsoft Exchange Online, Microsoft SharePoint Online, and Microsoft Dynamics CRM Online.

■ **Note** You do not have to use these offerings in isolation. You can combine IaaS, PaaS, and SaaS. You can also combine your on-premises IT infrastructure with Microsoft Azure to create a hybrid solution. This enables you to meet unique and diverse business needs by combining on-premises and cloud-hosted deployments, while using the same set of servers, tools, and expertise across these environments.

Microsoft Azure has two options for hosting SQL Server workloads:

- *SQL Server on Azure virtual machines (IaaS)* – As the name suggests, here SQL Server is installed on Microsoft Azure virtual machines hosted in the cloud. This falls into the industry category IaaS. Microsoft provides an availability SLA of 99.95% that covers just the VM. This SLA does not cover the processes such as SQL Server running on the VM and requires that you host at least two VM instances in an availability set. For SQL Server HA within VMs, you should configure one of the supported HA options in SQL Server, such as Always On Availability Groups as discussed in detail in chapter 18.

- *Azure SQL Database (PaaS)* – It's a relational database-as-a-service (DBaaS) hosted in Microsoft Azure cloud. It falls into the industry categories of PaaS and is optimized for SaaS app development. The database software is automatically configured, patched, and upgraded by Microsoft, which reduces your administration costs. For SQL Database Basic, Standard and Premier service tiers, Microsoft provides an availability SLA of 99.99%. There is a small subset of SQL Server features that are not available with Azure SQL Database. For more information, refer to Microsoft article title "Azure SQL Database General Limitations and Guidelines" at https://azure.microsoft.com/en-us/documentation/articles/sql-database-general-limitations/.

How to Start Using Microsoft Azure

In order to start using Microsoft Azure, you will need to have a subscription and create an Azure account. Here are the options to create an Azure account at the time of writing this chapter:

1. Start a '30-day Azure free trial' at https://azure.microsoft.com/en-us/free/. During this trial, subscribers get up to $200 of Azure credit.

2. Use your MSDN subscriber benefits. If you have a Visual Studio Professional with MSDN subscription, you will get $50 in free Azure usage credits per month. Those with Visual Studio Premium with MSDN subscription get $100 in credits, and those with Visual Studio Ultimate with MSDN subscription get $150 in credits. These monthly figures add up to $600 per year, $1,200 per year, and $1,800 per year, respectively. Let's take an example to illustrate how the benefits could be used for development and testing. A developer with a Premium-level MSDN subscription and $100 in Azure credits can run three virtual machines for 16 hours per day or can use 80 virtual machines for a 20-hour load test.

3. Buy a subscription. They are multiple ways to buy Azure services as detailed at the Microsoft Pricing site at https://azure.microsoft.com/en-us/pricing/purchase-options/.

Summary

In this chapter, we introduced you to Microsoft Azure and discussed the three main categories of Microsoft Azure compute offerings, namely, Infrastructure as a Service (IaaS), Platform as a Service (PaaS), and Software as a Service (SaaS). We also discussed the options to host SQL Server workloads using Microsoft Azure. In the next chapter we will help you get started with Microsoft Azure for your Always On Availability Groups deployment.

CHAPTER 18

■ ■ ■

Availability Groups in Microsoft Azure

Always On Availability Groups on Microsoft Azure can be created manually or by using the Microsoft Azure Marketplace image. Azure Marketplace provides preconfigured templates for software deployment in Azure. It automates the deployment of an SQL Server Always On Availability Group for high availability of SQL Server. It provisions two SQL Server replicas (primary and secondary) and one witness file share in a Windows Cluster. It also provisions two Domain Controller replicas (primary and secondary). In addition, it configures an availability group listener for clients to connect to the primary SQL Server replica.

This template deploys an Always On Availability Group such that after deployment is complete, the user has a fully available availability group. The template implements performance, security, and availability best practices. This template is called SQL Server Always On Cluster. The name is misleading as it gives the impression that you would be installing an SQL Cluster. However, the fact is that this template would deploy Always On Availability Groups for you in Microsoft Azure. The Always On label for the clustering and availability group technology has already caused a lot of confusion and calling the availability groups deployment template on Azure as an Always On cluster just adds to the confusion. Let's walk through the steps for deploying availability groups on Azure using the Marketplace image.

Step 1: Select Template

Using your Internet browser, navigate to http://portal.azure.com. You will be prompted to sign in using a valid Azure account. Once logged in, click on the "+ New" option in the left navigation pane on the screen.

Figure 18-1 shows the portal.azure.com web site. Once you click on the "+ New" option, the New blade opens up with the search bar. Type in SQL Always On and then hit enter.

© Uttam Parui and Vivek Sanil 2016
U. Parui and V. Sanil, *Pro SQL Server Always On Availability Groups*, DOI 10.1007/978-1-4842-2071-9_18

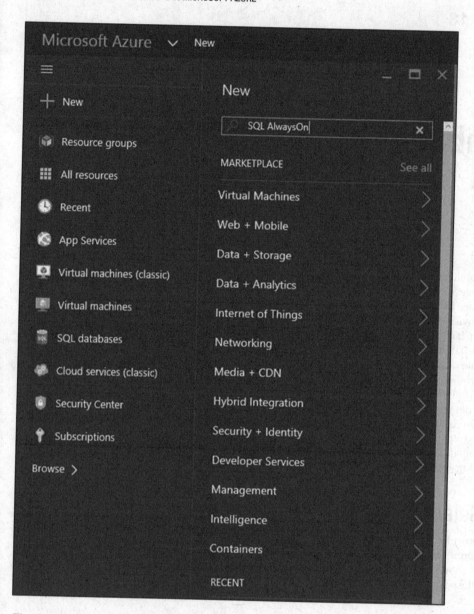

Figure 18-1. *SQL Always On search in Azure Marketplace*

Figure 18-2 shows the SQL Server Always On Cluster template that shows up in the search results.

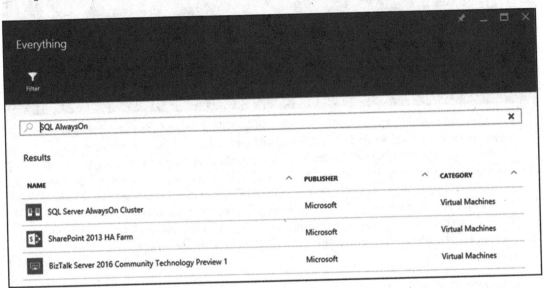

Figure 18-2. *Always On Dashboard*

Select the SQL Server Always On Cluster template.
Figure 18-3 shows the SQL Server Always On Cluster configuration wizard.

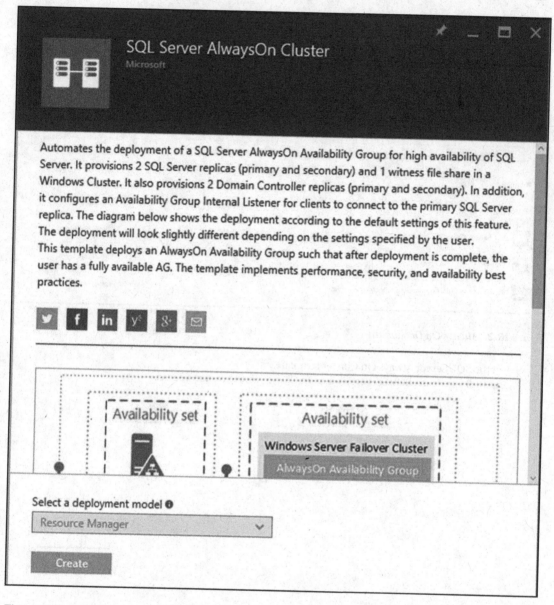

Figure 18-3. SQL Always On Availability Groups deployment configuration wizard

Resource Group: It is a container that holds related resources for an application. It helps you to deploy, manage, and monitor all of the resources for your solution as a group, rather than handling these resources individually. So this new availability group deployment will be grouped under a resource group. Later on, you will have the option of specifying a new resource group or an existing resource group.

> ■ **Note** Resource Manager is the recommended deployment model for new virtual machines. The SQL Server Always On Cluster deployment template does not allow you to change the deployment model and uses resource manager as the default.

Next let's review the availability group setup configuration.

Figure 18-4 shows the deployment according to the default settings of this feature. The deployment will look slightly different depending on the settings specified by the user.

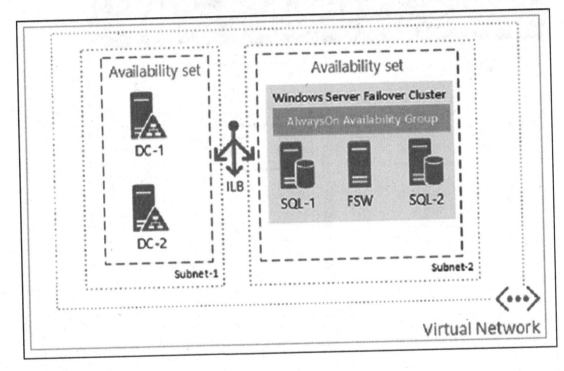

Figure 18-4. *SQL Always On Availability Groups deployment*

Availability Set: During downtime such as maintenance, an availability set helps keep the virtual machines available. When two or more similarly configured virtual machines are placed in an availability set, it creates the redundancy needed to maintain availability of the applications or services that the virtual machine runs. For example, in this availability group deployment, DC1 and DC2 are placed in one Availability Set, whereas SQL 1, SQL 2 and the File share witness are placed in another. Hence during maintenance, DC1 and DC2 will not be unavailable at the same time; likewise SQL 1, SQL 2, and FSW will not be down at the same time.

Internal Load Balancer (ILB): The availability group listener name is mapped to a load-balanced IP address and Azure's load balancer directs the incoming traffic to only the primary server in the replica set. The ILB can only be accessed by resources inside the cloud service or via VPN that connects to the Azure infrastructure. This enables internal applications to run in Azure and be accessed within the cloud or from on-premises.

After reviewing the deployment architecture, click on Create.

Step 2: Configure Basic Settings

The portal opens the basic setting configuration blade. Provide the Administrator user name, password, select subscription and location, and provide the new or existing resource group name.

Figure 18-5 shows the basics blade.

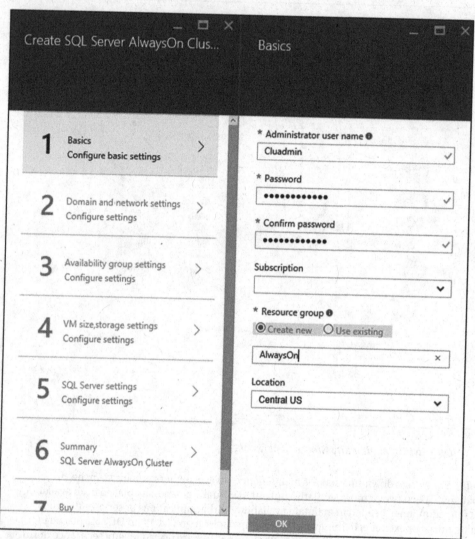

Figure 18-5. *Configure basic settings*

■ **Note**   The administrator account will be for all the virtual machines. It will also be the domain administrator for the new domain deployment.

Using a new resource group is helpful if you are just testing or learning about SQL Server deployments in Azure. After you finish with your test, delete the resource group to automatically delete the VMs and all resources associated with that resource group.

Click OK.

Step 3: Configure Domain and Network Settings

The portal opens the domain and network configuration blade. Provide the forest root domain name, virtual network name, domain controller subnet name, and SQL Server subnet name.

Figure 18-6 shows the domain and networks settings blade.

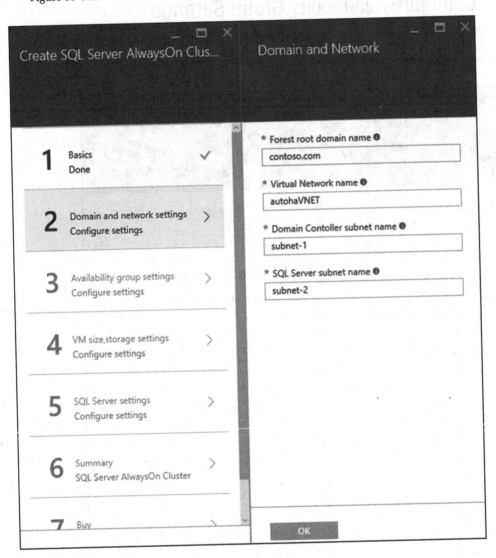

Figure 18-6. *Configure domain and network settings*

The domain controllers and the SQL Servers will be on separate subnets. All the VMs in the deployments will be under one virtual network.

■ Note The virtual network address range will be 10.0.0.0/16. The DC subnet address prefix will be 10.0.0.0/24, whereas the SQL subnet address prefix will be 10.0.1.0/26.

Click OK.

Step 4: Configure Availability Group Settings

The portal opens the availability group settings configuration blade. Provide the availability group name, listener name, and port number.

Figure 18-7 shows the availability groups settings blade.

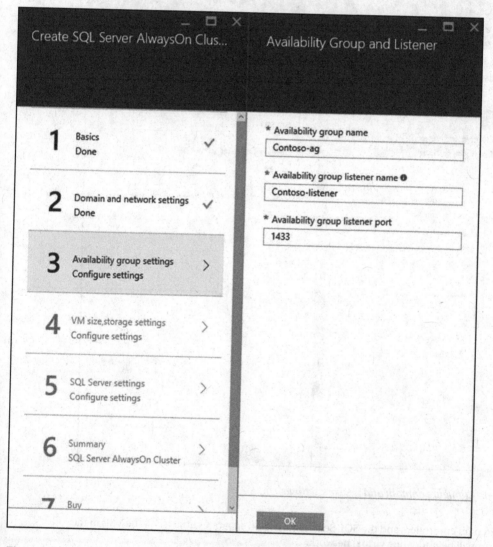

Figure 18-7. Configure Availability group settings

A listener will be created with the availability group listener name that you provide.

■ **Note**   If you choose to use port 1433, you do not need to provide a port number in a connection string. If you choose a port other than 1433 for your listener port, you will also need to explicitly specify a target port in your connection string.

Click OK.

Step 5: Configure VM size and Storage Settings

The portal opens the configure VM size and storage settings blade. Select the SQL Server, DC and file share witness VM size, configure the SQL storage account and the SQL data disk size, and also select the storage optimization option.

Figure 18-8 shows the VM size and storage settings blade.

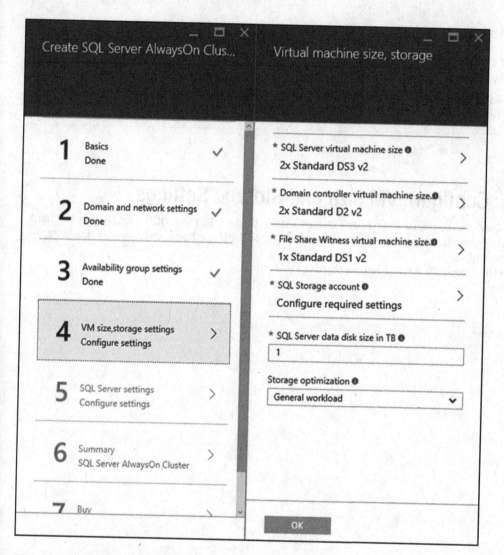

Figure 18-8. Configure the VM size and the storage settings

Click on the SQL Server virtual machine size option. The portal opens the size blade on the right side. The standard VM sizes consist of several series: A, D, DS, F, Fs, G, and GS.

D-series VMs are designed to run applications that demand higher compute power and temporary disk performance.

- Faster processors

- Higher memory-to-core ratio

- Solid-state drive (SSD) for the temporary disk

Dv2-series is a follow-on to the original D-series, features a more powerful CPU.

- About 35% faster than the D-series CPU.

- Based on the latest generation 2.4 GHz Intel Xeon® E5-2673 v3 (Haswell) processor with the Intel Turbo Boost Technology 2.0, which can go up to 3.1 GHz.

- Same memory and disk configurations as the D-series.

F-series provides the best value in price-performance in the Azure portfolio based on the Azure Compute Unit (ACU) per core

- Based on the 2.4 GHz Intel Xeon® E5-2673 v3 (Haswell) processor, which can achieve clock speeds as high as 3.1 GHz with the Intel Turbo Boost Technology 2.0.

- Same CPU performance as the Dv2-series of VMs.

G-series

- Most memory

- Run on hosts that have Intel Xeon E5 V3 family processors

DS-series

- DSv2-series, Fs-series, and GS-series VMs can use Premium Storage, which provides high-performance, low-latency storage for I/O intensive workloads.

- Use solid-state drives (SSDs) to host a virtual machine's disks and also provide a local SSD disk cache.

- Premium Storage is available in certain regions.

■ **Note** The following VM sizes are recommended for SQL:

SQL Server Enterprise Edition: DS3 or higher

SQL Server Standard and Web Editions: DS2 or higher

A-series

- Can be deployed on a variety of hardware types and processors.

- The size is throttled, based upon the hardware, to offer consistent processor performance for the running instance, regardless of the hardware it is deployed on.

A0

- Size is over-subscribed on the physical hardware.

- Other customer deployments may impact the performance of your running workload.

■ **Note** The size of the virtual machine affects the pricing, processing, memory, and storage capacity of the virtual machine.

Figure 18-9 shows the SQL VM size blade.

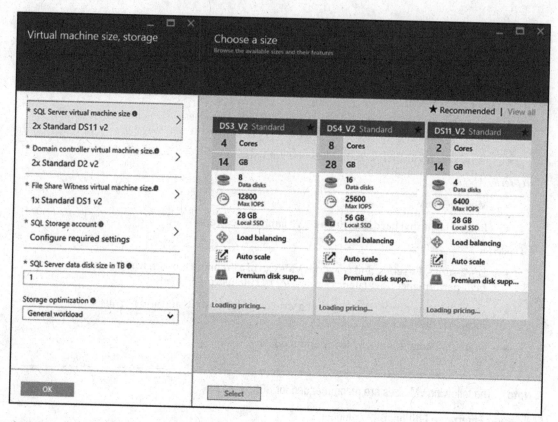

Figure 18-9. Choose a size for the SQL VMs

The blade initially displays recommended machine sizes. It also estimates the monthly cost to run the VM. The virtual machine size is the Azure virtual machine size for both SQL Servers. Choose a virtual machine size appropriate for your workload. For production workloads choose a virtual machine size that can support the workload. Many production workloads will require DS4 or larger. The template will build two virtual machines of this size and install SQL Server on each one. Click on the View All button, which shows all machine size options.

■ **Note**   The Marketplace image will install the Enterprise Edition of SQL Server.

Choose the machine size, and then click Select.

■ **Note**   At the time of writing this book, the Marketplace image provided the option for choosing SQL VMs with only premium disk support. As a result, the only SQL storage type available was *Premium locally redundant storage* (Premium_LRS). We will be discussing the all storage types in detail, later in the chapter.

Now click on the Domain controller virtual machine size option. The portal opens the size blade on the right side.

Figure 18-10 shows the size blade.

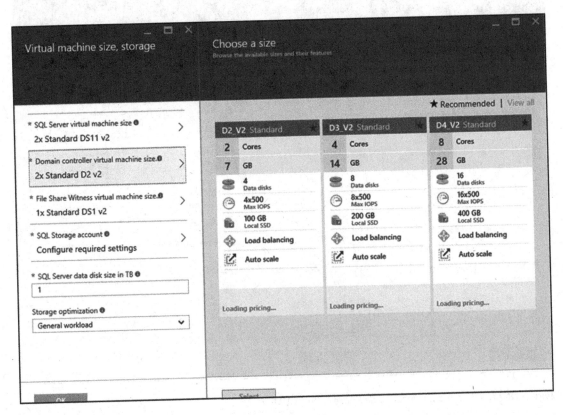

Figure 18-10. *Choose a size for the Domain controller VMs*

Like the SQL VM size blade, this blade initially displays recommended machine sizes. It also estimates the monthly cost to run the VM. Click on the view all button, which shows all machine size options.

Choose the machine size, and then click Select.

Now click on the File Share Witness virtual machine size option. The portal opens the size blade on the right side.

Figure 18-11 shows the size blade.

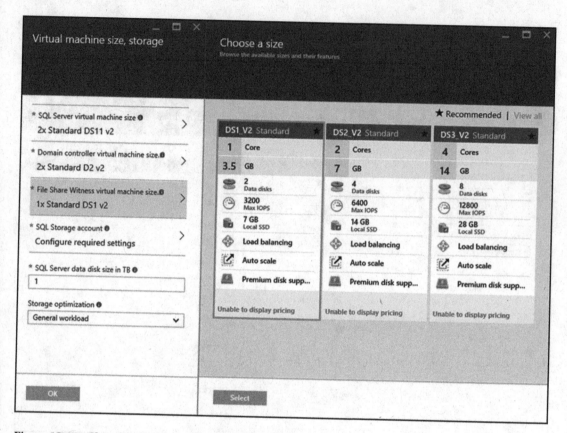

Figure 18-11. Choose a size for the File Share Witness VMs

Choose the machine size, and then click Select.

Now click on the SQL Storage account option. If no existing storage account exists, then it opens the create storage account blade on the right side.

Figure 18-12 shows the storage account creation blade.

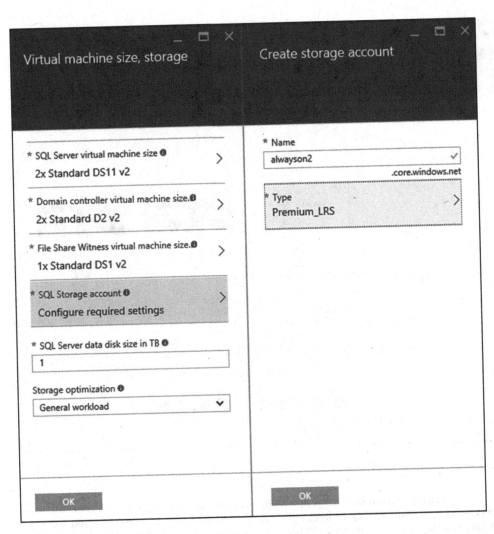

Figure 18-12. Create storage account blade

Provide a unique name for the storage account and click on Type. The portal opens the choose storage type blade.

Figure 18-13 shows the storage account creation blade.

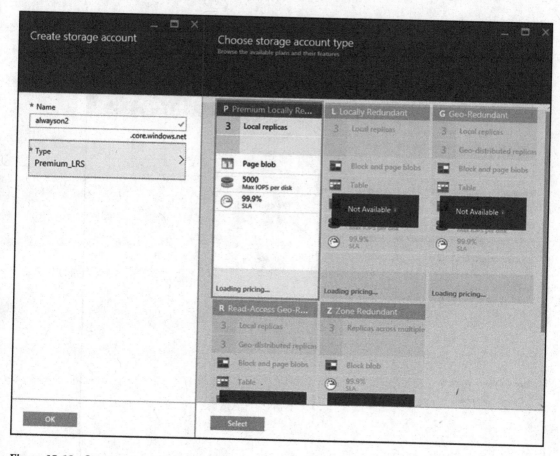

Figure 18-13. *Create storage account blade*

As mentioned earlier, the Marketplace image provided the option for choosing SQL VMs with only premium disk support. As a result, the SQL storage type available is Premium_LRS. However, if you are building the VMs manually then you can choose VMs without premium disk support, and that will make the different storage types available.

■ **Note** The data in the storage account is always replicated to ensure durability and high availability, meeting the Azure Storage SLA even in the face of transient hardware failures.

Types of storage:

Locally redundant storage (LRS)

Data is replicated within the region in which the stored account is created. The data is replicated three times. A transaction is considered successful only once it has been written to all three replicas. These three replicas each reside in separate *fault domains* (FD) and *upgrade domains* (UD). The three replicas are spread across UDs and FDs to ensure that data is available even if hardware failure impacts a single rack and when nodes are upgraded during a rollout.

■ **Note** FD is a group of nodes that represent a physical unit of failure and can be considered as nodes belonging to the same physical rack.

UD is a group of nodes that are upgraded together during the process of a service upgrade.

Zone-redundant storage (ZRS)
Data is replicated across two to three facilities, either within a single region or across two regions, providing higher durability than LRS.

Geo-redundant storage (GRS)
Data is replicated to a secondary region that is hundreds of miles away from the primary region. Data is durable even in the case of a complete regional outage or a disaster in which the primary region is not recoverable. An update is first committed to the primary region, where it is replicated three times. Then the update is replicated to the secondary region, where it is also replicated three times, across separate fault domains and upgrade domains.

■ **Note** Write data is replicated asynchronously to the secondary region. Since asynchronous replication involves a delay, in the event of a regional disaster it is possible that changes that have not yet been replicated to the secondary region may be lost if the data cannot be recovered from the primary region.

Read-access geo-redundant storage (RA-GRS)
Availability for the storage account is maximized, by providing read-only access to the data in the secondary location, in addition to the replication across two regions provided by GRS. The application can read data from the secondary region, in the event that data becomes unavailable in the primary region.

Premium local redundant storage (P-LRS)
Azure Premium Storage is the next generation of storage that provides low latency and high throughput IO. It works best for key IO intensive workloads, such as SQL Server on IaaS. Premium Storage account only supports LRS as the replication option and keeps three copies of the data within a single region.

Click Select and then click OK on the create storage account blade.

Next provide the SQL Server data disk size in TB. You can specify a number from 1 through 4. This is the size of the data disk that will be attached to each SQL Server.

Figure 18-14 shows the SQL Server data size in TB option in the VM size and storage blade.

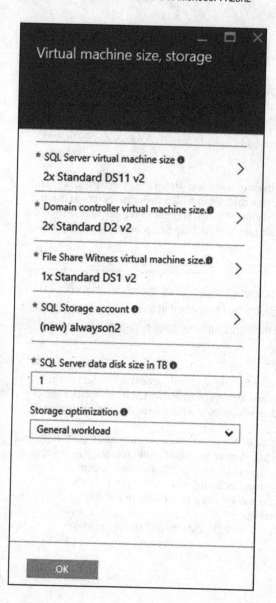

Figure 18-14. *Provide the SQL Server data size in TB*

Next choose the Storage optimization option for your workload. All the SQL Servers in this deployment use premium storage. In addition, you can optimize SQL Server settings for the workload by choosing one of these three settings:

- *General workload* sets no specific configuration settings

- *Transactional processing* enables trace flag 1117 and 1118 on the SQL Server instances

- *Data warehousing* sets trace flag 1117 and 610 on the SQL Server instances

Figure 18-15 shows the storage optimization in the VM size and storage blade.

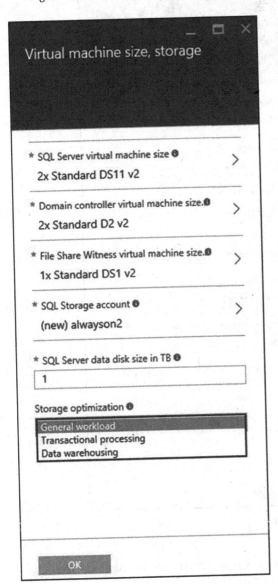

Figure 18-15. *Select the storage optimization option for the workload*

Then click OK.

Step 6: Configure SQL Server Settings

The portal opens the SQL Server settings blade.
    Figure 18-16 shows the SQL Server settings to configure.

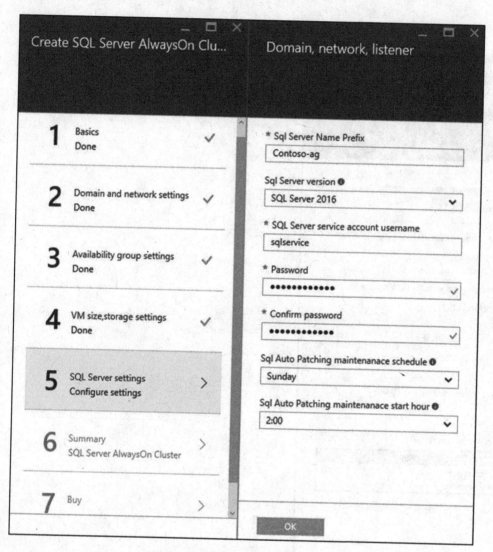

Figure 18-16. Configure SQL Server settings blade

SQL Server Name Prefix is used to create a name for each SQL Server. If the default contoso-ag is used, then the SQL Server names will be Contoso-ag-0 and Contoso-ag-1.

SQL Server version is the version of SQL Server that you want to use.

SQL Server service account user name is the domain account name for the SQL Server service.

Password is the password for the SQL Server service account.

SQL Auto Patching maintenance schedule identifies the weekday that Azure will automatically patch the SQL Servers.

SQL Auto Patching maintenance start hour is the time of day for the Azure region when automatic patching will begin.

After providing and selecting the required options, click OK.

The portal opens the summary blade as Azure validates the settings.

Figure 18-17 shows the summary page for review.

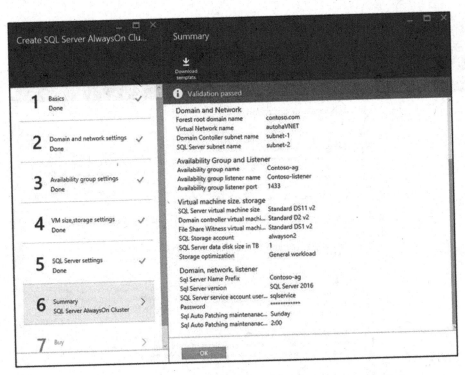

Figure 18-17. *Azure Marketplace Always On image deployment summary blade*

Review the summary and then click OK.

The portal opens the buy blade, which is the final blade that contains Terms of use, and privacy policy. Review the information and click purchase to start creating the virtual machines, and all of the other required resources for the availability group.

Figure 18-18 shows the buy page.

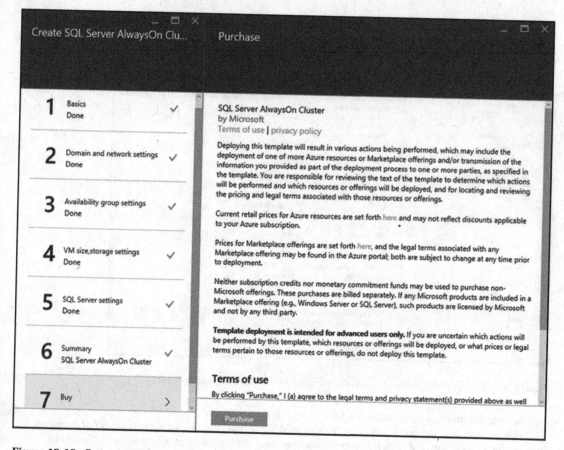

Figure 18-18. Buy page with terms of use and privacy policy

Post deployment, review the deployment by accessing the deployed resources.

Performance Best Practices

Let's take a look at some best practices for SQL in Azure VMs for optimal performance. Most of the standard best practices that apply for on-prem SQL instances would apply here as well. However, performance in Azure depends on certain factors in Azure.

Choosing VM size

- DS3 or higher **is recommended** for SQL Enterprise edition.

- DS2 or higher **is recommended** for SQL Standard and Web editions.

Choosing Storage

- Premium Storage is recommended for production workloads.

- Standard storage is only recommended for dev/test environments.

- Storage account and SQL Server VM should be in same region.

- If you are not using premium storage, then disable Azure geo-redundant storage (geo-replication) on the storage account.

- Disks

  a. Use at least two premium Storage disks (one for log and the other for data and tempdb).

  b. The temporary storage drive (D drive), is not persisted to Azure blob storage. Hence user database files or transaction log files should not be stored on the temporary storage drive.

  c. If using premium disks, enable read caching on data and TempDB data disks.

  d. Do not enable caching on transaction log disks.

  e. Do not enable caching if not using premium disks.

- Stripe multiple Azure data disks to get increased IO throughput.

  a. For more throughput, add additional data disks and use disk Striping.

  b. Analyze the number of IOPS available for the data and log disks to determine the number of data disks.

  c. For Windows 8/Windows Server 2012 or later, use Storage Spaces.

■ **Note** Storage Spaces is a new functionality introduced in Windows Server 2012 R2. It allows provisioning storage based on a pooled model. It also provides sophisticated storage virtualization capabilities.

---

  d. For OLTP workloads set the stripe size to 64 KB.

  e. For data warehousing workloads set the stripe size to 256 KB.

  f. For Windows 2008 R2 or earlier, use dynamic disks, that is, OS striped volumes.

  g. Create one storage pool for the workload that is not log intensive and does not need dedicated IOPs.

  h. Otherwise, create two storage pools: one for the log files and another storage pool for the data files and TempDB.

  i. Set column count to equal the number of disks in pool for maximum performance.

I/O optimization

- Enable database page compression.

- Enable instant file initialization for data files.

- Disable auto shrink on the database.

- Consider compressing any data files when transferring in/out of Azure.

- Apply the latest SQL Server I/O performance fixes.

Extend On-Prem Always On Availability Groups to Azure

We just looked at how to deploy Always On Availability Group in Azure. Another practical availability group scenario is to host a hybrid cloud solution, that is, to extend the On-Prem AG setup to Azure. You can extend an on-premises availability group to Azure by provisioning one or more Azure VMs with SQL Server and then adding them as replicas to the on-premises availability group.

Prerequisites for extending an On-Prem availability group to Azure

- An active Azure subscription.

- An existing availability group on-premises.

- Connectivity between the on-premises network and the Azure virtual network. A site-to-site VPN would need to be configured between the on-prem site and the Azure infrastructure to achieve this.

Figure 18-19 shows the add replica to availability group wizard. The Add Azure Replica button will allow you to add an Azure replica to an existing on-prem availability group.

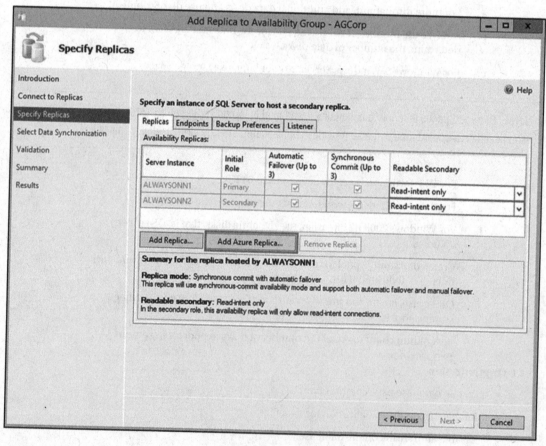

Figure 18-19. *Add Azure Replica to an existing on-prem availability group*

On clicking the Add Azure Replica button, it opens up the Add Azure Replica page. Figure 18-20 shows the Add Azure Replica page.

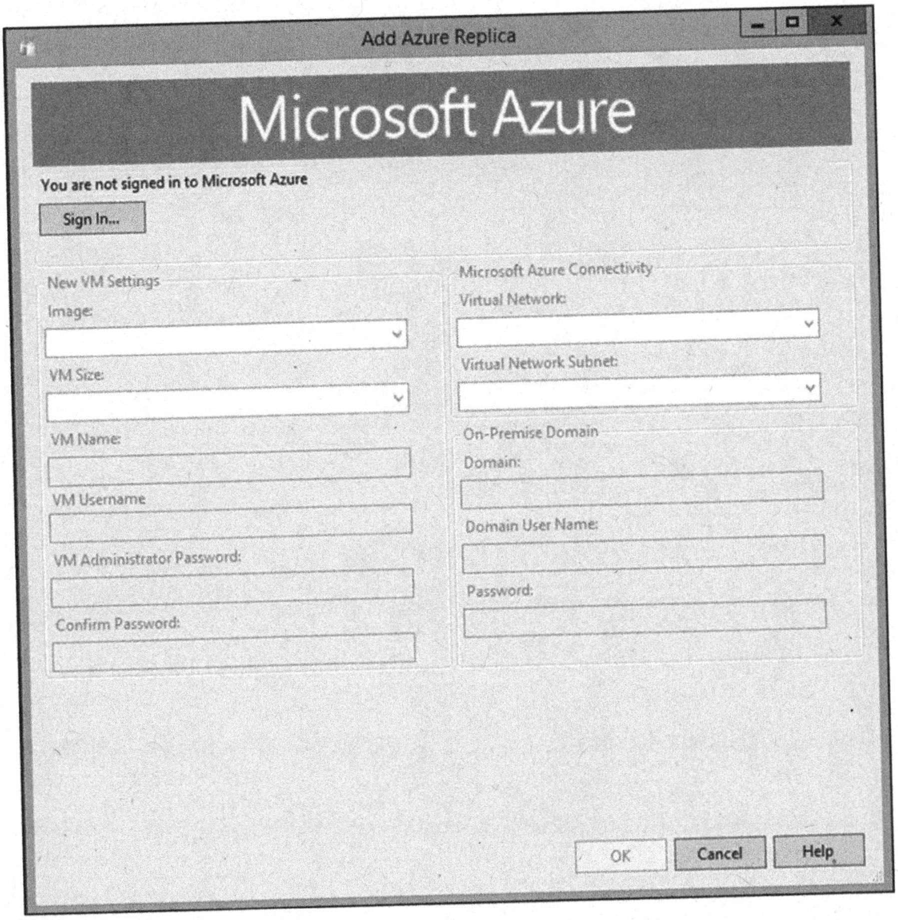

Figure 18-20. Add Azure Replica

After signing in to the Azure account, select the New VM image, size and provide the name and user credential information to be created. Also select virtual network and subnet for Azure connectivity and provide the on-premises domain name and user credentials.

Summary

The information in this chapter should help you get started with Microsoft Azure for your Always On Availability Groups deployment. Throughout this book, we have seen the amazing improvements that have been made to Always On Availability Groups in SQL Server 2016 and the ability to easily deploy it to Microsoft Azure, providing unparalleled flexibility. We have thoroughly enjoyed writing this book, and we hope that it has empowered you to put the knowledge gained from this book to practical use.

Index

© Uttam Parui and Vivek Sanil 2016
U. Parui and V. Sanil, *Pro SQL Server Always On Availability Groups*, DOI 10.1007/978-1-4842-2071-9

Get the eBook for only $5!

Why limit yourself?

Now you can take the weightless companion with you wherever you go and access your content on your PC, phone, tablet, or reader.

Since you've purchased this print book, we're happy to offer you the eBook in all 3 formats for just $5.

Convenient and fully searchable, the PDF version enables you to easily find and copy code—or perform examples by quickly toggling between instructions and applications. The MOBI format is ideal for your Kindle, while the ePUB can be utilized on a variety of mobile devices.

To learn more, go to www.apress.com/companion or contact support@apress.com.

Printed in the United States
By Bookmasters